THE
ELEPHANT
IN THE
LIVING ROOM

 RODALE
LIVE YOUR WHOLE LIFE™

Every day our brands connect with and inspire millions of
people to live a life of the mind, body, spirit — a whole life.

MAKE TELEVISION WORK
FOR YOUR KIDS

THE
ELEPHANT
IN THE
LIVING ROOM

DIMITRI A. CHRISTAKIS, MD, MPH
AND FREDERICK J. ZIMMERMAN, PhD
DIRECTORS OF THE CHILD HEALTH INSTITUTE
AT THE UNIVERSITY OF WASHINGTON

RODALE

© 2006 by Dimitri A. Christakis and Frederick J. Zimmerman

Rodale books may be purchased for business or promotional use or for special sales. For information, please write to: Special Markets Department, Rodale Inc., 733 Third Avenue, New York, NY 10017.

Printed in the United States of America

Rodale Inc. makes every effort to use acid-free ♾, recycled paper ♻.

John's story in Chapter 1 was reprinted with permission from *Pediatrics*, Vol. 113, pp. 708–13, © 2004 by the American Academy of Pediatrics. Dan Cook's story in Chapter 7 was reprinted from *Stay Free!* Issue #20, Fall 2002 (stayfreemagazine.org) with permission from the publisher.

Illustrations by Sandy Freeman and Joanna Williams

Book design by Joanna Williams

Library of Congress Cataloging-in-Publication Data

Christakis, Dimitri Alexander.
  The elephant in the living room : make television work for your kids / Dimitri A. Christakis, and Frederick J. Zimmerman.
    p.   cm.
  Includes bibliographical references and index.
  ISBN-13 978–1–59486–276–2 hardcover
  ISBN-10 1–59486–276–1 hardcover
    1. Television and children.   I. Zimmerman, Frederick J., date   II. Title.
HQ784.T4C545   2006
302.23′45083—dc22
                                                                        2006018441

Distributed to the book trade by Holtzbrinck Publishers

2   4   6   8   10   9   7   5   3   hardcover

For Lenna, with whom It all began, and for Aleco, who taught me about high levels of abstraction, but most of all for Danielle Zerr, Alexi, and Ariana—my inspiration and my best friends at family movie night.

—D.A.C.

To Sarah Stein and to our sons, Ira and Julius—who make everything work in our family.

—F.J.Z.

This instrument can teach, it can illuminate;
yes, and it can even inspire. But it can do so only to the
extent that humans are determined to use it to those ends.
Otherwise it is merely wires and lights in a box.

Edward R. Murrow, keynote speech at the
1958 convention of the Radio-Television News Directors Association

CONTENTS

ACKNOWLEDGMENTS

This book owes much to a whole host of people who in various ways and at various times were instrumental in making it happen.

The final version, such as it is, could never have come about without the thoughtful comments and careful edits provided at various stages by Dick Stein, Sarah Stein, and Danielle Zerr, each of whom patiently read one or more versions of the entire manuscript. Others also offered their helpful advice, including Howard Yoon, Stacey Prohaska, and Jennifer Freeh. Our editor at Rodale, Mariska van Aalst, patiently edited the later versions and made many useful contributions.

We are fortunate to work in a field with many dynamic, thoughtful, and generous researchers. Their work has been underrecognized in the public sphere, and we hope this book goes some way toward redressing that problem. We are gratified to be working in such a collegial field. Many of our colleagues (too many to mention) have helped us in various ways in our research and have influenced our thinking. Several research colleagues warrant explicit thanks for their generous response to specific questions about the book. Joanne Cantor was kind enough to read drafts of an early chapter and to generously give us advice on many aspects of the writing and publishing of it. Kris Harrison, Tom Robinson, Amy Jordan, Caroline Oates, Juliet Schor, Jessica Taylor-Piotrowski kindly engaged us in discussions or responded thoughtfully to e-mail queries about specific aspects of their research. To them all, we are grateful.

Our ongoing research is made possible by Lyn Bassett, Tasheda Navarro, Joe Leonard, Michelle Garrison, Andrea Richardson, Darcy Thompson, Becca Calhoun, Tori Lollemont, Jane Yoon, and Melissa

Zent. But first and foremost, it relies on the generous assistance and invaluable contributions of the many families that have and continue to participate in our studies. We are grateful to all of them.

We owe a special debt of gratitude to Fred Connell, who has served as a mentor and friend to both of us.

Each of us, in turn, has personal influences that are reflected throughout the text.

For Fred, this project has been a wonderful opportunity to reflect on the thoughtful, loving, and always engaged parenting of his mother and father, Joanell and Fred M. Zimmerman. Their love of children and appreciation of the value of childhood have been profound influences. Fred's siblings, Carita, Christina, Brigitte, and Hans, are much-loved companions and friends. None will reveal the secret of the spontaneously malfunctioning television of 1975. In his professional work, Fred is never far in one form or another from the advice and philosophy of Michael Carter, and he can only try to live up to the guidance of Edward Cronin, that Irish teacher of English.

For Dimitri, his beloved siblings, Nicholas, Anna-Katrina, Quan-Yang, and Nora, with whom he negotiated control of the television as a child, were an enormous influence on his understanding of its role in families. In thinking about parenting, he continues to draw on the memory of his mother, Lenna Saranti, whose courage and dedication to that art in the face of extraordinary adversity remain a standard he can strive for but never reach. Finally, his friends Evan Westerfield, James Forman, and Ted Vial have always been willing to tell him what they think of everything he says. That assistance has become something he cannot live without.

Our most important acknowledgments are to Danielle Zerr and Sarah Stein, each of whom has displayed unstinting support and patience in the long process of pulling this book together. They are amazing people, wonderful mothers, and the ideal co-parents. We are eternally grateful for their intelligence, wit, wisdom, help, and love.

CHAPTER 1

LOOKING AT THE ELEPHANT

When television is good, nothing is better. When it's bad, nothing is worse.

Newton Minow, chairman of the Federal Communications Commission in the 1960s

The many shower gifts that Elizabeth and David received on the happy occasion of the imminent birth of their son included the usual mix of sleepwear, crib toys, and a book about the first year, plus something unexpected—an "educational" baby video. "A real lifesaver," their friend Kara said as she gave it to them. "My baby just loves it, and it gives me some time during the day to myself." Elizabeth and David graciously accepted it, looking at the cover image of a brainy-looking—or rather, nerdy-looking—baby with spiked hair and wire-rimmed glasses. It gave them pause. They had discussed many facets of their lives that would affect their child, including their house, the school district, and their religion, but they really hadn't thought about what role television would play in their new baby's life.

Television is the elephant in the American living room. It is a massive presence in childhood, and yet, as for Elizabeth and David, its importance seldom seems to merit discussion. Children watch an average of 3 hours—and sometimes more than 8 hours—of television per day, and typical schoolchildren spend as much time in front of the television as they do in class. Children too young to go to school are old enough to be

1

schooled by TV, typically starting their TV-viewing careers as early as 6 months old. Children under the age of 3 spend up to 20 to 30 percent of their waking hours watching TV and videos, despite the fact that at this age, their attention span is only a few minutes at a time.

If you're like most parents, you'll have a strong, visceral reaction to numbers such as these. Either you'll be glad that your children don't or won't watch much TV, or you'll feel guilty about how much they do watch, or you'll feel good that you are highly selective about what they watch, or you'll be convinced that the whole concern with TV is overblown. When our friends found out that we were working on a book on the effects of television on children, reactions varied. Some responded as our friend Caroline did: "I know I've probably ruined my kids already—they watched a lot of *Scooby-Doo* when they were little." Others, like Kim, said things like, "Good. Finally someone can tell us that it is fine for them to watch as much as they want."

While it's true that most parents (and grandparents) have strong feelings about television, it's also true that they seldom share them with other people when they're not sure others agree with their position. Television, like religion and politics, needs to be discussed with great caution. It's understandable that the topic of television and children is fraught with strong emotions, generating more heat than light. After all, parents have had to rely on their own opinions because high-quality, scientifically based information and advice about television haven't been readily available—until now.

As parents, we came to our research on TV with the same kinds of emotional responses to the topic most parents have. As scientists, we've put those emotions on the back burner as we've delved into the rigorous work of painstaking data collection and careful statistical analyses. And we've discovered that our initial reactions were wrong—or partly wrong, for as you'll see in this book, our scientific research and that of many other TV researchers tell us that television can be both worse than we'd feared and better than we'd thought possible. For this reason, we no longer think of TV as inherently good or bad. Instead, we see it as a tool.

Much like a food processor or a power saw, television can be dangerous. But properly used at the appropriate age and with the requisite adult supervision, it can produce wonderful things. As you read this book, we ask you to set aside initial emotional reactions, as we have, and join us in exploring how TV—with all its promise and pitfalls—can work for your child.

WHY THIS BOOK?

Open up your favorite parenting book and look through the index. How many references to television are there? Five? Ten? None? The lack of good-quality information for parents about television is all out of step with the enormous role TV plays in children's lives. There is a strong need for thoughtful and accurate information on what effects it has on children as well as what effects it doesn't have.

This need for information is now being met by important new research, including our own. In this book, we will introduce you to some of the fascinating research we have been engaged in regarding the issue of television and its effects on children. In Chapter 2, we'll explain the rationale and results of our study of television's impact on children's ability to pay attention. In Chapter 3, we'll discuss the implications of our study that looked at how watching TV at an early age affects school readiness—a study that for the first time highlighted the real disadvantages of too much television before children are ready for it. In Chapter 4, we'll outline our work on the effects of television on bullying behavior, a major concern in elementary schools.

All of these studies have garnered worldwide media attention. While the press coverage is gratifying, it hasn't always appropriately conveyed the important messages for parents. It has focused more on the dangers—which are real—than on what parents can do—which is important. Although between us, we had spent more than 20 years conducting research and had published well over 100 articles related to children's health, it wasn't until we had children of our own that we directed our scientific inquiries at television.

We wrote this book in part because we were eager to learn more about how this pervasive medium might affect our children. This book is the resource we *wanted*; it is the resource that the parents of our patients—and friends—*need*. It does something that is routinely avoided: It dispassionately and carefully discusses the "elephant in the living room." Its purpose is to inform and empower parents so they can take charge of their children's viewing. Many parents feel incapable of doing so. More than half are worried about the effect of television on their children. Many are concerned about how much time their children spend watching TV but feel they can do nothing to reduce it. Many parents would get rid of their sets altogether if they felt they could tolerate the absence of TV. Even among parents who aren't concerned, the majority have mixed views about TV's place in their children's lives, and a sizable percentage feel guilty about their reliance on it.

Parents should not feel guilty, powerless, or even indifferent about television, however; its effects need not be adverse, and they are most certainly remediable. Television viewing can be beneficial. It can be entertaining, broadening, and educational. It just has to be used properly.

THIS ISN'T YOUR PARENTS' TELEVISION

Consciously or unconsciously, Elizabeth and David, the couple in the story at the beginning of the chapter, will use their recollections of their parents' childrearing strategies as a template for their own. Sometimes they will use them as examples of what not to do, but more often than not they will fall back on them as being the right approach. Remember all the things you swore as a child you would *never* do to your children? You are probably doing more (or will do more) of them than you care to admit. While our own upbringings usually provide a good starting point for decisions about how to raise our children, television has changed so dramatically in a generation that old models are not necessarily useful guides for parents. One of the reasons Elizabeth and David never discussed television is that they thought it wasn't yet relevant. They were having a *baby,* after all; television surely didn't yet figure into his life.

Like most of us, they probably started watching television at age 3 or 4, when *Mister Rogers' Neighborhood* was on for just a half hour a day. We watched this and other truly commercial-free programming on PBS for a few years, then transitioned gradually to *Shazam!, The Mary Tyler Moore Show,* and reruns of *Gilligan's Island* as available on three channels in the family room. The family television—there was only one—was situated where our mothers could see us. The simple truth is that as much as we may have wanted to watch television, there frequently weren't any programs of interest to us. As recently as 20 years ago, VCRs were not widely in use. Holiday programs or favorite movies had to be seen when they aired or were missed altogether.

What a difference 20 years make! A typical child born today will probably watch videos first, starting as early as 4 to 6 months old, often sitting in a car safety seat if she is unable to sit on her own. She will quickly graduate to a bewildering array of shows laden with stressful cartoon violence and commercialism, which she may start watching as early as 9 months old. Yes, we enjoyed our share of *Tom and Jerry* cartoons when we were young, but today's children watch more realistically violent programs, which are no longer limited to Saturday mornings. Not only have cartoons become more violent over time, and not only are they more regularly available, but as we will show, the type of violence in cartoons particularly promotes aggressive behavior among children. What's more, the explosion of cable channels, cartoon networks, DVDs, and recording devices now makes such cartoons available 24 hours a day.

Children today are also more targeted by advertisers than they were a generation ago; television, including public television, has become much more commercialized. Marketing to children has ballooned from a $600 million industry in 1989 to $15 billion today—about a 25-fold increase in just 17 years! Reruns of shows from our childhoods are edited down to make room for more commercials, and it's no longer possible to consider making a children's television show—even an educational show to be aired on PBS—without carefully considering and making advance deals for its merchandising opportunities.

New content has also changed the landscape of children's viewing. A generation ago, MTV and VH-1 didn't exist or were in their infancy, yet today, music videos are far more sexual and more violent than regular TV programming. Seeing the video of a song has become as important as hearing it on the radio once was. Many parents are appalled when they become aware of the lyrics of the songs their children listen to. Usually, this entails reading them on liner notes, as most don't listen to lyrics, and when they do, they often can't discern the words. But those words come to life on the screen, and the rise of music videos has been a major reason for the maturing of content as viewers have become younger.

Reality television is also new, in all its bewildering variety, including game-docs like *Survivor* and *The Amazing Race*, celebrity shows like *America's Next Top Model* and *Dancing with the Stars*, teenage gross-outs like *Fear Factor* and *Jackass,* competitions like *American Idol*, makeovers of home (*Extreme Makeover: Home Edition*) and body (*The Biggest Loser*), and many others. What these programs have in common is that they are inexpensive to make; depend on psychodrama rather than plot, dialogue, and acting to attract audiences; and are hugely popular. Many of these shows are old-fashioned entertainment in a new wrapper, but a few of them, as we'll show in this book, pose genuine threats to children by offering models of behavior that are made more dangerous by their veracity—sometimes fatally so.

To be sure, the news is not all bad. Children now also have a much wider variety of educational programming to choose from than we did.

Even more important, parents can use new technologies such as TiVo and DVDs to maximize the benefits of educational shows. It may surprise parents to learn this, but children are happy to watch reruns of educational shows, often up to five times in row with no decrease in their attention to a program! As you'll see, this repetition actually helps them to better master the concepts involved.

We believe that there is a right amount of television for every child, and it is different for each one. The right amount depends on the child and what the show is. Parents know their children better than anyone else, which is why we're not fond of age-based television ratings. But if parents have part of the puzzle, they're missing part of it, too. We recently conducted a survey of parents of young children about educational programming on TV. Ninety-two percent of them knew that *Sesame Street* is educational, and 97 percent knew that *The Lion King* is not. But parents were more confused about many shows, with about 20 percent rating both *Big Comfy Couch* and *Teletubbies* as educational (*Big Comfy Couch* is, *Teletubbies* isn't). Yet our jaws dropped when we found that only 35 percent of parents recognized *Blue's Clues* as educational. As you'll see, *Blue's Clues* is not only educational, it also represents a uniquely successful approach to educational television that keeps it both highly educational and consistently entertaining.

THE DIGITAL REVOLUTION IS TELEVISED

What has led to these changes? In most cases, the answer lies in technological change: cable TV, videos, DVDs, TiVo, tiny video screens in cars and airplanes, giant televisions in home theaters—all new developments since we were children. There are now six networks and at least 15 national television channels with children's programming, with five cable networks completely devoted to it: Cartoon Network, Disney Channel, FOX Family

Channel, Nickelodeon, and Toon Disney. As this book went to press, a new satellite channel with 24-hour programming targeted at children under age 2 was just announced. Truly, we are immersed in television as never before. These developments have led to a preponderance of cartoons (instead of live-action shows) for children; they've also led to an increased emphasis on fast pacing, violence, and sex for keeping children's attention rather than high-quality, positive-themed programming, which is much more expensive to produce. There are exceptions, however—some wonderful bright spots—and we will discuss those as well.

HOW CAN TV HELP?

We know parenting is hard—oh, do we know it! Like any parents, we could probably fill a whole book just with our own anecdotes of parenting episodes gone awry. Parents who hear about the ill effects of TV on children often have a rising sense of panic, perhaps mixed with fear, guilt, frustration, and anger.

Relax. We aren't going to tell you to kill your television. On the contrary, we'll show you some of the more positive sides of TV.

Consider Cory, the son of a colleague of ours. When he was an active, likable 9-year-old, Cory was diagnosed with a debilitating illness that kept him in bed for weeks at a time. During this period, he began to watch a lot of TV. One day, he was flipping channels and came upon a cooking show. He was mesmerized. A man was flattening out pizza dough with his hands, and Cory loved the low-key theatricality of it. Something in the pacing and the patter appealed to his reduced energy. He became a regular viewer of *Ciao, America!* and soon added *Good Eats* and *America's Test Kitchen*, a strangely scientific cooking show on PBS. Cory soon carried his interest into the kitchen, and while he didn't become a gourmet chef—not yet, anyway—he quickly mastered deviled eggs and other simple dishes, much to his family's delight. His parents had never imagined he would be interested in cooking, and even if they had, they probably couldn't have coaxed him into trying it on their own.

At its best, TV can educate and inspire. High-quality documentaries offer insights into history that no book can equal. Nature programs do more than teach us facts about the science of weather or animals' native habitats; they take us to places many of us will never be able to visit. They capture scenes that take literally hundreds of hours of patient camera work and use technologies to take us to venues that it is not humanly possible to visit. Children's educational shows have the proven ability to help children learn to read, to be kind, and to share. In short, when used appropriately, television has the power to expand horizons and help children's cognitive, social, and emotional development.

HOW CAN TV HURT?

Now, the bad news. Too much TV, or the wrong kind, can have lasting, damaging effects that no parent would welcome. In this book, you'll see how television has influenced children to put their own lives and the lives of others at risk—along with their futures, their grades, and their imaginations—by depressing healthy development and encouraging early alcohol use, unsafe sex, and other dangerous activities. Teenagers are often at greatest risk for dramatic consequences, but the effects of television on younger children—even babies—are just as real, if more subtle. We'll show how watching certain kinds of television too early can impair language development or lead to symptoms of hyperactivity and how certain viewing habits can make for fat bodies and thin wallets. Still, we've tried to keep lurid tales of serious consequences in the background in this book. While acts inspired by TV do sometimes land children in the hospital, such dramatic and direct effects tend to be rare. More common are experiences involving poor use of TV, with results that aren't fatal or irreversible but are still unhappy at the time.

I quit my job 9 months ago to be a stay-at-home mother with my 3-year-old son, John. At the time, I was 7 months pregnant, and as each day passed, my son seemed to demand more and more attention . . . play with me, hold me, read to me. Before the baby was born, I would give in to his demands, or I would take him places like Story Time or have other children come and play. After the baby was born, I could not run all over the place, so again I tried to keep up with his demands . . . nothing worked. On top of that, my infant would only nap 30 to 45 minutes at a time. So eventually I put John in front of the TV anywhere from 1 to 3 hours per day. Since there was not always much on when we needed it, he watched a lot of cartoons. It gave me a little bit of sanity but only for the time he was actually watching a show. Then, when I would turn it off, things would be worse. I noticed that when I would read a book to him, he lost interest after about 15 minutes. Finally, we cut TV down dramatically. I now think that all of his demanding behavior was caused by jealousy and that putting him in front of the television not only made him dependent on something else to entertain him but actually did shorten his attention span immensely. Only time will tell if we can undo the damage. Until then, our TV will be off.[1]

Television used poorly can make children anxious and depressed and can lead to sleep disturbances and aggression. We will review all of these effects and tell you how to protect your child from them.

THE MODERN TELEVISION CHILDHOOD

The stories of Cory and John are compelling because although both children watched a lot of TV, the results were dramatically different. How do you use television to achieve the effects on your child's behavior that you are comfortable with while at the same time avoiding the effects you fear?

Each of the chapters that follow focuses on the three aspects of television viewing that we believe are most salient:

- *How much* is being watched (quantity)
- *What* is being watched (quality and content)
- *How* it is being watched (context)

Because these three dimensions critically inform the effects of TV viewing on children's development, we will focus on them as we examine these effects throughout the book.

Too much television or video watching can affect children's behavior and development—all experts agree on this fundamental fact. But how much is "too much"? It depends on what the children are watching, so our measurement of the *quantity* of television and videos should really be informed by their *quality*. And what does that mean? To some extent, just as for adult programs, the quality of children's television is defined by production values, the cleverness of the dialogue, the believability of the characters, and so on. But much more important for children, quality is determined by the content—the underlying message of the program. Educational programs such as *Sesame Street* and *Blue's Clues* usually have the potential to improve children's reading ability and vocabulary and to promote cooperative, kind, and tolerant behavior. Noneducational programs such as cartoons usually have the potential to promote aggressive and disrespectful behavior in children. Some may even inhibit development of reading ability and vocabulary.

However, this general observation also depends heavily on how the programs are viewed. As we will discuss, watching even high-quality educational programs at the wrong ages can slow a child's academic development. And some children with very busy or distracted parents can benefit from even noneducational television. Co-viewing is one important aspect of how television is watched. We'll discuss how the opportunity to be aware of and discuss a show's content can flip TV's effects on a child's behavior from negative to positive. When our children watch, we try to watch with them, and we encourage all of our patients' families to do so as well. We'll explain more in later chapters about why this single change can have such a powerful influence on your kids.

In the story above, the mom related that her son John watched 3 hours of TV a day. True, that is more than ideal, but in itself, it's not so excessive as to be damaging. But he watched exactly the kind of programming that would be likely to "ramp him up" and make him more unmanageable rather than any of the several shows that might help him become more understanding and supportive of his little brother. Believe it or not, there are such programs! Most important, though, was *how* he watched. John was set in front of the television so that his mother could focus on his sibling. When she pointed to his jealousy as a reason for his behavior, she was spot-on. As is so often the case, the context of the TV viewing profoundly shaped its effects on John's behavior. Leaving him alone with the television as a distraction bought his mother some time with her newborn, but solving one problem exacerbated another.

Cory, on the other hand, was bedridden, bored, and sad. Physically unable to do the things he liked most, such as playing sports, he gained a new creative outlet that required minimal energy to enjoy—watching cooking shows. In large part, this positive outcome was possible only because his parents knew what he was watching, and they encouraged him to step into the kitchen when he was able. In this book, you'll see again and again that all of these elements—the amount of TV children watch, what they watch, and how they watch it—are crucial to determining its effects on them.

Consider how dramatically these three elements have changed. In the early days of primetime programming, television brought families together as they gathered around a single, centrally located TV set to watch general-interest programs such as family-oriented variety shows. When Fred was in grade school, he wouldn't have chosen to watch *Little House on the Prairie* every week, but growing up with two sisters and one

TV, it was his only option on Wednesday nights. Over time, it became a family tradition and something to look forward to.

Now, television often keeps families apart. More than 80 percent of U.S. households have more than one set, and family members frequently watch TV separately. Television sets have become so affordable that typical families find it irresistible to increase the number of TVs they have—TVs now outnumber family members. They even outnumber toilets in the United States! As a result of the proliferating screens, more and more children watch alone or in isolation from their parents, who sheepishly concede that they rely on television and videos as electronic babysitters.

TAMING THE ELEPHANT

Our purpose in writing this book is to help you attune your children's TV viewing to your own needs and goals. Television is a part of our lives, and it is here to stay. We believe that the unexamined TV is not worth watching. As they say on Nick at Nite, "You wouldn't suck green ooze from a tube if you didn't know what it was—*would you?*" We espouse what we call *mindful viewing.* Engaging in mindful viewing means that you think about what you're watching and understand the underlying motivations of characters and advertisers. You can promote mindful viewing in your children by actively critiquing programs, both as you watch them and afterward, in other settings. The critique doesn't have to be all negative—positive comments about portrayals you like can contribute wonderfully to mindful viewing. The goal is to get your children to see television not as just a neutral presentation of what the world is like but rather as a medium with a particular point of view to sell, one to which you can be sympathetic or unsympathetic and one that can be realistic or unrealistic with regard to consequences of behavior. Above all, TV is a source of influence that, with mindful viewing, one can tap selectively and actively.

We address questions that all parents have but that have been unfortunately obscured by extreme or unrealistic rhetoric from both pro- and anti-TV camps. We'll cover not only questions about how much TV should kids watch but also others, including the following.

- At what ages should children watch different kinds of TV?
- How can kids get the most educational value out of television?
- What needs and desires motivate children to watch TV, and how are those needs exploited by both educational and noneducational shows?
- Does TV advertising really have an effect?
- Does watching TV lead to obesity?
- How much of the benefit of television depends on the ways in which it is watched and with whom?
- Are children truly passive when they watch TV, or is something else going on in there?
- Does television displace dangerous activities and keep kids out of trouble, or does it displace useful activities and deprive them of important experiences?
- How do the answers to these questions differ at different ages and with different parenting styles?

This book is organized by specific areas that TV has been shown to impact—attention, education, sleep, obesity—and covers the full spectrum of behaviors and outcomes that television is known to affect in these areas, both positively and negatively. Finally, it concludes with a program that will teach you how to improve your children's relationship with television. It includes step-by-step instructions as well as easily incorporated practical tips. You'll learn how to determine how much is enough (and how much is too much), how you can make the best choices for your children, and how you can increase the positive aspects of those choices, generally improving the ways television is used in your home. For our pragmatic approach, we draw heavily on many anecdotes and tips from parents we've worked with in our research, but we also rely on our own experience as parents. We'll show you how to identify your personal goals for TV viewing: What do you hope your children will get out of it? What are you concerned about? What do you want out of it for yourself? Then we'll help you take these goals and develop a plan to make television work for you and your children.

By providing a scientifically sound conceptual framework about television and child development, this book will help you understand that the subject of television and childhood development is one of the most important topics of discussion for parents. We want this book to open both eyes and minds, to teach you to use the power you have as a parent to make the most of this very important tool. So when someone gives you a baby video for your newborn or invites your 15-year-old to a *Sex and the City* slumber party, by all means, react emotionally—then respond rationally. After reading this book, you'll have the information you need to know when you should listen to your parenting gut and when you can just relax.

CHAPTER 2

STAYING IN FOCUS: TELEVISION AND ATTENTION

The only factor becoming scarce in a world of abundance is human attention.

Kevin Kelly, "Twelve Dependable Rules for Thriving in a Turbulent World," Wired, September 1997

Until I had Nevaeh, I had no idea how much time children take. I enjoy being with her, but sometimes I need a break. A little break every day. So I put her in front of the TV for a while, and I go do something else. She watches good stuff— like Clifford *or* Sesame *or sometimes a* Baby Einstein *video. She likes it, I think. She sure pays attention to it, and I can go do what I like. I guess it's good for her; it's supposed to be. But she's only 8 months old, and when I think about it, I can't imagine what she would be getting out of it. But I like it.[1]*

When David Sarnoff, president of RCA, presented the newly invented medium of television at the New York World's Fair in 1939, he had grand visions. Television, he proclaimed, would be "an art which shines like a torch of hope in a troubled world."

Thirty years later, after television had completed its rapid colonization of the developed world, the vision had tarnished. According to Jane Healy, author of *Endangered Minds*, in the early 1970s, teachers started complaining that they were noticing changes in their young students' ability to pay attention.[2] Teaching to children with 5-minute attention spans became the norm. Many teachers reported that they felt that they were expected to compete with educational television, to be as entertaining as *Sesame Street* characters in or der to keep pupils' minds focused on them— a tall order for even the most talented among them.

They weren't alone in thinking that television was bad for kids' brains. References to television as the "idiot box" or "boob tube" or to children becoming zombies in front of the TV have long popularized the notion that television viewing shortens children's attention spans. Does this popular conception have any merit? Does television really contribute to poor concentration, and if so, what is it about the medium that causes such problems? In this chapter, we discuss how television may influence the way the brain develops from the earliest ages and how viewing shapes children's capacity to pay attention. We also offer some suggestions for diminishing any possible negative effects on your children.

PAYING ATTENTION TO ATTENTION

As teachers or parents or casual observers, we know that some children pay attention better than others. From a practical standpoint, paying attention involves allowing certain information to be prioritized in the brain and excluding other, distracting information so it doesn't get in the way. Attention requires filtering so that what's most important is filed away in the appropriate areas of the brain. Paying attention, however, is more than just staring at something; we are all aware that it's possible to stare at an object, or even read a paragraph, without really focusing our minds on it. We can go through the motions of being attentive without bringing to bear the full power of our minds. Think of the once-popular *Where's Waldo?* books. Finding Waldo in a sea of other images requires that the visual center of the brain is alerted to be on the lookout for him and him alone. True attention involves selection ("I am looking for Waldo."), exclusion of distractions ("I am not looking at other potentially interesting images."), and concentrated thought ("Where is he?").

Thought is the component of attention that is most difficult for an outside observer to assess. You know when your child is looking at an object, and you know when he isn't being distracted, but how can you tell when he is looking at an object *and* thinking about it? The thought component is crucial for attention. As every sleep-deprived parent knows, there is a big difference between staring at something and examining it. *Looking* is not *seeing*. Or, in technical terms, *fixation* is not *engagement*. When Dimitri plays the game Concentration with his 4-year-old daughter, Ariana, her facial expression tells it all. When she's studying the cards, never averting her gaze from them as the two of them take turns flipping them in search of matches, she performs well.

The difference between looking and seeing is essential to a child's development. You have probably developed some intuition for this distinction in regard to your own children, but it can sometimes be difficult to know for sure. Psychologists have determined that attention (or thought while looking) deepens as a child looks at an object. Children usually take a few seconds to grasp an object visually before they can begin to think about it.[3] A toddler looking at a picture of a dinosaur sees just a meaningless blur of color until it resolves into an image of something that can be studied.

Psychologists don't have your intuition about whether an infant is looking (fixating) or thinking about (engaging) something he sees. Instead, they measure changes in heart rate to assess the extent to which infants are fixating or engaging. Careful experiments have shown that engagement reaches a maximum after about 20 seconds of looking at an object or a scene. Shorter looks are less likely to produce thoughtful looking and more likely to result in rapid distraction.[4] In this sense, rapid scene changes on television can keep a child looking but not thinking.

As a general rule, young children can be expected to pay attention to a task (such as looking at a book or playing with a toy) for a period of approximately two times their age in minutes (that is, a 5-year-old can be expected to pay attention for 10 minutes), although there is wide variation in what is considered normal. When trying to stay focused on a task, children with attention problems can be very easily distracted by other stimuli they may detect. They can become more interested in the green car on the street in the city where Waldo is hiding or the real car driving down the street outside as they are searching. Easy distractibility is a cardinal feature of attention deficit hyperactivity disorder (ADHD or sometimes ADD). Children with this disorder filter poorly and can't stay focused, especially when there is something else going on.

THE RISE OF ADHD

Over the past 20 years, there has been a 10-fold increase in diagnoses of attention deficit hyperactivity disorder. ADHD has become the most common behavioral problem in the United States and is currently estimated to affect somewhere between 8 and 12 percent of children. As American children watch more and more television at younger and younger ages, many observers have expressed concern that TV has played a major role in the sharp rise in diagnoses of ADHD.

ADHD has a strong genetic component: Children of parents with the disorder are at higher risk of developing it than the general population is. However, genetics go only so far in explaining ADHD. If one sibling of an identical twin pair (who have identical genes) has ADHD, there is an 80 percent chance that the other sibling also has it. If ADHD were entirely genetic, we would expect the probability to be 100 percent. According to a 1999 Surgeon General's report that reviewed the evidence for the heritability of ADHD, "For most children with ADHD, the overall effects of these gene abnormalities appear small, suggesting that non-genetic factors also are important."[5]

As with most personality, behavior, and physical traits, we are born with certain genetic predispositions in regard to attention, but the environment in which we live plays a critical role in determining how those predispositions materialize. Researchers in this area have moved away from descriptions of traits as either genetic or environmental and are instead focusing their attention on understanding how gene-environment interactions shape us. It is no longer a matter of nature *or* nurture but rather nature *and* nurture.

Among the simplest examples of such interactions is adult height. At birth, our genes set a ceiling on how tall we may become, but how we eat determines whether we reach that ceiling. For example, severely malnourished toddlers who are adopted into U.S. families grow rapidly as they begin to eat higher-calorie, more nutritious diets. In their native environment, they may not have reached their genetic potential, but in their new one, they will. Differences in height within the developed world, where almost everyone is well fed, are largely genetic; differences in height between those in the developed world and those in the developing world are largely environmental.

ADHD develops fully only when there is a very strong genetic predisposition with a small environmental contribution or when there is a moderate genetic risk coupled with a moderate environmental risk. And while you can't change your children's genes, you *can* modify their environment.

TELEVISION AND ATTENTION

Television is mesmerizing for young children. Even children with ADHD, who can pay attention to little else for meaningful periods of time, can stay focused on TV programming for hours. Much of what we know about children's attention to television comes from the makers of *Sesame Street,* who devoted considerable resources and energy to determining what makes children stay focused on the screen.[6] Researchers for *Sesame Street* even employed a "distractor" test in which a screen was placed at a 45-degree angle to a television and displayed images at fixed intervals. If a child was distracted (i.e., if she took her eyes off the TV to look at the slides), it was deemed that the program content wasn't sufficiently interesting.

For example, early research during the development of *Sesame Street* found that children will focus on the letter *J* on the screen for longer periods of time if it is animated than if it remains static. This research drove many programming decisions for *Sesame Street*. One of the reasons the show adopted a magazine format was that frequent short clips held children's interest better than longer ones. In its early shows, there were as many as 30 segments in an episode.

The producers of *Sesame Street* were determined to find ways to teach young children, particularly those in the inner city who don't have access to high-quality nursery schools or kindergartens. Doing so required capturing their attention, or at least directing their gaze toward the television. As Harold Howe, U.S. commissioner of education in 1968, mused, "Can a daily television program filled with elements of learning attract and hold the attention of 4- and 5-year-olds—particularly those from deprived homes—in free competition with animated cartoons and 'shoot-'em-ups'?" To succeed in this gamble, the producers turned to the same tricks that had become increasingly common in children's commercial fare: quick cuts and flashy graphics.

One of the central ways that television succeeds in maintaining the gaze of children is through the orienting response. First described by Ivan Pavlov (the guy with the famous dogs) in 1927, the orienting response can be thought of as the "what's that?" reflex, a manifestation of the brain's keen interest in something new or unexpected. It's easy to see why this is (and more important, was) critical to humans' survival. A new sight or sound could be a sign of imminent danger, and the brain quickly evolved to give that input instant, undivided attention until it could be reassured that the new stimulus did not pose a threat. A sudden rustling of grass could be a predator creeping up on the savanna: Stop gathering food and check it out!

By design, television programs exploit our orienting response. In contrast to the pace at which real life unfolds, television programs constantly change scenes, sounds, and images. Commercials frequently have disconnects between the visual images and the soundtrack in order to challenge and therefore refocus the brain on their content. Purveyors of children's television programming are keenly aware of this response as well.

Consider the immensely popular *Baby Einstein* series. The testimonial section of its Web site states, "Simply put, these videos are miracle devices for calming crying, fussy babies," and "We first introduced *Baby Einstein* to our daughter when she was only 6 months old . . . she was totally mesmerized by the images." The truth is, babies *are* transfixed by these videos, and the rapid scene changes are a big part of the reason.

We recently purchased a baby video that makes educational claims and viewed it to ascertain the pace of scene changes. A random 20-second segment of the video, which was billed as a depiction of farm life, had five scene changes, or one every 4 seconds. Think about your last visit to a farm. Were you in the barn 1 minute and in the middle of a cow pasture 3 seconds later? In the midst of that visit, did a cartoon cowboy emerge out of nowhere riding a bucking bronco? Adult viewers frequently find the pacing of such videos discombobulating because the content is incoherent. Young infants aren't capable of understanding the content, and they don't try to create a narrative from these images. For them, it isn't a day on the farm at all; it's just a series of stimuli coming at them full throttle. They will sit in front of the 30-minute feature not because they are interested in the content but because they are biologically programmed not to look away.

In contrast, early television, including children's programming, grew out of radio shows. Most early TV shows were slow paced; they involved few scene changes and very little editing for quick cuts. Children's programs were often just films of the live performances of colorful characters such as clowns, cowboys, and cops. Among the most popular were shows like *The Howdy Doody Show* and *Captain Kangaroo*, which involved short skits and songs. (Think of the character of Woody in the popular *Toy Story* movies—his entire plotline centers on his being a cast-aside relic of this bygone era of children's television.)

Mister Rogers' Neighborhood, which first aired in 1968, featured a primary character speaking slowly and deliberately. His show predominantly relied on two sets: his living room and the Land of Make Believe, with the transition from one to the other made via a train. The first episode featured Mr. Rogers visiting a neighbor to see the collection of lamp shades in her home. Yet the show kept its viewers' interest because of Mr. Rogers' natural appeal. As Fred Rogers himself said, "I'm not a character on *Mister Rogers' Neighborhood*. I don't think of my time away from the studio as my 'real' life. What I do in the studio is part of my real life, and the person on camera is the real me. I think children appreciate having a real person talk with them." As you'll see in Chapter 4, the "real life" presented by Mr. Rogers on screen helps children learn to share and be kind, but it also, by design, takes place in real time.

Mister Rogers' was an exception to an emerging trend. In the 1960s, as television matured as a medium, producers began to rely less on live performers and puppets and more on quick cuts, rapid scene changes, and especially animation. By substituting animation for the plodding process of creating content that would interest and appeal to children, the producers were able to keep children's attention while reducing costs. *The Howdy Doody Show* was replaced by *The Flintstones*.

With the new production techniques came new concerns. As we mentioned at the beginning of this chapter, by the early 1970s, educators, researchers, and children's advocates began to theorize that television might overstimulate developing brains, laying a foundation for subsequent inattention when the "real" world was too slow paced and boring by comparison. In the intervening years, research has shown that those preliminary theories had some merit.

Before we turn to the evidence on the relationship between television viewing and attention span, it's worth taking a moment to consider how such a relationship may work. As we discussed in Chapter 1, the overall impact of TV on children's development is directly related to three things: how much television children watch, what they watch, and how they watch. A child's degree of attention to television is part of *how* he watches it. And how might watching TV consequently reduce the child's ability to stay focused and pay attention? There are three possible mechanisms for it: structural changes in the brain, habits of mind, and language acquisition.

THE YOUNG BRAIN: A WORK IN PROGRESS

To determine a child's ability to pay attention, we must first consider the age of the child. The first 2 to 3 years of life are critical periods for the development of young children's brains. A newborn's brain triples in size by age 2. By age 7, it has reached 90 percent of adult size. As the brain grows, connections between cells called neurons form at a very rapid pace. These connections, or synapses, can be thought of as the wiring of the mind, and they form the basis for the processing of thoughts. Think of all the extraordinary changes that infants progress through in those early years of life—from being unable to walk or speak to becoming freely mobile and understanding and producing language. All of these changes occur in the context of, and in response to, external stimulation.

When you think about it, it makes perfect sense that infants are born with underdeveloped brains. Unlike having their brains develop in utero, a place with a steady state of conditions quite different from the diverse situations presented by the "real" world, this unfinished quality allows the postnatal fine-tuning of children's brains to happen within the very world they will continue to inhabit. The basic structure of children's brains, therefore, can be adapted for the demands of their particular world.

For many children, television is a big part of their world from a very young age. Children under the age of 3 are awake for only 10 to 12 hours per day. If they watch 2 to 3 hours of television during that time, 20 to 30 percent of their waking hours are spent in front of a screen. The question is, can this much stimulation from television have a direct effect on brain development?

Scientists can't look closely at children's brains, but we can look at rats' brains. When we do, we see that they actually look different depending on how much visual stimulation they got as pups. The more stimulation, the more dense the neuronal connections, or synapses, are. In fact, if rats are kept entirely in the dark for long enough during this critical window, they will be permanently blind. In other words, rats' brains adapt to their environment early on, and this adaptation quickly becomes irreversible.

The same is true for human beings. As a child watches television at an early age, his brain is being conditioned to take advantage of the particular kind of stimulus that television affords. That conditioning may prove damaging when the child tries to process stimuli from other, slower-paced sources.

HABITS OF MIND

Shaping structural changes in the developing brain is one way television may impact children's emerging attention spans. Another, less dramatic but equally important way is that television viewing may change children's habits of mind. The ability to stay focused is not entirely determined by a person's brain structure or genes. Interactions with the environment can also play a role in *teaching* focus. Children's natural inquisitiveness can have its own special rewards—rewards that can foster that inquisitiveness and greater persistence with a task. For example, once she is shown the toy's marvel, a 2-year-old will turn a Jack-in-the-box handle to experience the thrill of Jack popping out. She may do it again and again—both for the rush and to further solidify the causal relationship between turning the handle and having Jack appear. The longer a child looks at the toy and the longer she plays with it, the more engaged she can become. In fact, she can become downright studious. This training can carry over to other things, so once presented with a new, different toy, she may explore it more fully to see what she might learn from it and figure out what it might do.

Interest begets attention, which begets further interest, in a self-reinforcing and positive cycle. But this is not true of all stimuli. If a Jack-in-the-box catches your child's fancy, he can explore it for as long as he wants. If he likes a book that is being read to him, he can signal that he wants to pause on a page longer. But he can't keep the television set from switching scenes; it's entirely out of his control. Television viewing may therefore cheat children of the opportunity to practice concentrating. Instead, it provides them with a model of rewarded distractibility that they carry with them to other tasks as they get older.

To get a sense of the importance of how different a child's own pacing is from that of television, try a simple experiment. Read a picture book to your young child, but don't turn the pages when you finish reading the text on each page. Let your child turn the pages or indicate when he is ready for you to turn them, and pay attention to how long your child examines an image. We did this informal experiment with an 18-month-old boy named Julius while reading *Goodnight Moon* and similar board books. Julius looked at the images carefully, waiting anywhere from 5 seconds to over a minute, with an average of 15 to 30 seconds, before reaching to turn the page. Unfamiliar pictures provoked longer looks. By contrast, television shows change images every 7 to 8 seconds on average for educational shows like *Sesame Street* or *Barney & Friends* and every 3 to 4 seconds for noneducational shows like *Winnie the Pooh* or *Scooby-Doo*.[7] As mentioned above, rapid scene changes may keep children's focus, but they don't allow them to devote their full attention to the scene.

Television foreshortens a child's natural drive to control and achieve long looks at a specific scene. It also prevents interaction with the world. Children are born with brains keenly interested in the stimuli around them. They love to look at their parents and caregivers, who smile in return; they stare in wonder at their own hands as they move; and they listen and react to sounds. Babies just a few weeks old begin to imitate facial expressions. As children age, they begin to interact with the world around them, and these interactions help to form identity and personality. When a large part of a baby's environmental influence comes from television or videos, her brain will develop in response to that influence, particularly if television is very different from other environmental influences to which she is exposed. Ask yourself what types of environmental influences seem more important for your baby's brain to adapt to: a book, a toy, or a television screen?

Many people complain that television is inherently passive, that children don't seem to do anything while watching it. While this observation is not entirely wrong, it may be misplaced as a criticism. As we'll discuss in Chapter 3, children who watch television are capable of actively thinking about what they're watching, and they frequently engage in other activities while doing so. To an outside observer, being read to also seems to involve the passive participation of the child, although no one has ever suggested that books may be bad for children's attention span. One major difference between being read to and watching television is that *television keeps the child's attention for long periods without the need for adult interaction.*

When a child watches television on her own, she can't ask questions. Her attention is less often drawn to things that she may personally be interested in or are appropriate for her developmental stage. She is typically not encouraged to repeat words or to answer questions (although high-quality educational shows do incorporate this). Yet these elements of child-directed control and interaction are all present when a parent reads to a child.

Television holds a child's attention through the orienting reflex—through rapid scene changes, fast action, and a dramatic soundtrack.

When you read to your child, she is kept engaged by personalized interaction. When your son plays on his own with pots and pans in the kitchen, he is kept engaged through the excitement of self-directed discovery. When your daughter climbs on the jungle gym, she is kept engaged by the joy of physical accomplishment. By contrast, the one feeling that is never expressed (or for that matter, felt) when a child watches television is *"I did it!"* Yet this simple experience is among the most important in a child's developing sense of self.

TELEVISION, LANGUAGE DELAY, AND ADHD

Another way television may shorten attention span is by delaying language acquisition. Some researchers hypothesize that language delay or language deficits may be to blame for the development of ADHD.[8] According to this theory, young children use language to direct themselves as they engage in tasks. A 2-year-old, for example, may say, "I'm making a pile!" as she stacks up pebbles at the beach. This verbal self-direction, whether said aloud or to herself, improves her concentration by reminding her what the current task is and by cutting down on distractions. "I'm making a pile" means "I am *not* looking at the seagulls flying overhead" and "I am *not* listening to the sounds of the surf." But television may delay or inhibit this kind of verbal self-direction. Think about it: Can you imagine a kid proclaiming, "I'm watching TV!" with the same gusto as when she congratulates herself for stacking pebbles on the beach?

This effect is particularly pronounced with TV viewing early in life. In fact, even shows like *Sesame Street* are good for 3- to 5-year-old children's cognitive development yet harmful to their cognitive and linguistic development when viewed prior to age $2\frac{1}{2}$.[9, 10]

How can this be? It could be simply a matter of displacement—television interaction is not human interaction. Parents use a special language when talking to babies and toddlers (what linguists call motherese or parentese) that uses simpler syntax and sounds and more repetition than normal speech. Amazingly, this type of speech comes naturally not just to parents but to all humans. Even 6-year-olds use it when talking to infants. With the exception of a very few educational shows, this kind of language is absent from television. When trying to teach infants language, taped voices don't seem to be adequate to the task.[11] A colleague of ours at the University of Washington, Patricia Kuhl, PhD, conducted an experiment in which she asked native speakers of Mandarin Chinese to go to daycare centers to read Mandarin books aloud and chat in Mandarin while playing with 9-month-old babies from English-speaking households. Another group of babies was read to and spoken to only in English. This was done three times a week for 4 weeks.

After several weeks of this, the two groups of babies were tested to see whether they turned their heads to pay attention to someone speaking Mandarin, using words that were completely unlike any English words. The babies who had been read to in Mandarin turned their heads when they heard the Mandarin words, while those who had been read to only in English were completely uninterested in the Mandarin words and didn't turn their heads. Dr. Kuhl then repeated the experiment with a new group of babies, this time using carefully produced DVDs of Mandarin speakers or English speakers reading books and playing with toys. The DVDs were produced to realistically mimic the interaction with the children as much as possible. This time, after the completion of the 4 weeks of reading and playing, the babies who had viewed the Mandarin DVDs showed no greater interest in the Mandarin words than did the babies who had viewed the English DVDs.

Dr. Kuhl's conclusion—and we agree—is that the format of video somehow interrupts the language-learning mechanism inherent in the process of an adult reading aloud to a child.[12] This disruption may delay the child's ability to verbally direct himself, a skill that's a critical part of focusing attention.

Television viewing can displace time with adult caregivers and thereby delay language acquisition, and for some children, these language problems could lead to the development of ADHD. Truthfully, there is no substitute for real human interaction in this age group.

WHAT SCIENCE TELLS US: TELEVISION VIEWING AND ATTENTION SPAN

Repeated studies have found that children with shorter attention spans watch more television than do children with longer ones. This fact probably will not surprise the parents of any child who has been diagnosed with attention deficit disorder. Many such parents tell Dimitri at his clinic, "All we can do to keep our child calm is set him in front of the television." These studies tell us little except that there is an association between watching television and having a shortened attention span. It may be that television causes short attention span, or it may be that it is soothing for children who already have short attention spans (or it may give their beleaguered parents a much-needed respite!).

Some experimental studies have suggested that television reduces attention span. In the very first study of its kind, conducted in 1973 by Lynette Friedrich, PhD, and Aletha Huston Stein, PhD, of the University of Texas, 93 preschool children were randomly divided into three groups. Each group watched a specific show three times a week for 4 weeks. The first group watched *Batman*, the second watched *Mister Rogers' Neighborhood*, and the third watched other "nonviolent commercial television programming"—the equivalent of *Dora the Explorer* today. After the study period, research assistants observed the children in a simulated classroom environment. Children who watched *Batman* were noted to have considerably less tolerance for delay and were more impulsive. These children exhibited symptoms similar to characteristics of ADHD.[13]

In 2000, a similar experiment was conducted by Eugene Geist, PhD, and Marty Gibson of Ohio University, who randomly placed 62 children in three groups. One watched *Power Rangers,* another watched *Mister Rogers' Neighborhood,* and a control group engaged in age-appropriate play.[14] After spending 30 minutes doing these activities, the children who watched *Power Rangers* were observed to have shorter attention spans than those in the other two groups. This group of kids spent *50 percent less* time on a given task than the group who had not watched television (3 minutes compared to 6 minutes). There was no difference between the children who played or watched *Mister Rogers',* which isn't surprising given that the show takes place in real time.[15]

If the true effects of television viewing occur over long periods of time with repeated exposures, they may not be well measured by such short experiments, which typically last an hour or less. Perhaps it's necessary to expose children to more than 30 to 40 minutes of television over many days (as parents often do) to show the true effects. But again, it's not only the "how much" but also the "what" that determines the effects. These experiments further suggest that perhaps it isn't *any* television that affects children's attention but rather certain *kinds* of television. Remember, in the study mentioned above, the effect on children's behavior of watching *Mister Rogers' Neighborhood* was indistinguishable from that of playing, while the effect of watching *Power Rangers* was striking.

Finally, as we have discussed, given the special and important development of the brain in the first few years of life, it's certain that watching television as a preschooler has different effects than watching it as an infant under the age of 2. And it is in the under-2 age group that "how much" television can have an especially marked impact.

These observations formed the basis for a study we conducted, previously mentioned in Chapter 1, which was published in the respected journal *Pediatrics.* We looked at 1,354 children from across the United States, more than 10 times the number in the largest previous study. Our hypothesis was that television viewing during that critical window of brain development, before the age of 3, would lead to subsequent attention problems. In our study, when the children were 1 year of age and again when they were 3, each mother was asked how much television her child watched on a typical day. Then, when the children were 7, the mothers were asked a series of questions about their children's ability to pay attention, including whether they were impulsive or restless, had difficulty concentrating, or were easily confused. (These are some of the core symptoms of ADHD.[16] However, we must note that we did not have data on formal ADHD diagnoses.)

What we found was that for each additional hour per day of television (including videos) that children watched during the first 3 years of their lives, the chance of having a level of attention problems consistent with ADHD was increased by 9 percent. Put another way, a child who watched 2 hours of television a day before age 3 would be almost 20 percent more likely to have attention problems at age 7 than a child who watched none. A child who watched 3 hours was 30 percent more likely, and so on.

Our study also found that reading to children, taking them to museums, or telling them stories was associated with increased attention at age 7. As discussed earlier, attention is something that develops well in response to child-directed activity and interaction with adults, and the newborn brain conditions itself to its environment. Please use this window of opportunity to help your child's brain maximize its capacity for these all-important life skills!

STARTING MINDFUL VIEWING EARLY

We've seen how current research suggests that television viewing early in life can shorten children's attention spans. What can you do to help make

TV a positive influence on your own children's growing mind and attention? As always, the answer boils down to what your children watch, how much they watch, and how they watch it. In 2001, the American Academy of Pediatrics recommended that children watch no television in the first 2 years of life and that subsequent viewing be both carefully selected and minimized.[17] And despite television's allure as a "lifesaver" for new parents—and we do know how alluring it can be!—we must agree that you should avoid letting your children under 2 watch TV. There is no proven educational value at this age, and as we've shown in this chapter, there is considerable cause to be concerned about potential harm. But we know how rough it can be when you're almost at the end of your parenting rope, so in Chapter 9, we'll talk about alternative ways of handling situations when you absolutely need a break.

For older children, choose shows that engage them through challenging and interesting content, not flashy graphics, rapid scene changes, or a noisy soundtrack. Pay attention to how rapidly images cycle on the screen—in general, longer segments tend to be better. You want your children to *think* about what they see, not just look at it. Look for signs of engagement and ask them what they liked about a program when it's over. Did they get something positive out of it? Try to determine if they were paying attention well enough to tell you what it was about. If not, think about how you can help them pay better attention next time.

The possible dangers of television for children's attention spans are real, and while any potential for risk should be taken seriously, it need not be overblown. If you limit television viewing for young children and choose carefully for older children, you will avoid the worst of these dangers. As babies become preschoolers and then grade-schoolers, an important part of your television decisions will lie in choosing appropriate, educational content. As you'll see in the next chapter, parents typically have a lot to learn about both the potential and the pitfalls of educational television.

HOW TO MAKE TV WORK FOR YOUR CHILDREN'S ATTENTION

- Avoid television viewing for children age 2 and under.
- For children 2 and older, choose shows that engage through challenging and interesting content, not flashy graphics or a noisy soundtrack.
- Choose shows that aren't rapidly sequenced.
- Be sure to provide real-time cognitive stimulation for your young children (reading, singing, playing with blocks, and so on) to offset the effects of television viewing.

CHAPTER 3

GOING TO SCHOOL: TELEVISION AND EDUCATION

All television is educational television. The question is: What is it teaching?

Nicholas Johnson, University of Iowa law professor, former federal communications commissioner, and author of How to Talk Back to Your Television

Caitlin is loudly imitating a snoring person one morning as she comes into her parents' room at 5:30 a.m. "I'm sleepwalking!" she announces gleefully. Her now-awake parents chortle ruefully and haul themselves out of bed to begin the day. At 3½, Caitlin is an active, happy child, eager for learning at every opportunity. She sees these opportunities as beginning before 6:00 in the morning, and she doesn't stop to nap. By the time she goes to sleep around 8:00 p.m., her parents are completely exhausted. Although they try to keep up with her enthusiasms, the arrival of Caitlin's younger sister, Sophia, has recently tapped out their energies. With considerable hesitation and some guilt, they have begun putting her in front of the television for a half hour every day. They try to choose high-quality shows, but they're not sure exactly what that means. They steer clear of what they consider to be the worst cartoons, but beyond that, how to choose? Sesame Street *is okay, but what about* Winnie the Pooh? *What about* Scooby-Doo?

Is Caitlin's exposure to television helpful, harmful, or neutral for her cognitive development? Can her viewing be improved? In this chapter, we'll discuss the enormous potential of television to be educationally beneficial. We'll also discuss some of the pitfalls and common mistakes parents make concerning educational TV. You'll see how the quantity of television viewed (how much), its content (what), and the context in which it is viewed (how) interact to determine whether or not it will help your children learn to recognize numbers, letters, and abstract concepts like the grouping of similar items into sets.

Parents turn on educational television for many different reasons. Some have specific learning objectives in mind, such as reading; others are trying to satisfy their children's general curiosity; and still others, like Caitlin's parents, turn it on to keep an active child engaged and to buy themselves some time. Whatever the disparate reasons, very few parents know how to make educational television really work for their children.

THE UNEXAMINED TELEVISION IS NOT WORTH VIEWING

Most parents recognize that there is some "good" television for young children, but few actually know what makes a good show, and fewer still know how the value of good shows can be enhanced. It may surprise some parents to learn that television is not absolutely good or bad for a child's intellectual development; its effects depend on what is watched and how it is watched.

Preschoolers and other children are not passive when they watch television, and parents can do several things to influence how actively their children are engaged by the content they view. When watching television, children rarely devote their full attention to the screen. On average, preschool children look at the screen about 60 percent of the time, even when they're actively watching a show.[1] What determines when children pay attention to the screen and when they look away? When they're very young, they pay attention to the salient features—the flashy graphics and quick cuts, as you saw in Chapter 2. As they get older—into their preschool and elementary school years—they begin to pay attention to content that is challenging and informative.[2-5] Like adults, children pay attention when something interesting is happening and look away when there's nothing worth paying attention to. (Of course, even older children and adults continue to be captivated by cheap tricks!)

When children hear other children's voices on TV, they look because they assume that other kids—the ones on the screen—will be interested in the same things they are. They are less interested in adult voices. They pay attention to loud noises and to music. Flashy screen graphics and quick edits get their attention, but so does a calm discussion of things that they can understand. Like adults, children also pay attention to content that is somewhat challenging: They like things that they can understand but that are new or different to them. In short, *children want to learn from television and will focus their attention most when they can learn the most.* Content that's too difficult to understand turns them off; content that's too simple or easily understood can become boring.

Children, like adults, have the capacity to be actively engaged in choosing which content they pay attention to and which they turn away from. Finding shows that are at just the right level for your children takes some effort, and later in this chapter, we will show you how to do it.

As much as children want to try to learn from television, TV is also a form of entertainment, and children can be induced to watch it for hours purely to be entertained, without learning anything. A major determining factor of how children approach television is how they are taught to think of it. If you teach your children that TV is primarily entertainment, they will have low expectations of the demands that it will make and will consequently invest less mental effort in watching it. As a result, they won't retain or understand as much of what they see. But if you teach them that television is a fun, educational, and informative way to experience the world, they will want to invest some mental effort in the experience, and they'll expect to learn something exciting from it.[6-10] You needn't view the television as the idiot box in your house any more than you would the computer. In fact, viewing it as more than just a means of entertainment will enhance its value to your children's cognitive development.

Much research has demonstrated that kids' degree of investment in their activities improves their learning. For example, Gavriel Salomon, PhD, of the University of Haifa in Israel, had half of a group of elementary school–age children watch a film called *A Day of a Painter;* the other half read the story. Not surprisingly, kids in the reading group showed much better comprehension of the story than those in the watching group. One important reason was that those who watched the film invested less mental effort than those who read the story. A major determinant of how well the children did was how much effort they thought they would have to invest in either the print or television version. The more effort they thought was needed, the more they put into it, and the more they learned. Dr. Salomon found that it was possible to induce children to invest more mental effort in the TV version simply by telling them it was important and that they should pay careful attention.[11]

For younger children, literally telling them to pay attention and learn from TV probably won't work. The best way to convey this message is to take an active and obvious interest in what your children do learn and to reinforce not only the content of what they're learning but also the learning process itself. Actively modify the context—the "how"—of your children's viewing. If your children see you watching documentaries and the news and then commenting on what you've seen, they'll pick up the message that television is informative and takes some concentration. Conversely, if they see you watching only entertainment shows, they will come to view TV as a relaxing pastime that doesn't make any demands on their attention or intelligence. If they see you watching rarely and selecting shows carefully, they will learn that television is to be used selectively. If you turn on the TV and surf aimlessly in search of anything that catches your attention, they will come to see television as worthless fluff. When you talk about programs with your partner and your children, you add substance to the medium, and the kids will begin to see that it's worthy of conversation, like their schoolwork or friends or feelings.

The perceived function of television (for education or for entertainment) has even been studied at a national level. One study compared two countries: Israel, in which the primary view of television was as a source of information, and the United States, where the primary view of TV was as entertainment. The researchers found that in Israel, children invested more mental effort in watching television and as a result not only remembered better what they saw but also understood it more deeply than did kids in the United States.[12]

TUNE IN FOR LEARNING

We recently queried some parents of preschool children about how they viewed specific shows. It wasn't surprising that almost 100 percent thought of *Sesame Street* as educational, but it is surprising that only 35 percent thought of *Blue's Clues* that way. This is a common problem. Most parents are unaware of the variety of high-quality educational programs that are available, and many can't even say whether their children's favorite shows are educational or not. A survey of parents' views of television done in 2000 found that the seven shows most likely to be cited as educational for children included *Oprah* and *Who Wants to Be a Millionaire*.[13] More surprising, 16 percent of parents of children ages 8 to 16 considered *The Simpsons* to be educational, and 33 percent actively encouraged their children to watch the Cartoon Network on the grounds that it was educational. (Homer Simpson himself speaks cogently to the educational value of many cartoons, pointing out that "if *The Flintstones* has taught us anything, it is that pelicans can be used to mix cement.") Not surprisingly, children are no better in their judgments. Many of them rate *Judge Judy* as an educational show, and we can only guess that's because it features an inside look at the school of hard knocks.

These shows are not educational as defined by researchers. No doubt *The Simpsons* and *Oprah* have much to teach us about human nature and American culture, but they are not designed primarily to educate children, and their value as educational TV has never been tested. Similar shows, such as *Power Rangers* and *Teletubbies*, have been tested, however, and have been shown to slow children's development in vocabulary, reading, and math skills.[14]

Parents and children are not to blame for their ignorance of educational TV; information about which shows are educational is inconsistent and hard to find. Sometimes the shows themselves are hard to find: One Philadelphia station complied with the FCC rule to have regularly scheduled children's educational programming but preempted it 50 percent of the time.[15] And on the FOX network, *The Magic School Bus* aired before 3:00 p.m., when most children have not yet boarded the real school bus for home.[16] Although the networks identify which of their programs are children's shows, these ratings are almost useless for parents. FOX and NBC, for example, have both claimed that sports shows are children's educational television. One local station listed *The Jetsons* as educational on the grounds that it teaches children "what life will be like in the 21st century."[17] Here we are in the 21st century, and we're still waiting for our floater cars.

Experts in child learning classify television programs as educational if their primary intent is to educate and if they have a curriculum—that is, if they have some specific educational objectives for the children who watch their shows. *Sesame Street*, for example, has a long list of carefully considered and specific instructional goals developed by experts, including everything from "I.A.2. Given a printed letter, the child can select the identical printed letter from among a set of printed letters" to "IV.A.1.b. The child can specify whether he or she will grow up to be a mother or a father."[18]

These strict and explicit criteria read like a teacher's manual—and that's what they are. Why shouldn't the standards for educational shows be just as rigorous as classroom curricula? They have been shown to be instrumental in helping producers both develop and test content against an objective standard: Do children learn the lesson from the television show or not? Specific criteria such as these are necessary if television is to serve the educational needs of children.[19] Children need shows designed with specific criteria because they are literalists—they take everything on television at face value. They aren't good at extracting general lessons from a mass of material, and even content that would seem obviously educational to adults may have no take-away points for children. Just because your favorite children's book has been turned into a television show doesn't make it educational.

A case in point: One study assessed the educational value of a film produced in Sweden about Finnish immigrant children. The film's producers thought they were sending a clear message that the Finnish children were, on the whole, much like Swedish children and that they should therefore be accepted and not ostracized by the Swedes. Yet when the film was shown to a group of 5-year-olds, the children could accurately report details of the film but had no idea what the message was.[20] When the producers of *Sesame Street* tested a show about divorce with a group of children, they found that the kids took away the idea that if their parents fought, they would get divorced. (Not surprisingly, the show never aired.) Similar research on children as old as 12 has found that children are generally unable to understand an overarching message from a television program—or even to grasp the notion that there could be a message. If children are to learn anything from programming, the messages have to be extremely explicit and direct.

In 1998, a group of educational experts and psychologists got together through the Annenberg School for Communication at the University of Pennsylvania to review the educational value of television shows, with a particular emphasis on shows rated as educational and informative (E/I)

by the broadcasters. Shows on cable television were not formally evaluated because cable networks aren't bound by the same educational programming laws as broadcast networks are. According to the criteria used
by experts to define educational television (having an explicit curriculum
or set of age-appropriate learning objectives and being designed around
this curriculum), only about one-quarter of shows whose networks listed
them as educational truly were. About half were somewhat educational,
and one-quarter were not at all educational.

The best shows were ones with a clear educational approach, such as
Bill Nye the Science Guy and *Beakman's World*, both of which featured
wacky, live hosts who taught kids about specific principles of science, such
as how air pressure inflates a balloon or how momentum keeps objects in
motion. The minimally educational shows were those like *Wheel 2000*, a
version of *Wheel of Fortune* in which the contestants were preteens, and
Oscar's Orchestra, an animated series about mute musical instruments that
attempted to expose children to classical music. In between were a variety
of children's animal shows and animated series like *101 Dalmatians* and
Winnie the Pooh.[21]

Ignorance about the educational value of television is unfortunate
because there are some wonderful educational shows—including many
that deserve much wider recognition. The oldest and one of the best is, of
course, *Sesame Street*.

SWEEPING THE CLOUDS AWAY

The beloved children's show *Sesame Street* has been shown to improve
children's reading, vocabulary, attitudes toward school, acceptance of differences from others, and cooperation with other children. The show is
targeted at children 2 to 5 years old, and many studies show that children
in this age range who watch *Sesame Street* for an hour a day often benefit
from the experience.[22-28] The idea for *Sesame Street* was hatched in the

1960s, when few nursery schools existed and even kindergarten was not universal, particularly for disadvantaged children in the inner city. The idea was to create a show that would give kids a heads-up and a head start that would promote a smooth transition to school. But to achieve its goals, it had to be entertaining enough to hold kids' interest. From the beginning, the producers and founders built both solid education and entertainment into the makeup of *Sesame Street*. The educational content was built around learning objectives that emerged from the careful deliberation of a panel of experts. This panel included academic experts in child development and education as well as practicing teachers, community activists, musicians, and artists (such as Maurice Sendak, author of many beloved children's books and incidental cartoon chronicler of the experts' deliberations).[29]

Each episode of *Sesame Street*, and each segment of each episode, was carefully tested with a group of children before being broadcast. Imagine the scene: A group of 3-, 4-, and 5-year-olds sat facing a television, watching the antics of a big, yellow bird-puppet or a man carrying two strawberry cream pies down stairs, while nervous researchers watched from behind a one-way mirror, clutching their clipboards and feverishly taking notes on every aspect of the children's reactions. The scientists wanted to make sure that the children were interested, relaxed, and amused. This was hard work for the researchers and nerve-wracking for the producers. By the time the segments were tested, each had been written and produced at considerable expense. But if the children didn't like a segment, it was out. Many segments were significantly changed because the children didn't like them or didn't understand them (like the divorce episode), and some were thrown out altogether—at a loss of large amounts of scarce production dollars and time.[30]

The results were wonderful and worth it. Children who watch *Sesame Street* average a smile or a laugh every 2 minutes, and most parents and older siblings are happy to sit down and laugh along with the 3- to 5-year-olds in the target audience. A whole generation has learned from *Sesame*

Street, and the beneficial effects reach beyond learning basic skills, extending to improved confidence and more positive attitudes toward school in 1st grade. Compared to nonviewers, *Sesame Street* viewers in one study were better able to recognize letters, recognize and name shapes, and sort objects into like and unlike categories. The biggest improvement was in sorting objects (a 20 to 40 percent improvement for viewers as opposed to a 2 to 10 percent improvement for nonviewers), no doubt because of the segment with the memorable ditty "One of these things is not like the other . . ."[31]

 Sesame Street succeeded beyond anyone's wildest dreams. It is a wonderful example of how quality in production can serve educational content. Its success is a testimony to the faith of its creators in the ability of a few dedicated people to make the media environment of children a better place. The show stands as one of the greatest achievements in all of television.

SITTING IN THE THINKING CHAIR

Another great success is the Nickelodeon show *Blue's Clues*. Like *Sesame Street*, it was designed from the ground up, based on modern educational theories, and like *Sesame Street,* it represented a major step forward in children's educational programming. The show features a live host (first Steve and later Joe) and an animated dog (Blue) in an animated set. Each episode revolves around a puzzle that the host must solve with hints and clues from Blue and the help of the viewers. In one episode, for example, the viewers have to help Steve figure out what is Blue's favorite part of bedtime. The clues, which come gradually throughout the episode, are a mirror, a toothbrush, and toothpaste. Along the way, viewers are asked to identify parts of the body during Blue's bath and to shout out which pajamas have certain combinations of colors and patterns. The show boasts several features, such as repetition and interaction, that make it an especially good vehicle for learning.[32, 33]

Experts in child learning have long recognized the importance of repetition and interaction in the learning process. Tell a child something once, and she will probably forget it, but tell her the same thing five times, and she'll probably remember it. Even better, tell her something five times over 5 days, and then you are really teaching. Learning is facilitated all the more if the child is active in the process—not only mentally but also physically. These principles were taken up by the producers of *Blue's Clues* and pushed to the maximum extent possible.

They recognized that television is a natural medium for repetition. By design, the same episode airs five times each week, which makes the show unique among children's educational programs. Children who are regular viewers watch the same content repeatedly and therefore are not only exposed to new knowledge but also have this knowledge reinforced several times.

Repetition is one thing, but it's more challenging to use television to get children actively involved in learning. *Blue's Clues* encourages kids' participation by asking for their help in solving the puzzle around which each episode revolves. Here too the repetition of episodes helps. In our studies, we sometimes encourage parents to have their children watch educational shows such as *Blue's Clues, Sesame Street,* and others. The results are striking: Parents are not only delighted with the content but are pleased with how their children become completely invested in the learning that can take place through these shows. Kids jump up and shout out answers and run to the screen to point out clues. Fred's son Ira sometimes watches *Blue's Clues* on a DVD player with headphones on long airplane and car trips, and it's amusing to hear his periodic joyful shouts along the way. Every once in a while, a word punctuates the silence: "Toothbrush!" "Cows!" "Seven!"

When children watch an episode of *Blue's Clues* several times over the course of a week, they become more actively involved as they develop mastery over the new content in the episode. Research on repeat viewings of the show suggests that children's increasing involvement in the interactive parts of the show probably helps them to remember the content better.[34]

As with *Sesame Street*, the content of *Blue's Clues* is carefully laddered so that children of different ages and skill levels can participate. This laddering is especially important in keeping the interest of children as they watch over the course of the week. For children across a wide age range, the show is just challenging enough to engage them—neither so easy as to be dull nor so difficult as to be off-putting.

Blue's Clues was produced not by public television but by a private network, Nickelodeon. Its success both with children and as an educational vehicle shows that not only is ongoing innovation in children's television possible, it can produce wonderful results as well.

Other educational shows include *Mister Rogers' Neighborhood*, *Dora the Explorer*, and *Barney & Friends*, each of which has been shown in careful research to improve vocabulary, reading skills, cooperative behavior, physical activity, and other important aspects of school readiness. In Appendix 1, we provide a list of many popular shows categorized by the types of educational content at which they excel for children of a variety of ages.

HABITS OF HEALTHY VIEWING

Parents can do a lot to improve the learning value of the educational shows their children watch. First and foremost, pay careful attention to the appropriate age range. Preschool-age children, 3 to 5 years old, can benefit from a host of great educational shows, but children under 2 may suffer by watching the same shows. Between ages 2 and 3, there is a gray zone in which some kids benefit from some shows and others are harmed. The particular effects depend on the specific show and the specific child. For example, in one study, children under the age of 2½ who watched an older version of *Sesame Street* that was designed for 3- to 5-year-olds had a *slower rate* of language acquisition than those who didn't watch it.[35] The reasons for this adverse effect aren't clear, but they may have to do with the fact that children's needs are changing so quickly at this age that a show directed at 3- to 5-year-olds is worse than useless for 2-year-olds. (*Sesame Street* has recently been retargeted for 2- to 4-year-olds.) Very young children are still trying to master the basic sounds of English, and some of the *Sesame Street* characters—especially the Muppets—speak in altered voices. These voices may have been so difficult for very young children to understand that they ended up being confusing. This is just one example of why we advise parents to exercise caution in exposing young children to even educational television.

As we discussed in Chapter 2, age-appropriate viewing is an important part of the context of viewing, or *how* television is viewed. Parents are the best judges of age appropriateness for their children because they know their strengths and weaknesses. Many shows offer age guidelines, but these are loose and often preposterously generous. Many educational shows listed on the otherwise excellent PBS Web site, for example, claim that they are educational for children ages 2 to 7! Parents of 2-year-olds will have to think carefully about whether they want their children watching content designed for children as old as 7, and parents of 7-year-olds would be right to wonder if their children can get anything out of content designed for 2-year-olds.

How do you know if content is age appropriate? The first step is to choose shows with specific educational objectives that you can easily identify. When an episode of *Sesame Street* is "brought to you by the letter *K*," there's no doubt what the objective is. You should ask yourself if this is something that your child can benefit from. Is he ready to start learning letters, or are letters not even on his radar screen yet? Is he still trying to master letters? Has he known all his letters for a long time? The next step is to observe your child watching the show. Does he pay particular attention to the segments where *K* words are used? Does he show any interest in pointing out the letter *K* in books after watching an episode about *K*? Is he perhaps ready to try writing the letter? By paying careful attention to questions like these, you can get a pretty good idea of whether a show is pitched at the right level for your child.

In 2005, we were working on a study about how to redirect children's viewing toward more developmentally appropriate content. One girl (whom we'll call Isabel) in the study was a 5-year-old who watched a lot of TV. Her mother thought this was good because she watched only high-quality educational shows. When our research assistant, Sara, discussed Isabel's viewing habits with her mother, however, it turned out that Isabel wasn't paying all that much attention to the television when she watched and that she "fiddled around a lot" while viewing.

Sara suggested that Isabel was a bright child who had perhaps tapped out the potential of the preschool shows that she had been viewing. Sara and Isabel's mother came to the conclusion that it would be good to try to cut back on Isabel's overall viewing and to redirect it toward content that she would find more challenging. Sara suggested some nature shows on PBS.

The shows were a big hit. Isabel paid much more attention to the TV when she watched and fiddled around less, and her mother consequently benefited from more of a break. Isabel's love of the nature shows began to spill over to other areas, stimulating her interest in the nature topics covered, and she soon acquired new books about African wildlife and endangered sea mammals.

This example shows that sometimes all it takes is a periodic reassessment of a child's needs to make TV a more positive experience for everyone. In Chapter 9, we discuss how you can approach such a reassessment.

Finding shows that are age appropriate (or better yet, developmentally appropriate) is important because by doing so, you not only use your and your child's television time well, but you also send a positive message about the purpose of television. Since children pay attention to appropriately challenging content, if you have them watch TV programming that is "too old" or "too young" for them, you send a message that television is mere time-filling fluff, with nothing of interest or importance to teach them. How much better it is to show children how many marvelous things there are to learn in the world and how television can help introduce them to these wonders—whether reading and counting or, later on, science and geography. You can use television content to motivate children's natural interest in learning in ways that go beyond the show immediately in front of them.

You can help your children's learning even more by tailoring what they watch to what you want them to learn. Different educational shows emphasize different skills. For example, *Sesame Street* excels at teaching basic reading skills; *The Magic School Bus* series teaches about elementary-level science; *Mister Rogers' Neighborhood* teaches pro-social values, such as cooperating and playing well with other children; and *Barney & Friends* and *The Wiggles* are great at getting kids up and moving around. If you're concerned about reading, *Sesame Street* would be a good choice. If you take your active preschooler to the park regularly, *Barney* or *The Wiggles*, which emphasize movement, may not make as much sense.

While children's educational television has been shown to have beneficial effects when viewed by children in the right age range, noneducational television has the opposite effect. Unfortunately, much of what children watch is noneducational. Twenty-three percent of children ages 1 to 5 watch 2 or more hours per day of noneducational television and videos. Sometimes this viewing is counterbalanced by educational viewing, but more frequently, it isn't: 42 percent of children regularly watch no educational television. The TV regimen most likely to improve school readiness, as we mentioned earlier, is to watch only educational television, but fewer than 20 percent of children do so.[36-42]

While watching an enormous amount of educational television has dubious value, watching an enormous amount of noneducational television has clear disadvantages. It may be that parents see noneducational television and videos as a kind of "dessert" to reward their children for consuming their educational fare. If so, this is just as misguided as allowing children to eat more dessert than nutritious food. Nor is it necessary.

Beginning with *Sesame Street*, many of the modern educational programs are highly entertaining and enjoyable for children. There is really no good reason for children to watch noneducational programming when educational shows are so entertaining and widely available on video and DVD.

It may shock you to know that one study found that viewing *Teletubbies* was associated with reductions in both vocabulary and the complexity of language children used.[43] The research isn't clear about exactly why noneducational television is bad as opposed to just neutral. One theory that has gained some currency is that when kids watch a heavy diet of cartoons or other noneducational TV or videos, it takes time away from either better TV or better alternative activities, such as reading or playing with blocks. Research has shown, for example, that parental conversation with children is the major determinant of child language acquisition. A heavy diet of television that displaces this interaction without replacing it with something at least somewhat similar, such as discussions with teachers at preschool or other kids on the playground, would be likely to slow down a child's language development.

CARTOONS: DOING VIOLENCE TO LEARNING

Much of noneducational TV is violent, including that targeted at children—particularly animated shows. Viewing stressful or violent content may alter children's ability to pay attention to content that is not highly charged emotionally.

Violent television is particularly harmful for educational outcomes, even more so than noneducational, nonviolent television. One study found that the adverse effects of watching violent content in preschool continued all the way to high school: Those who had watched a lot of violent TV at age 5 had high school grade point averages 0.07 to 0.29 lower (on a 4.0 scale) in English, math, and science than those of children who hadn't

watched such shows.[44] These children didn't watch adult late-night dramas; they watched cartoons and G-rated animated films. Changing to
more wholesome TV habits early on will pay dividends your preschooler
will continue to realize for years to come.

A LITTLE OF EVERYTHING IS A LOT OF NOTHING

If educational television promotes learning and noneducational TV inhibits it, what happens when kids watch a mixture of educational and noneducational TV, as most kids do? Are the beneficial effects of educational
TV powerful enough to overcome the adverse effects of noneducational
TV? Experts believe that the effects of both types are probably additive,
meaning that a child who watches an hour a day of *Sesame Street* and then
an hour or two of cartoons is probably worse off than a child who watches
no TV at all.

We recently tested this proposition directly, and our findings under-
score the importance of limiting educational viewing to age-appropriate
content.[45] We looked at how much total TV children watched in two age
ranges: under age 3 and from ages 3 to 5. We then assessed the independent effects of this viewing on reading and math outcomes at age 6, when
the children were in 1st grade. (At that time there were no TV programs
or videos for children under age 3 with proven educational value, so all of
the viewing in the under-3 group is by definition noneducational.) We
found that viewing before age 3 was associated with worse scores on tests
of reading and math ability at age 6 and that viewing from ages 3 to 5 was
associated with better scores. The children who watched little television
before age 3 had the best scores in reading and math at age 6, regardless of
how much they watched at ages 3 to 5. The magnitude of the effects of
these different outcomes was great: It was comparable to the effect of the
child's mother having a lower versus a higher IQ. Since there's little proven

educational content for kids under age 3, the safest option for parents is to not allow any television or videos before this age.

This effect is also found in older kids. One New Zealand study found that each hour per day of viewing time for kids ages 5 to 15 was associated with a 30 percent reduction in the likelihood of obtaining a college degree, taking into account the children's IQ and the parents' level of education.[46] With so many parents of preschool children losing sleep over where their kids will go to college, perhaps they should look at the tremendous disadvantage they're not only allowing but in some cases encouraging!

PARENTS' ROLE

Just as important as what and how much TV children are watching is how they are watching it. Parents and other adult caregivers make up an important part of the context of children's television viewing, and parents' attitudes and actions with regard to viewing—even the simple presence of a parent in the room—can transform television viewing from a passive activity with little educational value into one that helps teach children letter recognition, basic math concepts, and, later on, about the wonders of the world around them. Beyond supervising and influencing how much and what kind of television or videos your children watch, what can you do to ensure that they benefit from the experience? How can you encourage mindful viewing of educational content by your children?

You've already seen that whether the parent frames the television experience as primarily educational or primarily entertaining makes a big difference in how much mental effort children invest in TV and accordingly how much they get out of it. We have also discussed the importance of watching age-appropriate educational programs. These are two aspects of the context of television viewing that are important in determining how much children benefit from it.

Another important aspect is interaction. Asking children to recount what happened in a program or quizzing them on what they may have learned helps them understand the educational potential of television and offers a good opportunity for parent-child interaction that in itself can be quite important. One father reported that he set up his own exercise for "which of these things is not like the other" and quizzed his daughter after she watched *Sesame Street*. A busy (but slightly guilty feeling) mother of three parked her twins in front of *Dora the Explorer* while she made dinner and chatted with them about the show while they watched. Her original motivation for chatting with them was to distract them slightly so they wouldn't get hooked on some solitary, nonsocial activity, but she found that as she watched, her questions became more relevant to what they were watching, and they were paying closer attention. Whatever her original intent, this mother inadvertently created a context for viewing the program that enhanced its learning potential for her children.

When you sit and watch educational shows and discuss them with your children or point out things happening on the screen, this interaction can help turn television from a "boob tube" into a teaching tool. But busy parents who are unable to engage in this level of hands-on mediation needn't despair. Although intensive interaction while viewing is helpful, it is not necessary. One fascinating study from the early years of *Sesame Street* found that children learned more from the show when their mothers were in the room while they were watching than when they were absent—even when the mothers were instructed to remain silent throughout![47] It's as if the mere presence of a parent signaled to the child that here was something important and worth paying careful attention to. Something as simple as moving the television into the same room where a parent is making dinner or folding clothes or paying bills can help enhance its value.

This effect can work in the opposite direction, too. Some evidence suggests that the ill effects of noneducational and violent television or videos may be exacerbated when parents watch with children, since the parents' watching is a way of validating the content kids see, whether it's aggressive interactions, advertising, or learning letters. In this sense, *how* you watch magnifies the effects—good or bad—of *what* you watch. You can do a lot to improve the context, but it all comes back to the amount and types of shows children watch. As they get older, these effects persist.

We have a young friend named Bridget who became fascinated with the violin while watching an educational show. Her parents no longer remember what show it was, but it made a big impression on Bridget at the time. When she was ready to begin music lessons, she was very excited, in part because of what she had seen about the violin on TV. Not fully realizing the depth of Bridget's interest in the violin, her mother tried to sign her up for piano lessons—a move that Bridget firmly and loudly rejected. Apparently, her brief exposure to violin music had made a profound impression on her. She subsequently took violin lessons and played for many years, eventually becoming first violin in her city's youth orchestra.

THE GRADE SCHOOL YEARS AND BEYOND

There are no special educational benefits of television for children in grade school and beyond, although the potential for deleterious effects continues. Some shows have educational value—especially science and nature shows, including children's shows such as *3-2-1 Contact*, *Cyberchase*, *Zoom,* and *The Magic School Bus.* Older children may also benefit from watching certain adult documentaries on shows such as *Nova* or *National Geographic.* But parents should be cautious with television and videos when their kids are between the ages of 5 and 15. As you saw earlier, children who watch a lot of television during this time are significantly less likely to pursue higher education, even when IQ is taken into account.

A modest amount of age-appropriate, carefully examined educational television can expand a child's horizons and spark his own interests. But this is the age when many children begin to assert their television independence, and the habits they develop during this period are important ones that tend to reinforce themselves over time.

The kinds of television or videos children watch, as well as their intent in watching—whether to learn or to be entertained—is determined by their interests. At the same time, though, watching particular kinds of shows can deepen this interest. Dimitri's son, Alexi, loves to watch nature shows (*Nova, Science, Nature,* and programs on Animal Planet are his favorites) because of his interest in science and ecology. Over time, continually watching such shows has given him the sense that he has special knowledge of these subjects that not all other children have and has helped him feel more confident in these areas—and this confidence has further spurred his interest. For Alexi, the topic is nature, but the same process can happen with sports, music, travel, cooking, foreign languages—indeed, just about any topic that can be and is regularly presented on television.

What we call a virtuous cycle can develop as children choose to watch challenging or informative content on television. Because they're watching challenging content that they have chosen, children invest more mental energy in their viewing and accordingly get more out of it. As a result of their learning, they excel in these subject areas and are validated in their efforts by teachers and others who see them as especially good in a particular domain. This validation is rewarding to the children, and they perpetuate it by choosing even more challenging and informative things to watch. This virtuous cycle works wonders for building children's confidence as well as their abilities.

Tapping into this cycle effectively takes some savvy selectivity on your part. One common trap some parents fall into is encouraging their children to watch news on television. In addition to the dangers of the violence that's prevalent on the news (reviewed in the next chapter), there is surprisingly little informational value to televised news. The individual news items are short and presented in a flashy, disjointed fashion. After 40 years in the business, Ted Koppel complained upon retirement that "the industry in which I have spent my entire adult life is in decline and distress."[48] Several studies have found that even adults are not able to draw much useful information from television news.[49–51]

One study recently surveyed adults about the main sources of their information about current events and their knowledge of these events. It found that television is the most common source, yet adults who rely exclusively or primarily on TV as a news source are among the least well informed. Their scores on a test of basic knowledge about current issues was below both those of readers of newspapers and magazines and those who got their news primarily from the radio or the Internet.[52]

Documentaries are another matter. They can be useful sources of specific information and can be enjoyed simultaneously by several members of the family to create a common bond. One 6th grader told a researcher the following story.

> *I'm Italian. So my dad caught this Italian show about how our culture was from babies to being grown up. So my dad told me to watch this to see if I wanted to see about my culture and stuff.*[53]

One can easily imagine parents and children pursuing mutual interests relative to Ken Burns's excellent documentaries *Baseball* and *Jazz*. But to be useful, documentaries must be well chosen. There are many high-quality documentaries on television and available for rent on DVD and video, and there are many more poor-quality ones. A television miniseries about Jon-Benet Ramsey, for example, would be a poor choice; *Roots* would be a good one.

When Fred was in graduate school, he had a friend from Brazil named Ricardo, who had two daughters in grade school. When the soccer World Cup started, it was a family event for Ricardo and the girls. They watched all of the final games on TV, which were all the more exciting because the tournament was held in the United States that year, and Brazil made it to the final match, for which Ricardo and his family hosted a party. When

Brazil won the match, beating Italy 3–2 on penalty kicks, the whole room erupted in cheers from graduate students and grade-schoolers alike. Ricardo's daughters, clad in their yellow Brazil uniforms, were clearly delighted to be included in a grown-up party, and they could certainly keep up their end of the soccer chatter. The World Cup helped to both gel and validate their already strong interest in soccer. They would certainly have been no less interested in the game—which they both played quite well, according to Ricardo—if they hadn't been able to watch it on TV, but doing so brought extra excitement and importance to their interest in the sport.

While the World Cup isn't a documentary, televised sports—in moderation—can help sustain interest in athletics and generate a lifelong commitment to healthy activity. (Unfortunately, one pitfall of televised sports that must be kept in mind is the advertising, particularly the heavy dose of beer commercials, a topic that we'll cover in more depth in Chapter 7.) As with any type of content, the quality and quantity also matter, but documentaries (on television or video) and televised sports offer fine opportunities for parents to have family time with their children that is both entertaining and educational.

A POWERFUL SOURCE OF LEARNING

The effects of television and videos are so varied in so many different circumstances that it can be confusing for parents who just want to do what's right for their children. Especially in high doses, TV exercises powerful effects on children's cognitive development, and as we've said, these effects depend on what is watched, how much is watched, and how it is watched. But if you use our suggestions on how to optimize your children's television experience, you can make TV into a powerful source of learning throughout childhood.

You've seen that much of the educational value of television is undermined when it's paired with a heavy dose of violent and aggressive content. But the effects of such viewing extend far beyond just its adverse effect on cognitive development, as we'll explain in the next chapter.

HOW TO MAKE TV WORK FOR YOUR CHILDREN'S LEARNING

- Seek out educational programs that may work for your children. We list some in Appendix 1. You can also refer to the media Web sites in Appendix 2 for more ideas. The networks maintain Web sites for their own shows, but their assessments of educational value are often overly rosy.
- Understand that the broadcast channels' E/I (children's educational and informative) ratings are not useful; don't rely on them to tell you what's appropriate for your children.
- Enhance the educational benefit of the shows your children watch by carefully choosing age-appropriate content. Watch a few episodes of each program with your children and observe whether the three elements of age-appropriate educational viewing are present.

  1. Are your children paying attention and interacting with the program?
  2. Can you tell what the educational objective of the episode is?
  3. After repeated viewing of the same episode, have your children made some progress toward learning the lesson?

- Encourage children to respond to the interactive parts of shows. Ask them afterward which ones they liked.
- For preschoolers, consider doing some of the tie-in educational activities available on the Web sites of most shows, but use your judgment. Some activities clearly have an educational purpose, and some clearly have a marketing purpose.
- For older children, find some tie-in activities of your own. If your children were interested in a documentary about lions, for example, get a

book about lions from the library or do a Web search for additional information. Encourage the curiosity that you see them developing because of TV shows they like.

- Don't invite young children to watch your shows with you, including quiz shows, talk shows, cartoons, and the nightly news. Tell them that just as some beverages (such as coffee and beer) are for grown-ups only, so are some television programs.

- Consider watching carefully chosen documentaries as good opportunities for entertaining learning time together.

- For preschoolers, rent or buy DVDs of educational shows to promote repeated viewing.

- For school-age children, don't expect kids to be able to multitask with homework and TV. Make it a rule that television is acceptable only after homework is done.

- Don't expect kids (or yourself!) to learn about current events from TV. Instead, use TV news as a springboard to reading the newspaper. Better yet, encourage children to learn about current events from the newspaper and save television for things the medium does better, such as documentaries.

CHAPTER 4

NAUGHTY OR NICE? TELEVISION'S EFFECTS ON AGGRESSION AND PROSOCIAL BEHAVIORS

One of the few good things about modern times: If you die horribly on television, you will not have died in vain. You will have entertained us.

Kurt Vonnegut, "Cold Turkey," In These Times, May 10, 2004

Tamara, a smiling, bouncy baby, settles into her mother's lap to watch a serious man on TV play with a toy. The man holds up the toy and begins to manipulate it in a way that would not occur to most babies. He pulls it and prods it, grabbing a little piece. He does this several times, and after a few minutes, the television goes off. Tamara is handed the same toy she has just seen on TV. Without hesitation, she pulls and prods it, grabbing a little piece just as she saw the man do. At just 15 months of age, Tamara is imitating what she sees on TV.

Tamara (not her real name) was participating in a groundbreaking research experiment in the late 1970s.[1] The experiment showed that children can imitate and learn from what they see on TV. The brilliance of this study lay in its simplicity: It used an experimental design to study a very specific behavior. But the experiment's simplicity also proved its limitation. After all, toddlers are mimics by nature; they don't censor what they see to determine whether it is worthy of emulation. The fact that very young children manipulate something as shown on television doesn't mean that older children will imitate other, more complex behaviors. For concerned parents, researchers, and policy makers alike, these facts raise fundamental questions: When and where does imitation stop? Do children imitate the full range of behaviors and actions they see on television?

Many parents wonder not only about whether television leads to aggressive behavior but also about what kinds of programs are most likely to do so. Will *Digimon* make children meaner? Will *SpongeBob SquarePants*? They also wonder whether TV can encourage the kinds of behaviors and attitudes they want to instill in their children. Can *Dora the Explorer* help children share? The role that television plays in promoting what researchers call prosocial behaviors—cooperation and kindness—hasn't gotten as much attention as the role it plays in promoting aggression and violence. This lack of attention in the laboratory and on the front pages is unfortunate because selected television programs can help young children develop these desirable behaviors. In this chapter, we will describe both the positive and negative effects of television, beginning with the negative: violence.

TELEVISION AND VIOLENCE: WHAT'S THE CONNECTION?

The advent of television occurred at a time of considerable social upheaval and a dramatic rise in violence in the United States. Discussion of the role that television may play in violent behavior began in the early 1950s with Congressional hearings on the impact of television violence on juvenile delinquency. In 1968, 5 days after Senator Robert Kennedy was assassinated, President Lyndon Johnson appointed the National Commission on the Causes and Prevention of Violence, which concluded that there was no single cause for the rise of violence but warned the television industry to be more careful in its portrayals of violence. In 1972, U.S. Surgeon General Jesse Steinfeld released a five-volume report expressing concern about the effects of television violence on children, stating that viewing violence "does have an adverse effect on certain members of our society."

How big an "adverse" effect? Who are those "certain members of society"? The notion of a vulnerable subset of the population for whom media violence poses a problem is perpetuated by dramatic news stories. You may recall the tragic story of Lionel Tate, a 12-year-old boy who imitated professional wrestling moves on a 6-year-old girl, with lethal consequences. Tate claimed that he put his friend Tiffany in a headlock and banged her head on a black lacquer table without intending to hurt her. The autopsy results revealed that part of the young girl's liver had detached, suggesting much more extensive and brutal injuries. At the trial, the defense argued unsuccessfully that Tate, who was an enormous fan of World Wrestling Federation telecasts, did not understand that the moves portrayed on television were staged. This tragic story is joined in the popular memory by the infamous one of Dylan Klebold and Eric Harris, the Columbine teenagers for whom the movie *The Basketball Diaries* served as inspiration for a murderous assault on their high school.

These dramatic stories suggest that the connection between media portrayals of aggression and actual aggression plays out in spectacularly tragic ways. In fact, the effects are subtler and therefore more insidious. The most egregious examples exaggerate reality, but they also cover it with a cloak of exceptionalism. Since our children haven't been moved to wield weapons at school, doesn't that mean that they're immune to the effects of media violence? Sadly, no. Aggressive behavior runs the gamut from being rude to a store clerk or cutting someone off on the freeway to committing assault and other violent crimes.

To be sure, television is not the sole cause of aggression. Put another way, the elimination of violent programming (or even the elimination of television altogether) would not put an end to murders and herald the emergence of an entirely congenial society. At the same time, television need not be the root of all aggression in order to represent a significant public health problem in the United States. Even if television violence only increases the chances that *some* people will act aggressively, its impact can be large. Suppose that 1 in 100 people who watch violent programming will be more likely to commit an aggressive act as a result. If 10 million people watch such a show, 100,000 aggressive actions may result. Given the sheer volume of televised aggression, the consequences of even a small effect may be significant. If your child is like the average American child, he will see more than 8,000 murders and more than 100,000 assorted other acts of violence on network television before leaving elementary school. If he sees half that many, it will be a major success on your part, but it would still represent an enormous exposure to violence.

Since the Steinfeld report was issued in 1972, several hundred additional studies (10 times more than had been conducted at the time of the original report) have examined the relationship between violent media content and aggression. Most of these studies have shown that violent programming begets aggression, while a few have shown that it does not. Some have found large effects and some have found small ones, thereby fueling what appears to be a lingering controversy about the effects of pervasive violent programming. But in reality, the controversy has been settled.

A comprehensive review of all existing studies was performed in 1994. Researchers used a statistical methodology called a meta-analysis to synthesize the results of all the studies to produce a single summary measure of the effect of violent programming on aggressive behavior.[2] They concluded that there is a moderate and statistically significant association between watching violent television and behaving aggressively. How big an effect is "moderate"? Consider the graph on the opposite page, which summarizes the relationships among several familiar behaviors and their putative effects. The length of the bars gives some sense of how confident we can be that the answer to each question is yes. Consider as your bench-mark the question about smoking causing lung cancer, something that all of us—including the tobacco companies—now accept as true. And, as you can see, the evidence that media violence leads to aggression is twice as strong as the evidence that doing homework improves academic achieve-ment—a core belief for many parents.

Does Violent TV Really Hurt?[3]

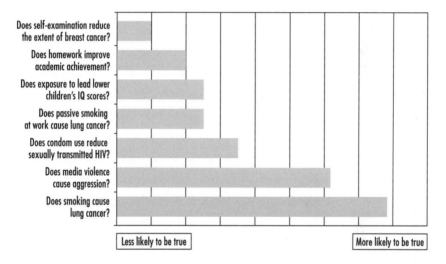

In scientific circles, these data have largely ended the debate about the connection between media violence and aggression, but it remains alive in the American public's mind. Although poll after poll confirms that the vast majority of Americans think that there is too much violence on tele-vision and that it is harmful for children, when asked if their children are being put at risk by televised violence, the majority responded that they are not. In a recent national survey, 80 percent of U.S. adults reported that they thought there was too much violence on television. When asked if they had seen something on television that bothered them, only 7 percent cited a violent portrayal.[4] This discordance may be explained by the fact that survey respondents avoid programming that is offensive to them.

However, when asked to name something that they disliked about programs that had been specifically targeted by Jerry Falwell in the 1970s and 1980s because of violence, only 5 percent of people mentioned violence as a problem with the shows.[5] This disconnect has been called the third-person effect: "Television violence is bad—very bad—but not for my children, only for someone else's." Many of us seem to feel that it's only the parents of the Lionel Tates of the world who need to be vigilant—the parents of "certain" vulnerable members of society. This is simply not the case.

The concern about the effects of violence has spurred some action, and there have been numerous attempts to tone down violence (relying on the industry to police itself), to rate programming to enable parents to make more informed decisions about what their children watch, and to provide technologies (most notably the V-chip, in which *V* stands for "violence") to help minimize children's exposure to TV violence. The V-chip warrants specific comment. Introduced amidst great fanfare and mandated on all new television sets larger than 13 inches sold after January 1, 2000, the V-chip promised a technological solution that would empower parents to control access to violent content. By all accounts, it has failed to deliver on that promise. The reasons are plentiful and include the lack of reliability of current rating systems as well as parental discomfort with the device itself. In 2002, researchers at the Annenberg School for Communication at the University of Pennsylvania gave more than 100 families V-chip-equipped televisions and information on how to use them. One year later, only 8 percent were using them and fewer than one-quarter had ever even tried![6] Surely this is not for lack of opportunity to do so.

Anyone who watches television can attest that there has been no effective reduction in the frequency or intensity of violent content. In fact, it's been shown that the amount of violence on television has remained high and steady. This is particularly true of content intended for young audiences. We had forgotten how much violence there is in children's fare until we had children of our own. We were surprised by how frequently a "family" video has aggression serve as an integral part of the plot. We shouldn't have been. Harvard researchers Fumie Yokota, PhD, and Kimberly Thompson, ScD, analyzed all G-rated animated feature films released in the United States between 1939 and 1999. It was a daunting task involving viewing and coding more than 74 full-length animated features, including such classics as *Bambi* and *Fantasia*; more recent hits, including *A Bug's Life* and *The Lion King;* and some box office bombs like *Little Nemo: Adventures in Slumberland* (not to be confused with the contemporary hit *Finding Nemo*). Every single film they studied had at least one act of violence. The least violent one was *My Neighbor Totoro* by acclaimed Japanese director Hayao Miyazaki, hardly a mainstay on the shelves of U.S. video stores. The researchers further found that the amount of violence portrayed, in terms of time on screen, increased significantly between 1940 and 2000—from about 3 minutes to 10 minutes on average per movie. Half of the films showed at least one character rejoicing in violence by either cheering or laughing.[7]

The situation is similar on the small screen. Between 1994 and 1997, the National Television Violence Study, a collaboration of researchers at four universities, sampled more than 8,000 hours of programming on cable and broadcast television between 6:00 a.m. and 11:00 p.m. Approximately 60 percent included violence, and fewer than 4 percent included an anti-violence theme. These numbers probably don't surprise you. In fact, you may be thinking that it's possible to avoid such problematic fare simply by steering clear of horror movies and news and sticking to good old family fare. Sadly, this is not true. While the nature of the material is entirely different, family series and even family-oriented sitcoms are chockablock with conflict and stress.

Consider *Desperate Housewives,* a show watched regularly by 870,000 children ages 2 to 11. The first two seasons featured scenes such as a woman throwing the contents of her shopping cart at a woman she thought was having an affair with her husband; a woman slugging her husband because he was reluctant to wear a condom; and a woman humiliating her husband by publicly announcing that "he cries after he ejaculates." The show is even more of a hit with the 12-to-17 age group, among which it is currently the fifth most popular show.[8] Many parents know to steer clear of *Desperate Housewives,* but it's important for them to take a careful look at what goes on in reality TV shows and even in family sitcoms, because these are staples of children's viewing. In fact, situation comedies are the most popular shows among elementary school children today.

At a time when children are learning about their own emotions, how to interpret others' emotions, and how to respond appropriately to emotional cues, the pervasiveness of TV viewing and of family sitcoms in particular makes television a cornerstone of children's emotional education. Of course, it's only one corner—along with parental interactions, peer relations, and formal teaching in books and at school—but it can have a major impact because of the emotional cues possible in the medium. Flashbacks, music, audience reactions, sound effects, and other devices enhance the emotional power of the on-screen portrayals and clearly communicate values about the emotional interactions depicted.

Unfortunately, much of what is depicted is not positive—literally. This truth is writ large in the person and commentary of Simon Cowell, *American Idol*'s famously cutting judge, who once said, "That was extraordinary. Unfortunately, it was extraordinarily bad." The fifth season of this show turned out to be its meanest: A heavyset woman with an extraordinary voice got a thumbs-up from the judges, but Cowell couldn't help adding that a bigger stage might be in order. And Cowell's comments are only one example. A 1989 study found that more than 40 percent of the interactions on family sitcoms consisted of criticism and nasty remarks.[9]

Another revealing study analyzed family interactions in the five most popular family sitcoms among children ages 2 to 11 in 1994: *Full House, Step by Step, Home Improvement, Family Matters,* and *Fresh Prince of Bel Air.*[10] If you recall these shows, you'll remember that their subject matter hardly seemed antisocial; on the contrary, each purported to be wholesome family fare. The researchers evaluated the main emotions presented by each character in every scene of several episodes of each show. On the basis of facial expression, tone of voice, posture, gestures, and context, the researchers were able to code all emotions into 12 categories—including happiness, humor, sadness, jealousy, and so on. They also recorded the responses of the other characters to these emotions—including discussing, comforting, yelling, ignoring, and so on.

One might assume that humor is a very common emotion in comedies, but in fact, it accounted for less than 3 percent of the emotions portrayed. In sitcoms, we laugh *at* the characters, not *with* them—and they aren't always happy about it. Although 50 percent of the emotions portrayed were positive, 47 percent were negative, with anger and fear representing the large majority of these. Situation comedies present emotions that are almost as negative as they are positive.

HOW DOES TELEVISION VIOLENCE LEAD TO ACTUAL VIOLENCE?

In 1980, 39-year-old director Sean Cunningham had a title for a movie and that was all. He sold *Friday the 13th* without a script, cast, or crew. The enormous success of the movie (it cost $500,000 to make and has grossed over $70 million to date) is credited with creating a Hollywood genre: the slasher movie. Scores of teens and preteens flocked to see it that year, and it has since become a cult classic. For the few who may be unaware, the original movie tells the story of Mrs. Voorhees, who exacts gruesome vengeance on a group of counselors at Camp Crystal Lake as retribution for the death of her son, Jason, who drowned there years earlier as a result of previous counselors' neglect. Urged on by the voice of her dead son, Mrs. Voorhees violently and methodically murders every counselor except Alice, who ultimately decapitates Mrs. Voorhees with a machete. But just as Alice relaxes, Jason emerges from the lake as an undead mutant in what *appears* to be just a nightmare.

According to Cunningham, Jason's cameo at the end of the movie was an afterthought, one last cheap thrill for the audience. As afterthoughts go, Jason emerging from the lake is as good as it gets. He returned in more than 10 sequels, wearing his trademark hockey mask, and is now an American icon.

Slasher movies are intended to horrify through violence, and parents may rightly make their children avoid them. But as you'll see, even less dramatic portrayals of violence also exert effects on children. In general, portrayals of violence and aggression on television can affect children in at least three ways.

1. They can *desensitize* children to violence by having them witness it repeatedly.
2. They can *induce* children to behave more aggressively by conveying the message—implicitly or explicitly—that aggression is acceptable, effective, or even desirable.
3. They can *teach* children to see the world as a fearful place and to initiate aggressive behavior as a way of protecting themselves against the perceived threats that constantly surround them.

We separate these effects on children not because they are unrelated to one another. In fact, becoming desensitized to viewing violence may well be one way to induce it. For example, some would argue that it was not naiveté that allowed Lionel Tate to batter his friend, for surely he should have known better. Rather, it was the fact that his heavy diet of television had made him callous to the effects of harm. The girl's screams of pain, her cries for help, fell on ears deafened by exposure to so much violence on television. To be sure, not everyone who is desensitized to violence will behave more aggressively, but desensitization itself is undesirable; it can make children less empathetic or compassionate, and it can simply be unseemly. Should we be concerned that our young children are trained to be amused by violence?

This early training of children's tastes results in the likes of the movie *Scream*. The *Scream* series harkens back to *Friday the 13th*. Part slasher movies, part comedies, these films make fun of the genre even as they replicate it. The idea that a movie is at once terrifying and amusing is odd indeed, but it's quite a natural one given emerging sensibilities. Jason himself pops up in all sorts of unlikely places. In the Nickelodeon series *All Grown Up,* Dill wears a hockey mask and holds up an ax, saying, "It's time!" Then Tommy says, "It's Friday the 12th, not Friday the 13th." In the animated show *Arthur,* Arthur and Buster go to the library, where they see Binky reading a book. He hides the book behind a comic book with a bloody hockey mask on the cover. What was once horrific is now funny.

As parents, we are repeatedly taken aback when we hear children recount the humorous movie scenes that involve someone being hit, run over, blown up, or shot from a cannon. How did the idea that these sorts of stunts are funny become part of the fabric of today's childhood? We begin their education early. For us, there were *Road Runner* cartoons; now it's *Yu-Gi-Oh!*, but the message is the same: Aggression is funny.

VIOLENT PORTRAYALS: ASSESSING THE RISKS TO YOUR CHILDREN

Knowing that violent programming can increase aggressive behavior, we need to understand what aspects of it are particularly risky. Do all portrayals of aggression pose the same risks? Must we eschew all violent programming and institute a zero-tolerance policy (which is a challenge in our culture), or is it sufficient to be especially vigilant about some types and less concerned about others? Many years of research have clarified some of the answers to these questions. Six factors influence whether and to what extent children mimic the violent behavior they see on television.

1. The likability of the perpetrators
2. The justification of the violence
3. How real it appears to be
4. How prolonged or intense the viewer's experience of aggression is
5. Whether the violence lacks consequences
6. The co-occurrence of violence and humor

LIKABLE PERPETRATORS: WHAT WOULD SUPERMAN DO?

Children as young as 3 begin to see the world in terms of "good guys" and "bad guys." This taxonomy serves many purposes. Bad guys embody children's amorphous fears and anxieties, but at the same time, their existence serves to reassure them. Most children don't actually know many (or any) bad guys, so the good guys seem to have them considerably outnumbered. The bad guys they do get to know are frequently on television. Whether it's Swiper on *Dora the Explorer* or Dartz in *Yu-Gi-Oh!*, the bad guys almost invariably lose. Again, this is reassuring. Although Dora frequently uses wit rather than brawn to shame Swiper into returning his ill-gotten booty, other "good" characters frequently resort to aggression to keep the bad guys in check.

When Dimitri's son, Alexi, was a preschooler, he sometimes had play dates with his friend Todd. A favorite playground activity of Todd's was imitating Superman. Alexi had never seen *Superman*, but he happily played along. Todd's parents willingly indulged this fantasy, and sometimes the boy would arrive in full Superman regalia. But by design, to be Superman, a child needs both "good" people to defend and "bad" people to defend against, in the form of Lex Luthor or others. Todd was generally a well-behaved child, but sometimes, unfortunately, complicitous or unsuspecting children on the playground were conscripted into the roles of bad guys—and attacked.

How on-screen aggression is perceived, and how likely viewers are to emulate the behaviors, depends on who commits the acts. Heroes or "good guys" who demonstrate violence or aggression may provide attractive models for children to imitate.

JUSTIFIED VIOLENCE: GETTING WHAT'S COMING TO THEM?

When Superman resorts to violence, it's with good reason. The notion that aggression is occasionally warranted seems harmless or even protective to many parents. Our 3-year-olds tell us that police officers carry guns to protect us from "bad guys." They understand, in other words, that the possibility of violence can be protective and that it exists only to be used against "bad" people. Most adults would agree with this assessment, but even portrayals of justified aggression legitimize violence in the eyes of children. Such portrayals even appear to increase the chance that children will feel that violence is an appropriate response to situations in which they find themselves.

Leonard Berkowitz, PhD, and his colleagues at the University of Wisconsin conducted an experiment to test the effects of justified versus unjustified violence on people's aggressive tendencies. To do so, they showed undergraduates a scene from *The Mod Squad* in which a motorcycle gang encircled a middle-aged man with their bikes. Each member of the gang then zoomed toward him in a threatening way, narrowly missing him each time. The video clip gave no indication of the motivation for this assault. The subjects were then randomly assigned to three groups. One group was told nothing more about the clip. A second group, the "justified group," was told that the targeted man had led an unprovoked attack on two members of the motorcycle gang (a husband and wife) and that he had personally beaten the man's wife. The third group, the "unjustified group," of viewers, was told that the targeted individual was an innocent victim whom the gang had singled out after vandalizing the town in which he lived. Not surprisingly, the justified group felt the actions of the gang were more warranted than the unjustified group did.

Next came the most interesting part of the experiment. After watching the clip and learning the motivation, members of each group were asked to conduct a test with a research participant. They were told that the purpose of the test was to see how someone functioned under stress, so they were supposed to shock a study subject when answered questions incorrectly. Unbeknownst to the participating students, the shocks weren't real, and the study subject to whom they were to administer them was actually a member of the research team, who consistently gave the same number of wrong answers. The group who had been told the motorcycle gang's attack was justified inflicted greater "pain" on their subjects than did the unjustified group, in terms of both the intensity and duration of the shock.[11] A heavy diet of justified violence, the central ingredient of good-versus-bad programming, may therefore increase the likelihood that children view aggression as a reasonable strategy for conflict resolution.

PROLONGED OR INTENSE EXPOSURE: MORE IS WORSE

Acclaimed director John Woo is considered the master of shoot-'em-up scenes. Woo, whose box office successes include *Face/Off* and *Mission Impossible 2,* explains, "I like to put a musical element into my action scenes; I shoot them like I'm shooting a dance scene." They are indeed well choreographed. Shot from many different angles, including from the perspective of a bullet, Woo's scenes are unmistakable and intense. Furthermore, they're sometimes shot in slow motion, allowing viewers to notice nuances that might otherwise elude them, such as the facial expression of someone who has been shot. This intensity may sell tickets, but scientific studies have proven that the more intense, frequent, and prolonged the exposure to violence, the greater the risk that viewers are desensitized to it both on the screen and in real life.

Victor Cline, PhD, and his colleagues at the University of Utah conducted a study in 1973 in which they recruited 40 heavy television viewers and 40 light television viewers between the ages of 5 and 12. Heavy viewers were those who had watched 25 hours or more of television per week for the previous 2 years; light viewers had watched fewer than 4 hours per week over the same period. The researchers' hypothesis was that given the amount of violence on TV, heavy viewers would be less sensitive to its effects than light viewers. To test this, they collected some physiologic data on the children's levels of arousal by attaching electrodes to their skin to measure galvanic skin response (GSR), or how well the skin conducts electricity. Skin conducts electricity better when it's sweaty, and being stressed or aroused leads to the proverbial sweaty palms. The children's GSR was measured while they watched three different programs: a ski movie without violence, violent fight scenes from a boxing movie, and neutral scenes (between rounds) from a boxing movie.[12]

Heavy and Light TV Viewers' Reaction to Screen Violence

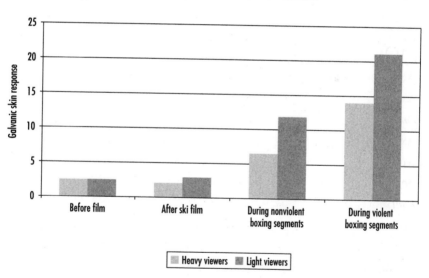

As can be seen in the graph of the study results, the arousal levels of light and heavy viewers were the same before any films were shown. After the ski film, light viewers were slightly more aroused than heavy viewers, while after violent sections, they were much more aroused. The heavy viewers had greater psychological tolerance for violence: Their thresholds for arousal had been raised. This finding exposes one of the more pernicious aspects of the heavy diet of media violence many children consume. The ante is continually being upped. As generations of viewers grow increasingly accustomed to intense violence, portrayals have to become more frequent and more intense in order to motivate viewers' reactions. The cycle of increasing media violence is both self-perpetuating and self-escalating.

REALISTIC VS. FANTASTICAL VIOLENCE: THE ALLURE OF REALITY TV

Wes Craven, a master of cinematic horror, got his start in the 1970s. His big hit then, *The Last House on the Left*, was considered to be an incredibly realistic portrayal of the rape, torture, and killing of two teenagers and the revenge exacted by their parents. The tagline it coined, "To avoid fainting, keep repeating 'It's only a movie . . . It's only a movie . . .'" is now part of horror movie lore. By today's standards, *The Last House on the Left* is a walk in the park. Online reviews by people who actually watch and review such movies describe it as "cheesy," "filled with fake blood," and "more annoying than realistic." Thus have the standards evolved for what is truly shocking. A movie that in its day inspired protests because of its realistic portrayals of rape and murder is today a cult classic because of its campiness.

But realistic (or today, real) portrayals of aggression and violence carry increased risks for young viewers. Charles Atkin, PhD, of Michigan State University randomly assigned 5th- and 6th-grade students in Lansing, Michigan, to three groups: a control group that watched no violence, a group that watched a realistic rendition of a classroom fight, and one that watched a fictional account. In the fictional account, the voiceover described it as a trailer for a late-show movie titled *Murder on Campus,* in which "some young Americans on a narcotics trip turn the classroom into a no-holds-barred battle." In the realistic account, it was billed as a news story. The fight scene was identical, but the voiceover was provided by an anchorman, who stated, "Channel 6 photographer Bob Ray was on hand this afternoon when young Congressional candidate Bill Thompkins addressed a political science class on the university campus, but he didn't plan on this development . . ."[13] Seventy percent of those watching the realistic version reported that they paid "a lot" of attention to the fight, compared to 32 percent of those who thought it was just a movie. Real violence is more interesting to viewers, perhaps because they are over-saturated with fictionalized violence.

The subjects of the Atkin study were then presented with some hypothetical scenarios that might anger them and asked how they would respond. They were asked, for example, "Suppose you were standing in a long line at a movie and some kid cut into line in front of you. What would you do?" Options included "I would shove the kid out of line," "I would yell at the kid," and "I would just let it go." People who had seen what they believed was real violence exhibited more aggression in the scenarios than people who thought they had seen fictional violence. Notably, members of both groups that had seen violence were more aggressive than those who had seen none. Those who had seen the fictional melee had aggression scores 30 percent higher than those who had seen no violence. Those who had seen what they thought was an actual event had scores 50 percent higher.

When this experiment was conducted in the 1970s, Dr. Atkin had to present a fictional movie as real in order to test his hypothesis. If the study were repeated today, it would be much easier to find an example of true-life violence. His study predated the meteoric rise of reality shows such as *Fear Factor* and *Jackass* and in-your-face, knockdown talk shows such as *Jerry Springer*, which included recent episodes titled "I Slept with Everyone in Your Family" and "Hillbillies and Gay Men in Shorts." Dr. Atkin's finding that "reality" held more interest was published in a psychology journal and read by academics, but it took the TV industry only a few more years to discover this fact on its own. It should come as no surprise, then, when your teens express keen interest in realistic portrayals of violence; those are the ones you should be especially wary of.

In one important respect, television portrayals are patently unrealistic: They almost never include consequences of the violent actions.

LACK OF CONSEQUENCES: BAD DEEDS GO UNPUNISHED

Children (and adults) are conditionable. They learn consequences and adapt their behavior accordingly. A 4-year-old child who has the misfortune of touching a hot stove learns a lesson not easily forgotten. As a parent, you reward certain behaviors and punish others as a way of modifying behavior and distinguishing between right and wrong actions. But much of the violence depicted on-screen goes unpunished, and often it's even rewarded. Portrayals of violence without consequences inspire kids to emulate them. By contrast, portrayals of violence with actual consequences—victims and families who are truly hurting or perpetrators who are punished and remorseful—can reduce the likelihood of viewers acting aggressively. Unfortunately, violence is rarely portrayed this way. According to the National Committee on Television Violence (NCTV), the majority of violent scenes (54 percent) neither reward nor punish the perpetrator. In 17 percent of scenes, violence is rewarded! And what of the victims? The graph on the opposite page uses data from the NCTV to show what happens to the victims of TV violence.

More than 40 percent of the time, there is either no harm or no target even depicted. It's as if children are being shown on a regular basis that touching a hot stove causes no injury. Think about that the next time your 4-year-old is in the kitchen. Lionel Tate's defense team pointed the finger at professional wrestling, but there was plenty of blame to go around.

FUSING PAIN AND LAUGHTER

The idea that on-screen "pain" can be funny is as old as the medium of movies. When Charlie Chaplin was bopped on the head and suffered no ill effects except some transient disorientation, audiences howled. Both the frequency and intensity of what is now considered humorous violence have increased considerably over the past few decades, whether in cartoon form (*The Incredibles*) or dramatic form (*Dodgeball*). Many of us have come to view violence as a legitimate vehicle for laughter.

How Often Violence on TV Is Depicted as Harmful

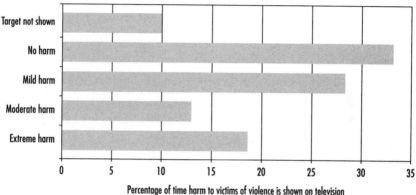

Percentage of time harm to victims of violence is shown on television

It's important to note that in order for violence to be humorous, it must be portrayed unrealistically and without consequence. For instance, if the characters in *Dodgeball* who were trained to act quickly by having metal objects hurled at their heads suffered the consequence that might be expected with such trauma—serious brain hemorrhage—normal people would be revolted, not amused. Several studies have found that the more hostile humor is, the more likely it is to provoke aggressive action. Conversely, nonviolent humor has been proven to be protective—capable of dissipating anger.

Robert Baron, PhD, of Purdue University conducted a fascinating study in 1978 that supports the existence of these relationships.[14] His experiment involved 41 male undergraduate students who were told that they were going to study how people's bodies reacted to stressful situations. A research accomplice (who participants thought was the study subject) was brought in. The undergraduates were to deliver shocks to him (the intensity of which they could determine) when he answered questions incorrectly. As in the Berkowitz study, the shocks were fake, and it was predetermined that in each case, the subject would make a consistent number of mistakes. Unbeknownst to the participants, they had been randomly assigned to one of three groups that would view either nonhumorous pictures, images of nonhostile humor, or pictures of hostile humor.

While they were "waiting" for the study subject in order to begin the experiment, the researcher told them that they could take a look at the pictures (each group looked at 10). The nonhumorous pictures were of scenery, furniture, or abstract art. Nonhostile humor was depicted in one of the pictures by two workers standing in a rice field, with one saying to the other, "I've always wondered what Rice Krispies taste like!" Such an idle and bizarre musing may not be that funny, and it's certainly subtle, but it is surely nonviolent. The hostile images included a cartoon in which a woman was shown speaking on the phone while in the background, a body dangled from a rope. She remarked, "It all turned out just as you said it would, Mother."

Afterward, the subject conveniently arrived, and the shocking occurred. The results are presented below.

Shocks Delivered after Being Exposed to Different Types of Humor

| Nonhostile Humor | No Humor | Hostile Humor |

As you can see, nonhostile humor may reduce aggression, so laughter may indeed be the best medicine! But as with any medicine, the wrong type can produce serious side effects. Hostile humor increases aggression: Those exposed to it in this study delivered greater shocks to the research subject.

AGE MATTERS: THE SPECIAL RISK TO YOUNG CHILDREN

Young children have their own ways of understanding and responding to televised violence. In fact, they appear to be the most susceptible to the effects of violent programming. Children's viewing habits and their limited ability to distinguish fiction from reality (which is true of most children under 7) puts them in a uniquely vulnerable position when it comes to violent programming. Bear in mind that 95 percent of the average child's viewing consists of programs not specifically produced for young audiences.[15] But much commercial programming intended for young audiences also contains a great deal of violence, and cartoons probably pose some of the greatest risk. Think of the classic *Road Runner*. The entire premise of the show is that Wile E. Coyote is out to kill and eat the Road Runner— not an unnatural scenario, although the means employed are hardly conventional. We're all familiar with the hijinks that follow, and I suspect we have all laughed at them, but as adults, we recognize that violence is being portrayed. Children do not. Fewer than 25 percent of 4- to 12-year-olds describe *Road Runner* as violent. Their reason? It isn't violent because it's "funny." Parents who think that cartoon violence or slapstick, á la the Three Stooges, is "safe" because it is so patently fake should think again.

Think about violent characteristics of the programming you select for your children. Use "The Aggression Matrix" on page 85 as a scorecard to help you evaluate the risks that a show poses to your children. Avoid high-risk shows or be certain to watch them with your children to help them process the events. If you're uncertain about a show's content, preview it on your own first. If your children watch a program without you being present, ask them what happened in it. Many children recount the storylines on their own, without prompting. Take the opportunity to look for examples of the portrayals discussed above. When the kids attempt to regale you about the time Mr. Incredible blew up Syndrome, for example, listen intently, then ask if they think that was the right course of action and if they can think of more reasonable alternative actions that may have been more appropriate. Here are some questions to get you started.

- What happened in the show?
- What did you like about the show? What did you not like?
- Do you think that could happen in real life? Why or why not?
- How do you think the character felt? Why did he feel that way?
- Did the character do anything that made other people feel happy?
- What do you think will happen next?
- Which character would you want to be?
- What would you do if you were that character?

It's especially important to talk with your children about the violence they see in television programs and videos, especially since some children are frightened by the violence, and some will try to imitate what they've seen. Once you've asked the basic questions above, here are some more things to ask.

- Are some characters sad, mad, or scared?
- Who might be hurt? How do you think they feel now?
- How do you think their mommy (or daddy or brother, etc.) feels?
- Did anyone break things? Who's going to fix the things that were broken?
- Would someone get hurt if they did that in real life?
- What was the scariest part?
- Why do you think the character hurt the other guy?
- What could he have done instead, without hurting anyone?
- What would you do if you were that character?

These kinds of questions will modify the context of your child's viewing of televised aggression and promote mindful viewing. They will allow you to mitigate the show's effects. What's more, they'll let you use the content of the programming to serve a better purpose: to explore feelings, develop your children's empathy, and reinforce the fact that violence has real consequences.

THE AGGRESSION MATRIX

The following chart summarizes the effects of different types of on-screen violence. Upward arrows indicate that the portrayal increases the chances of your children learning to be aggressive, becoming desensitized, or feeling greater fear. Downward arrows indicate that the portrayal decreases the chances.

Portrayal	Learning Aggression	Desensitization	Fear
Likable perpetrator	↑	—	—
Justified violence	↑	—	—
Unjustified violence	↓	—	—
Prolonged exposure	↑	↑	—
Realistic violence	↑	—	↑
Graphic violence	—	↑	↑
Punishment	↓	—	—
Humorous context for violence	↑	↑	—

PROSOCIAL BEHAVIORS: THE MR. ROGERS EFFECT

Despite appearances, bright spots on the TV landscape do exist. Although less heralded, there are *benefits* to children's behavioral development that can result from viewing selected programs. Researchers typically refer to such effects as being prosocial, that is, promoting development of cooperation and empathy. Positive behavioral effects are harder to define than aggression is. While we can all agree on what constitutes violent or aggressive behavior, it's more difficult to agree on what constitutes being nice to people. Nevertheless, just as television can model undesirable behavior, it can also model positive behavior, and children are quite able to learn the positive as well as the negative. (*Note:* The benefits we discuss here are not related to educational or intellectual achievement, which we discussed in Chapter 3.)

A meta-analysis of 34 studies of the effects of selective viewing on children's prosocial behavior (akin to the one done for television and aggression) found that the effect of good television in promoting good behavior was almost as large as the effect of bad television in promoting bad behavior. We showed earlier how the effects on aggression of viewing violent programming compared to several other common activities or practices and their outcomes. Let's look at that graph again, now with the positive effects of viewing good television included.

Does Prosocial TV Really Help?

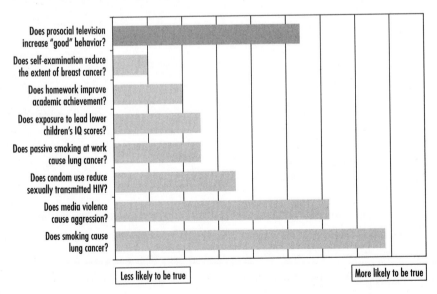

This chart sums up the evidence, and the message is clear: The evidence that prosocial television viewing leads to good behavior in children is almost as strong as the evidence in support of media violence leading to aggression.

TELEVISION VIEWING AND ALTRUISTIC BEHAVIOR

Parents are frequently flummoxed by the fact that a single utterance of a bad word by them can induce children to use it repeatedly, but hundreds of "pleases" and "thank yous" said in their presence may not be sufficient to make them more polite. The parents may conclude that children more readily model bad behavior than good. However, they do model good behavior.

Rita Poulos PhD, a psychologist at the State University of New York, and her colleagues did a study in 1976 that monitored the effect of television viewing on altruistic behavior.[16] They took 15 boys and 15 girls from a 1st-grade classroom and randomly assigned them to watch one of three programs: a prosocial *Lassie* episode, a neutral *Lassie* episode, and an episode of *The Brady Bunch*. In the prosocial *Lassie* episode, Lassie tried to hide her runt puppy out of fear that it would be given away. The climax involved the puppy falling down a mineshaft and Jeff risking his life to rescue it successfully. The neutral *Lassie* episode involved Jeff's attempts to avoid taking violin lessons. Lassie was in the show, of course, and as always was a good dog, but she and Jeff didn't help each other. The *Brady Bunch* episode depicted the youngest children trying to set a record for time spent on a teeter-totter. The family cooperated as they generally did on that show, but there was no human or canine heroism.

The children were told that they could watch the programs while the experimenter was getting ready for their next activity. They were then told that they would play a game in which they could press a button to earn points toward a prize—with more points leading to bigger prizes. They were also asked to monitor the care of some puppies in a distant kennel by listening to some earphones. When a dog barked, the children could choose between pushing a blue button that would earn them prize points or pushing a help button that would signal a helper in the kennel. The idea here was to measure altruism in the sense that children would forgo earning a prize to help a puppy. How long the help button was deployed was recorded for each group. Here's what the researchers found.

Children who watched Jeff risk his life to save a puppy were more than twice as willing to help at the expense of winning prize points than children who watched either the other *Lassie* episode or *The Brady Bunch*. This study isn't without flaws, however. For example, the targeted behavior—helping a puppy—is directly related to the content of the show. Watching a *Lassie* episode may predispose children to help dogs, but not necessarily to share better with their friends. But it does show the possible effect of prosocial programming and gives us reason to believe that watching sharing might lead to sharing.

Watching Someone Be Helpful Can Lead to Being Helpful

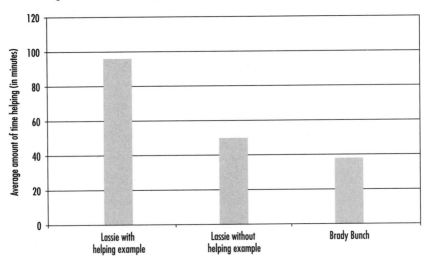

Other studies have focused more generally on the effects of programming that portrays prosocial interactions. Although *Sesame Street* has added some prosocial messages, its primary focus has traditionally been on children's intellectual development. Rigorous studies of the effects of *Sesame Street* on children's prosocial behaviors have come to mixed conclusions, although none have demonstrated harm as a result of viewing. *Mister Rogers' Neighborhood,* on the other hand, made positive behavior a central theme of its program. Kids have been shown to be more willing to be helpful, to share, and to express empathy for classmates after they watched the show.[17-19] Although Fred Rogers passed away in 2003, don't despair that you may have missed the boat with your kids. They still have a chance to enjoy his show, which lives on in books and DVDs and still airs on some PBS stations. Studies of current shows, such as *Barney & Friends*, have found similar results, showing that preschoolers who watch it play better with others.

In all these studies, how the shows were watched was almost as important as what was watched. The effects of the messages on the children were much greater when other prosocial activities followed, such as talking with teachers about what they'd seen. Here again, the critical role that context plays is evident, in this case as a means of supporting and enhancing the positive effects. An adult companion can help children label, understand, discuss, and reenact the situations they watch on TV. They can reinforce the positive message both during the show and afterward, simply by asking questions like, "Remember what we saw on *Mister Rogers*?"

TELEVISION AND RACIAL TOLERANCE

Using television to counteract existing racial stereotypes was a major motivation for *The Cosby Show*. Highly popular with black and white audiences, the show was unusual at the time for its portrayal of a two-career African American couple who lived an upper-middle-class life. Bill Cosby's intention was to use the show as a vehicle to help counterbalance existing societal stereotypes that were seen elsewhere during primetime programming. And his goals were probably realistic given the results of studies that looked at how positive portrayals can help dispel stereotypes.

In one study at McGill University that examined the effects of television on stereotypes, researchers randomly divided a group of 3- to 5-year-old white children.[20] Half of them watched *Sesame Street* segments that showed Japanese children playing together and Native American children playing together. The other group watched an animated cartoon, *Yogi's Gang*. Afterward, each group was shown two pictures, one of a group of white children and one of nonwhite children. They were asked which group they wanted to play with. Seventy-nine percent of the children who watched the cartoon chose the group of white children, compared to 52 percent of the children who watched the racially mixed program.

Interestingly, when asked the next day to choose who they wanted, the differences in preference were gone. What are we to make of this? As with many experiments of this kind, it's hard to know how to apply the findings to real life. Critics or cynics might note that the effects wore off remarkably fast, therefore indicating little evidence of any long-term benefit. But the exposure was also very brief, so it's not surprising that the positive effects wore off. In this case, prolonged exposure to positive stereotypes on TV just may induce more long-lasting tolerance or interest in other ethnic groups.

PROSOCIAL PROGRAMS: CHECK THEM OUT

Just as children can copy violence they see in television programs or videos, they can also learn good behaviors, such as sharing and staying safe. Here are some questions to help you determine which programs will be helpful for young children.

- Do the characters help other people who need it?
- Do they try to make other people feel better?
- Do they make a point of being safe? Do they wear a bicycle helmet or hold an adult's hand to cross the street?
- Do they try to stop other people from doing something wrong?
- Do they help with everyday tasks like cleaning up?

- Do they stop and talk about what might happen before they decide what to do?
- Do they work together as a group to come up with a plan that will work for everyone?
- Do they take care of their belongings?
- Do they try to understand how other people might feel?
- Do they find ways to solve problems without being mean or hurting anyone?
- Does the program have positive characters from different age groups, genders, or cultural backgrounds?

The more statements you can answer with a yes, the more good behaviors your child can learn from that program. These items are also good things to talk about with your child when you watch the program together.

THE NET EFFECT OF TELEVISION VIOLENCE

We now have a pretty good idea of what science tells us about the effects of TV viewing on children's behavior. Again, we can use the comparison with a power saw: As a tool, it can have positive as well as negative effects. But what does TV do in real life? What is the net effect of prosocial and aggressive programming? Do these effects cancel each other out? Unfortunately, no. In large part, this is because the volume of violent programming far exceeds the volume of programming espousing prosocial messages.

In Appendix 1, we give some examples of programs that model and promote prosocial behavior for children. In the interest of usefulness (not to mention space!), we decided not to itemize the negative programs—there are simply far too many. The National Committee on Television Violence, however, did provide a summary. They reviewed all of the available programs sorted by category and identified what times of day and what types of programming are "high risk" for promoting violence in children. They sampled from programs available in each category (drama, comedy, children's, and so on) and identified high-risk incidents based on the features of programming discussed above. The table below shows their findings.

Young Children: High-Risk Patterns for Learning Aggression by Genre and Time

Time of Day	Drama	Comedy	Children's	Movies	Music Videos	Reality-Based
Before school (6:00 a.m.–9:00 a.m.)	Minimal	No	Substantial	Minimal	Minimal	Minimal
During school (9:00 a.m.–3:00 p.m.)	Minimal	Minimal	Substantial	Minimal	Minimal	No
After school (3:00 p.m.–6:00 p.m.)	Minimal	Minimal	Substantial	Minimal	Minimal	No
Early evening (6:00 p.m.–8:00 p.m.)	Moderate	No	Substantial	Minimal	Minimal	Minimal
Primetime (8:00 p.m.–11:00 p.m.)	Minimal	Minimal	Moderate	Minimal	Minimal	Minimal

	No high-risk incidents
	Minimal number of high-risk incidents
	Moderate number of high-risk incidents
	Substantial number of high-risk incidents

Source: The National Committee on Television Violence Report (1997).

What is striking in this table is how dark the children's programming column is. Children's programming, as a rule, has the greatest number of high-risk incidents throughout the day. Why? In a word, cartoons. Cartoons are frequently violent, and with the advent of cable television, they're frequently available. And "cute" though they may be, some are far from innocuous fun.

In 2005, we completed a study examining the relationship between early television viewing (at age 4) and bullying behavior in elementary school.[21] When we did it, we didn't know what children were watching, only that they were watching TV and for how long. What we found was that early television viewing was strongly related to subsequent bullying, and the effect was significant. Going from no television viewing to the average amount of viewing for 4-year-olds represented a 25 percent increase in the risk of becoming a bully later on. This study accounted for other aspects of the home environment, such as how nurturing the parents were, how much they read to their children, and even whether the children showed any early signs of becoming bullies. We could therefore feel confident that the effect we observed was truly the result of television itself and not one of these other factors.

Bart Simpson says, "Cartoons don't have messages," but we couldn't disagree more. Most of this bully effect is probably due to cartoons. As you saw earlier, cartoons contain an enormous amount of violence, and it's precisely the types that we discussed as being high risk for children. On the other hand, educational shows such as *Sesame Street, Barney & Friends,* and *Mr. Rogers' Neighborhood* have a beneficial effect. Sadly, our study demonstrates that the typical television diet of an American 4-year-old is laden with enough violence to overwhelm the beneficial effects of any educational television they're watching. Therefore, parents really need to be selective and proactive and exert control over what their children watch; just because a show is animated doesn't mean it's safe—not by a long shot. (We'll discuss a thorough approach to viewing in greater detail in Chapter 9.)

Controlling access to what your children watch is the first step in assuring that you minimize the harmful effects of programming— again, underscoring the importance of content. But being present when they watch is also critical. As you've seen, the prosocial effects of television were considerably more pronounced when they were discussed with parents and teachers. And, the negative effects of violent programming can likewise be reduced. Context again is critical: Unattended viewing of violent content is much more likely to lead to negative rather than positive behavior, because of both the content and the importance of parents in mediating the messages, both good and bad. Remember that everything on the screen provides an opportunity for discussion. Use undesirable on-screen behavior as a launch point for discussion of alternative, more desirable, and appropriate strategies. Even at its worst, television can provide ample fodder to discuss better courses of action. In the next chapter, we will address some other effects of frightful sights on screen as we discuss television's effects on children's sleep habits.

HOW TO MAKE TV WORK FOR YOUR CHILDREN'S BEHAVIOR

3- TO 5-YEAR-OLDS

- Avoid news programs that include violence or reports of violence.
- Don't allow violent cartoons.
- Watch programs with prosocial messages.
- Emphasize the distinction between fantasy and reality.

5- TO 10-YEAR-OLDS

- Avoid portrayals of realistic threats and dangers.
- Minimize violent cartoons. Cartoons with rough-and-tumble play or fantasy violence are okay, but no depictions of violence that may result in serious injury should be allowed.

11-YEAR-OLDS AND UP

- Avoid horror movies, especially those that glamorize or sexualize violence.
- If violent programming is selected, make sure the violence has consequences.

ALL AGES

- Know what they watch.
- Discuss violence and its real-world consequences.
- Discuss positive behaviors you see on television.
- Present alternatives to violence you see on television.
- Watch with them whenever possible.

CHAPTER 5

ASLEEP AT THE SWITCH: TELEVISION AND SLEEP PROBLEMS

People who say they sleep like a baby usually don't have one.

Leo Burke

After a hard day at school, I like to come home and veg out in front of the TV for a while. It really helps me relax.

Todd, a 15-year-old in Seattle

Some of the most horrific testing on animals did not involve toxic substances or massive infusions of questionable food additives. Instead, it centered on sleep—or rather, the lack of it.

Rats that have been deprived of sleep suffer a terrible fate. Their body temperature plunges, sores develop on their tails and paws, and their body weight falls despite increased food intake. Within 3 weeks, they are dead.

Thankfully, no one has duplicated this study on humans, but there's no doubt: We need our sleep. Sleep is necessary for physical growth, mental health, and concentration—not to mention maintaining our inhibition. Children and adolescents who get inadequate sleep experience reduced creativity, poor coordination, memory lapses, slowed reaction times, impaired learning, depressed mood, and behavioral problems such as temper tantrums, increased aggression, and hyperactivity. They are more likely to make physical and mental mistakes; in fact, inadequate sleep is among the biggest risk factors for automobile accidents among teenagers.[1]

If you are new parents, you probably take a keen interest in your baby's sleep in part because your own sleep is inextricable from it. But even if your children are older and your sleep is unaffected by theirs, your duty to ensure proper sleep habits continues throughout childhood and into adolescence, since getting enough sleep is critical for children's physical, emotional, and cognitive well-being.

But how many of us fall asleep in front of the television each night? According to one national poll, as many as 9 out of 10 adults report that they often watch television before sleeping, and three-quarters of school-age children have television as part of their bedtime routines.[2] Furthermore, more than two-thirds of all children (69 percent) experience one or more sleep problems at least a few nights a week.[3] The fact that both sleep problems and nighttime viewing are so common begs the question: Might television viewing and sleep problems be related?

The relationship between sleep and television is made clear when you consider that sleep timers now come standard on most new television sets. These timers encourage viewing at bedtime by automatically shutting off the set after a preset interval. Falling asleep at the TV switch is surprisingly common. Before discussing what we know about television and sleep in children, it's worth briefly reviewing a bit of what we know about sleep and sleep regulation.

WHAT HAPPENS WHEN WE SLEEP?

A common misconception is that the brain rests during sleep. Although the body is generally relaxed, the brain can be highly active, especially during dreaming. Sleep itself is divided into two states: REM (rapid eye movement) sleep and non-REM sleep. REM sleep is active: Breathing and heart rate increase and are irregular; muscles are typically relaxed. It is during REM sleep that dreaming occurs. Non-REM sleep has four stages, ranging from drowsiness (stage 1), when one can be easily awakened, to deep sleep (stages 3 and 4), when awakening is more difficult and when the most positive and restorative effects of sleep occur. Anyone who has labored to awaken a 2-year-old to leave for a family vacation or tried to stir an adolescent on a weekend morning has experienced just how deep this sleep can be in children!

Both REM and non-REM sleep are crucial to getting enough quality sleep. Our bodies try to maintain the proper balance of each. For example, in the laboratory, if people are prevented from getting sufficient REM sleep (by being awakened every time they initiate it) and are then allowed to sleep, they quickly go into REM sleep and spend more time than usual in that stage to make up for the amount they were deprived of. Many of us have had the experience of beginning to dream as soon as our heads hit the pillow. On these occasions, we are in more desperate need of REM sleep, and our bodies ensure that we get it.

Although dreams occur during REM sleep, the only ones we can remember are those that occur just before we wake up. Sometimes, as with nightmares, dreams are so intense that they wake us up—and thereby deprive us of more REM. But even if they don't send your kids running to your bed in the middle of the night, frequent nightmares can prevent them from getting the right balance of sleep types or from getting enough deep non-REM sleep. Before we explore the role that television may play in those nightmares, it's important to know a bit more sleep physiology.

MELATONIN: THE SLEEP REGULATOR

To their parents' dismay, many infants are born nocturnal. This unfortunate occurrence is not a fluke; it happens because babies tend to be rocked to sleep in the womb as their mothers walk around during the day and then wake up at night when the moms finally lie down to rest. Over the first few months of life, babies acclimate to the real world and start to regulate their sleep. Although it can take a while for them to sleep through the night, they do start sleeping more at night than during the day over the first few weeks of life. They are able to do this with the help of a hormone that regulates sleep patterns: melatonin. Familiar to many frequent flyers as a supplement that claims to counteract jet lag, melatonin is a sleep-inducing substance secreted by the pineal gland, a pea-size structure that sits in the middle of the brain. Typically, we begin to secrete it as our natural bedtimes approach; the levels rise gradually, peak after about 6 hours, and disappear after about 12 hours. The normal rise of levels is shown by the dark line in the graph below.

Melatonin Levels During a Day

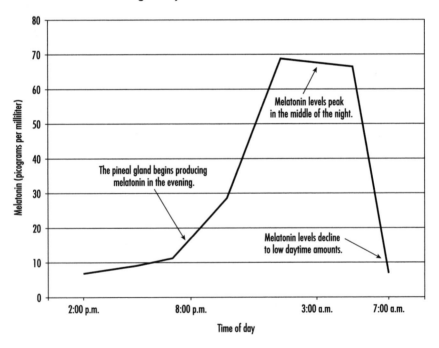

LIGHT: THE ANTI-MELATONIN
Special cells called retinal ganglion cells, which are found in the backs of the eyeballs, play a key role in melatonin release. Even brief exposure to intense

light can suppress or delay the secretion of melatonin, resulting in what is called a phase delay. Instead of melatonin rising normally, its release is delayed, and people don't get the natural sleep induction that the hormone produces. The effect of this is indicated by the broken line in the graph below.

Historically, this "phase shift" has functioned to help keep us more alert at times when natural light may be more abundant, such as during the summer months in northern regions of the world. Many parents have noticed that it becomes notoriously difficult to maintain winter bedtimes during the dog days of summer. Despite being more active outdoors during the summer, which might be expected to lead to exhaustion, children are able to stay up later. The bright sun late in the day suppresses melatonin release, and as a result, kids' energy levels remain high longer. Left to their own devices, kids would also wake up later, but frequently, wake-up times are fixed, at least while school is in session.

Melatonin Phase Shift from Light Exposure

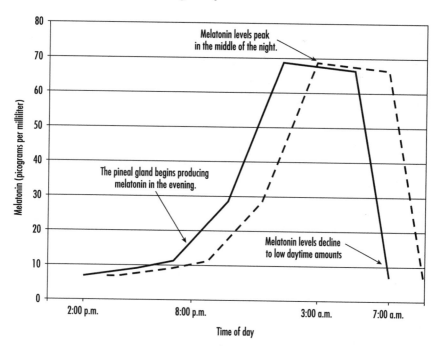

Whereas once humans depended entirely on the sun for light, more recently we have found alternative, readily available sources of nighttime light. At a societal level, the effects of this abundance of easy light have been dramatic. Before Thomas Edison invented the lightbulb, people slept an average of 10 hours a night; today, Americans average 7 hours of sleep per night.

Just how much light is needed to cause a melatonin phase shift? The answer isn't all that simple and depends on many things. The simplest of these is the intensity of the light that reaches the retinal ganglion cells. Light intensity is measured in units called lux, with 1 lux being as bright as 10 birthday candles burning in an otherwise dark room. Here are some examples of light intensity in various situations.

Sunny day: 50,000 to 100,000 lux

Cloudy day (even in Seattle): 1,000 to 10,000 lux

Bright, well-lit office: 400 to 600 lux

Most homes: 100 to 300 lux

Full moon: 0.2 lux

Lux are also determined by how close you are to the source. As you move farther away from a light source, the light intensity diminishes rapidly. When people use light therapy for seasonal depression, for example, they're encouraged to sit within 1 foot of a very powerful light source.

Research tells us that exposure to as little as 200 lux (the equivalent of a well-lit room) for 30 minutes can be enough to suppress melatonin secretion and keep you awake.[4] But not all colors of light are the same. For example, intense blue light is most effective at suppressing melatonin. Now think of the way your television gives off a blue glow in the darkness. Scientists have long speculated that watching television at night may interfere with melatonin secretion and therefore sleep.

DOES YOUR CHILD HAVE A SLEEP PROBLEM?

Parents of Dimitri's patients often ask him if their children are getting "enough" sleep. They typically do this after telling him precisely how many hours their children are getting and then questioning if that amount is normal. The "normal" amount of sleep varies depending on age. The table below summarizes the average amount of sleep children get at various ages.

Normal Sleep by Age

Age	Average Nighttime Sleep (hr)	Average Daytime Sleep (hr)
Newborn–5 months	8–9 (waking through the night to feed)	8
6–12 months	10–12 (usually sleeps through the night)	5
13 months–2 years	10–12	4
3 years	10	1
4–6 years	10	Usually none
7–12 years	10	None
13 years and up	7	None

Simply comparing whether or not a child gets as much sleep as the average child her age isn't enough to determine whether she's getting enough sleep. Each child's needs are different—your children may require considerably more or less sleep. Also, the amount of time they're asleep (or in bed, which is what most parents count) is only one measure of sleep. It may attempt to measure the *quantity* of sleep but doesn't measure the *quality*. Time in bed doesn't necessarily mean time asleep—or may not be any reflection of how restorative the sleep was.

Children who have difficulty initiating sleep may stay awake for long periods in bed. Children with nightmares may awaken frequently during the night and have difficulty getting back to sleep, and they may not get the requisite amount of REM sleep or enough deep non-REM sleep. Whether the quantity and quality of your child's sleep are sufficient depends on their behavior. Although, like adults, children with inadequate sleep experience daytime fatigue, they often do not yawn or act drowsy the way grown-ups do. In fact, hyperactivity may be a more common symptom, along with irritability and agitation. To help determine whether your child may have a sleep problem, ask yourself the following questions.[5]

- Does your child have any problems going to bed or falling asleep?
- Does your child have difficulty waking in the morning, seem sleepy during the day, or take more naps than other kids their age?
- Does your child wake up a lot at night?
- Does your child have irregular bedtimes and wake times?

If you answered yes to one or more of these questions, your child may have a sleep problem. Now let's explore whether television may be at least partly to blame.

"VEGGING OUT" ISN'T ALL IT SEEMS

Most people are surprised to learn that television may cause sleep problems, because watching television, at least initially, seems relaxing. The full story is more complex, however, and Robert Kubey, PhD, and his colleagues at Rutgers University have done some fascinating work exploring this. They asked subjects to carry pagers that beeped periodically at random times during the day. Whenever the pager sounded, the subjects recorded in journals precisely what they were doing as well as their current mood and feelings. Their reports were then compiled into montages to produce a more general sense of people's states of mind before, during, and after activities. In Dr. Kubey's studies, television was the most commonly cited activity used by participants to relax. However, the relaxing effects were shown to be short-lived.

Although people relaxed while watching television, they ended up less relaxed when they stopped than when they started. Other leisure activities, such as entertaining friends, doing artwork or hobbies, or watching a play, made them feel more relaxed, and for a longer time, than watching television. Consider this graph based on Dr. Kubey's results.

Although people started in nearly the same state of relaxation before beginning these activities, their relaxation level during the activity varied. As you might expect, when playing sports, people were less relaxed than when they were watching television or engaged in leisure activities. But what's interesting is that when the activities were over, the people who played sports relaxed, and those who did leisure activities continued to feel relaxed. But the people who watched television were less relaxed than they were during viewing and markedly less relaxed than before they started watching.

Relaxation Before, During, and After Selected Activities

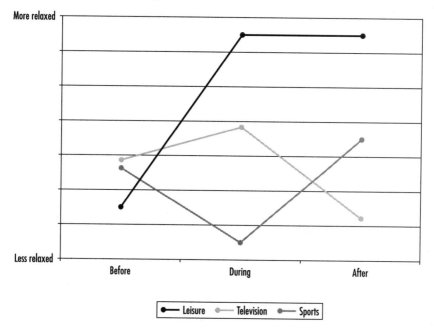

Although many of us try to use television to relax, we may not get what we're after. Relaxing is an integral part of inducing sleep, and watching TV can make falling asleep more difficult. What's more, we may come to associate watching television with relaxation (and not watching with being aggravated), which in itself can make us reluctant to stop watching. Thus, although people often fall asleep at the switch, they may stay up longer as a result of watching TV than they would if they just tried to fall asleep in the first place.

HOW MIGHT TV INTERFERE WITH SLEEP?

We know that adults and children who report having sleep problems watch more television than those who report not having sleep problems. However, disentangling the cause and effect is difficult. When we can't fall asleep, many of us turn on the television. In such cases, can we really say that TV caused our insomnia since, after all, we weren't able to fall sleep *before* we started watching? Indeed, most parents are skeptical of the connection between television viewing and sleep problems: 90 percent report that television does not negatively affect their children's sleep patterns.[6]

But how exactly does television impact sleep? We have a few theories. Some are related to *what* is watched (content), and others are related to *how* it's watched (context). These distinctions are important because each theory has implications for how to rectify television-related sleep problems. As you'll soon see, the problems that result from content can be fixed by changing which shows are watched; those that result from context require changes in the environment around the TV.

WHAT IS WATCHED: THE FRIGHTFUL SIGHTS ON THE SCREEN

I woke up in the middle of the night because I heard the heavy breathing that I associated with the killer in the film. I was very scared and

went into my parents' bedroom. I then realized that the noise I was
hearing was my dad's snoring. Even after finding this out, I was still
scared . . .[7]

—a Wisconsin teenager

Television portrays a lot of scary things, some real and some fantastical. From killers to car accidents to earthquakes, children are affected,
often deeply, by what they see on screen. Many children are frightened as
they watch and become trembly and weepy thereafter. The fear they
experience can often interfere with their sleep. Joanne Cantor, PhD, of
the University of Wisconsin has studied for years the effects of television
on children's fears. In her excellent and aptly named book *Mommy, I'm
Scared!* she details the ways in which television can traumatize children—
often with long-term consequences. Dr. Cantor discusses the examples of
several children who have been hospitalized with fear after watching
especially terrifying television shows or movies and recounts the story of
one boy in Great Britain who was so traumatized that he was hospitalized
for 2 weeks!

While few children experience such dramatic consequences, approximately two-thirds of children have a fright experience from watching
TV or movies that lasts more than a week. In one of the best studies of
television and nightmares done to date, Belgian researchers surveyed
more than 2,500 high-school-age children[8] and asked them how often
they had television-related nightmares. These results are summarized on
page 108.

Almost 35 percent of 8th-grade boys and girls reported having TV-
related nightmares at least monthly. While nightmares were less common
in 12th-grade boys, more than 25 percent of 12th-grade girls continued to
have them monthly. Looking at these data, it's easy to see why Dr. Cantor
argues that television and movies are the largest preventable causes of
nightmares among children.

TV-Related Nightmare Frequency in Boys and Girls

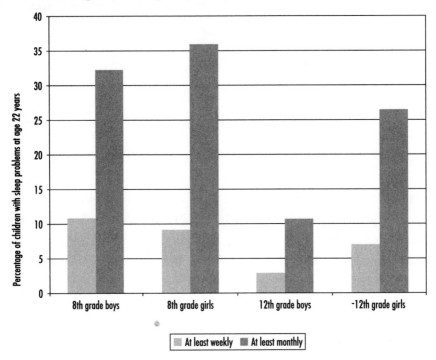

What scares children differs by age. Young children—before about age 8—are most frightened by the immediate sights and sounds on the screen. A scary-looking monster, a scream, a loud argument, and a fierce animal are all very threatening to young children and can affect them deeply.[9] For young children, an ogreish-looking mother—even if she is kind and well intentioned—is scary. Think of how many young children are frightened of clowns!

In part, young children's fears are based on their limited conceptualization of reality. By 4 or 5 years of age, they understand that television is not real; they know that if their mom or dad opened the back of the television set, little people and animals would not come spilling out. They understand that TV is a *representation* of reality. However, the difference between fictional and nonfictional representations of reality is quite subtle and often irrelevant to young children, whose job, after all, is to learn about the world as it presents itself to them, not to impose their own views on what they see.[10] A 4-year-old wants to know what life is like, and a mean dog on TV is a very scary part of life. It does little good to explain that the dog lived long ago, because preschoolers have only an approximate grasp of time. Nor is it useful to suggest that the dog is far away, because there are plenty of real dogs in the neighborhood. There's also no point in arguing that TV isn't real when the image of the scary dog on TV is just as real as the two-out, late-inning homer by Ichiro Suzuki that Daddy was so excited about yesterday or the home movie of the family's last vacation that they watch frequently.

The potential of television to frighten young children is also of concern because of the high proportion of frightening material in shows and movies designed for them. As we noted in Chapter 4, children's cartoons are violent. A 1985 Annenberg School for Communication study found that children's cartoons contain 29 percent more violence than adult primetime programming.[11] And don't forget, as we also discussed in Chapter 4, 100 percent of G-rated animated videos in the United States contain some violence.[12]

The violent content of cartoons and animated movies is supplemented by a heavy dose of similar content in commercials, which, as you'll see in Chapter 8, are part of 25 to 33 percent of children's viewing time. The worst offenders are often advertisements for TV shows or movies. For example, Dimitri watched the swimming finals of the 2004 Olympics with his son during primetime. Alexi, then 5, was an avid swimmer, and watching a swim meet take place in their homeland had the makings of a wholesome father-son moment. When the commercial break came, there was an ad for the season premiere of *ER*, featuring a car flying off a bridge into a river after the driver had been shot in the head—a rather dramatic and abrupt shift from the Olympic fare and definitely not what they had signed up for.

Violence isn't limited to commercials that promote shows on television or elsewhere. A 1994 study analyzed food advertisements aimed at children and found that the most common theme to emerge was violence, with fully two-thirds of ads involving some combination of violence, conflict, and trickery. In one example, Olive Oyl cried, "Popeye, space creatures are stealing Sweet Pea. Where's the spinach?" Popeye replied, "Can the spinach. I want my Instant Quaker Oatmeal," and then went on to fight and defeat the space creatures.[13]

Young children are very sensitive to all of this stressful fare. Researchers in Finland asked 20 5-year-olds to view approximately 5 minutes of children's television shows, such as *Tom and Jerry* cartoons or the equine classic *Black Beauty*. As the children watched, their faces were videotaped, and five independent judges later rated the emotions indicated by the children's expressions without knowing what they had been watching. The film clips that contained more physical and cartoon violence evoked significantly more fear, worry, and withdrawal than the nonviolent clips.

This study examined only the immediate effects of short video clips on children's emotions. While emotional consequences often persist for much longer, parents don't always know about their children's reactions to what they have seen. A survey of 6th and 10th graders asked whether they had ever been nervous about what they saw (and if it lasted for a long time), if they had trouble getting to sleep, or if they had bad dreams or nightmares about what they had seen. The children reported, on average, that this had happened "sometimes," while the mothers, on average, reported that it had happened "rarely."[14] This may not seem like a huge distinction, but it points to the fact that parents can be blissfully ignorant of how much impact TV has on their kids' sense of fear and safety.

Not all programs have scary images or themes, but many do. Why does the loss of a parent or sibling figure so prominently in so many of the movies that are specifically intended for young audiences, even those rated G by the Motion Picture Association of America? Why does Bambi's mother get shot? Why is the Lion King's father murdered (by his own brother, no less)? Why does Cinderella's kind father die, leaving in her in the hands of an evil stepmother? Why are Nemo and his father separated? As a general rule, these movies have happy endings that belie otherwise disturbing beginnings. Obviously, the makers of such programming put more stock in the destination than in the journey. It's as if all's well that ends well—as long as good ultimately triumphs over evil and the story ends in happily ever after. Yet children are not able to follow narratives well and often dwell on the details that make the greatest impression on them rather than on where the plot is going. For them, it's as much about the journey as about the destination. Many young children who watch *Finding Nemo* continue to ask what happened to his mommy long after adults have moved on to the more entertaining parts of the storyline.

To be sure, there is nothing new about the idea that children's stories are scary. The Grimm brothers' macabre fairy tales from the early 19th century might even rate a PG-13 by today's lax standards. Bruno Bettelheim argued that these fairy tales existed to serve a constructive purpose.[15] In the 1800s, parents often did die, people did get very sick, and children were frequently orphaned. What's more, children were well aware of the cruel vagaries of life, as they were all around. Fairy tales in those days typically were read or told to children while they were in the relative comfort and security of a caregiver's lap. Kids had the chance to be reassured by a hug or a talk about what had happened in the stories. These stories, then, were construed not so much to *create* anxiety in children as to alleviate it. But times have changed, and it would be hard to make the same argument for today's stories or shows. Parents, of course, sometimes do die prematurely today, but hardly with the frequency that they did back then, and certainly not often enough to make it necessary to teach children about the possibility at such an early age. Also, don't forget that, unlike stories or tales, which are told when parents and children are in physical proximity, movies are frequently watched by kids by themselves, so the children are left to process these terrifying moments on their own.

Unlike young children, older children tend to be more frightened by dramatizations of events that they perceive as posing a credible threat to them. In a study conducted after the nationally televised drama *The Day After*, in which a Kansas community is depicted after a nuclear attack, young children were surprisingly unaffected, whereas teenagers found it very distressing.[16] By the time children are in late elementary school and into adolescence, they are better able to intellectually cope with the fearsome aspects of what they see. They become able to tell themselves "it's not real," or "it's only a movie." However, this cognitive coping comes with a downside, since children at these ages can better understand, remember, and generalize threats. They're able to manage instances of bloody injuries or screaming or rabid beasts by comforting or distracting themselves. But the more able they are to cope with the graphic images they see on-screen, the more vulnerable they are to abstract threats that aren't directly portrayed. For older children, more realistic threats, such as war, disease, or child abductors, dominate their fears.

You might argue that fear of real risks is inevitable and perhaps even healthy in that these fears promote social awareness or safety consciousness. You might even argue that if television depicts real-life events, it can't be more harmful than reality. After all, wars do occur, people get seriously ill, and children are occasionally abducted.

But the problem is that television in general—even reality-based programs—exaggerates risks. For example, only 0.2 percent of crimes reported by the FBI are murders, whereas about 50 percent of the crimes in reality-based television programs are murders. Television news shows, especially local broadcasts, lead with sensational headlines about the latest local murder, accident, abduction, or assault. Watching the news can make the world—or worse, your city—seem like a very scary place to live.

Most of the time, fright reactions are completely manageable. But for most people, at some point and for whatever reason, watching a particularly scary and powerful scene leads to a deeply distressed emotional response. A study conducted in Wisconsin asked college students to report on a time when they had seen something on TV or in a movie that really scared them. Two-thirds of the students reported that they had had such an experience that lasted more than a week. The average age at which these students had their frightening viewing experience was just 14.

The immediate reactions included crying, screaming, shaking, nausea, clinging to a companion, feeling cold, sweating, and numbness. Longer-lasting symptoms included avoiding certain rooms or situations, prolonged nervousness, and avoiding certain movies. After seeing *Jaws*, one student reported:

> *I had fun watching the shark, but I was surprised at the effect it had on me when I went swimming in Wisconsin lakes. If someone yelled "Jaws!" and I was in the water, my heart would start racing and I would fly out of the water. It lasted a good year.*[17]

This student was not put off from swimming forever, but she did quit the swim team—in the middle of a race—the day after seeing *Jaws*. Many children modify their behaviors to avoid activities associated with scary things they've seen on television or in movies. An experiment with elementary school children found that those who saw 5-minute depictions of drownings or out-of-control fires on TV were more likely than those who saw neutral depictions of fire or water to say that those experiences could happen to them. Subsequently, they were also less interested in doing related activities, such as canoeing, swimming, building a fire, or baking a pizza.[18] One revealing part of this research is that the depiction of fire came not from some terrifying horror film but from *Little House on the Prairie*. Even when disturbing scenes are included in a mostly gentle, pastoral show, they can have a lasting impact on children.

Dr. Cantor's research has uncovered a bewildering array of long-lasting changes in behavior as children try to fend off the perceived threats they have absorbed from television and movies. Children report that for years, they sleep with blankets around their necks to foil the advances of vampires, lock the bathroom door while showering to keep psychos at bay, stay out of large pools to reduce the possibility of encountering concealed underwater shark tanks, stay out of small pools so as not to be sucked through the drain at the bottom, stay out of lakes with lily pads to give killer blobs a wide berth, and stay off ski slopes so as not to end up dangling by a ski from a lift chair. As Dr. Cantor puts it, "A few hours of entertainment have altered their lives."

While many of these fears stem from recognizable horror films, others come from sources as seemingly benign as *Willy Wonka and the Chocolate Factory* and *Rescue 911*. This observation suggests that it isn't just highly scary horror or crime genres that can frighten kids but also realistic depictions of real-world threats. Another student in the Wisconsin study reported:

> *It was a show about the effects of a nuclear war* [The Day After] . . . *I was, needless to say, completely terrified and obsessed with the idea that the world would soon come to an end. I had horrifying nightmares and experienced stomach pains to the point where my mother had to take me to the doctor. Still, however, I can feel the terror I had for those couple of weeks.*

Today, environmental disasters such as the Asian tsunami and Hurricane Katrina periodically dominate the airwaves, but terrorism has since displaced nuclear war as the ongoing global threat of the moment. Among New York City schoolchildren, those who watched a lot of coverage of the 9/11 attacks on television were three times more likely to exhibit post-traumatic stress reactions than those who did not.[19] That highly televised event was dramatic, but more mundane threats are everywhere, most particularly on the nightly news, which has put increasing emphasis on violence and sensationalism in recent years. The proportion of television news shows devoted to sensational and human interest stories—including crime, violence, accidents, and natural disasters—more than doubled between 1976 and 1992.[20] No doubt the degree of sensationalism has only increased in recent years.

Although elementary school children aren't regular viewers of television news, a significant number do watch occasionally—as many as half a million 2- to 11-year-olds on any given night. And what the news has to offer these children is unmistakably disturbing. A study of grade school children conducted in 1994 found that 25 percent of kindergarteners had been upset by news in the previous year, and the number rose to 45 percent for 6th graders. The specific threats that disturbed the children included:

- Stranger violence (35 percent of incidents)
- War or famine abroad (32 percent)
- Natural disasters (25 percent)
- Violence against children (19 percent)
- Animal violence (as victim or perpetrator; 6 percent)
- Acquaintance violence (4 percent)

Simply put, the stuff on the screen spills into the lives of children.

Fear is the best-studied mechanism by which the content, or the *what*, of programming can affect sleep, but it isn't the only one. Another way in which TV may interfere with sleep is by increased stimulation right before bedtime. The exhilaration that a teenage devotee of *Monday Night Football* may feel when his team wins, or the anguish he may experience when they lose, can inhibit his ability to fall asleep, even when the game ends after midnight. This arousal effect isn't limited to sports programs. At its best, educational programming promotes thought and action: Think of the dancing at the end of *Dora the Explorer,* the challenges posed by *Blue's Clues,* or the excitement of a deep-sea shark feeding frenzy on the Discovery Channel. Such excitement could interfere with your child's relaxation before bed and keep him keyed up way past his bedtime.

HOW IT IS WATCHED: THE CONTEXT
OF VIEWING CAN CAUSE SLEEP PROBLEMS

Beyond what is viewed, the *act* of viewing itself may contribute to difficulty sleeping. The simplest means by which television may affect sleep is by displacing it. Children of all ages, but particularly young ones, are apt to procrastinate and avoid going to sleep. Hunger, thirst, and additional hugs all take on renewed urgency as bedtime approaches, so why wouldn't television? Negotiations for later bedtimes are frequent occurrences in our households. Left to their own devices, children may easily forgo sleep to channel surf or watch the ballgame. In fact, as many as 30 percent of children of all ages (including those under 6) and 70 percent of teenagers have televisions in their bedrooms, placing temptation at arm's length. Parents may encourage this habit, particularly if they view television as an educational or otherwise worthwhile activity, as one in two parents report they do.[21] Think of the mother in a commercial for V-Smile (a television-based game for young children) who says, "You can stay up 1 hour later if you play your video game." Whether watching television before bed is a part of the routine or an optional evening activity for children, it can push bedtimes back.

Another way that the very act of viewing may affect sleep is related to what we discussed earlier: Turning off the set after watching for a while can leave you feeling agitated. As you saw, rather than being a relaxing activity—such as taking a warm bath or reading a book, the effects of which linger—television's relaxation effects don't last. The increased agitation you may feel after viewing can happen no matter what you've watched. Parents often report that their children are riled up or irritable after a long TV session, and it's obvious that being agitated makes going to sleep more difficult. These parents are simply experiencing what has long been scientifically documented.

This physical agitation brings us back to where we began, with the physiology of sleep deprivation, and a theory we've been investigating (although it has yet to be scientifically proven): Television may impede sleep by suppressing melatonin release, leading to the phase shift. While we know of no research to date that has focused specifically on the effects of television's glow on melatonin secretion, in theory, this light may be sufficient to suppress it. We've done some preliminary research to determine how much light there is when watching television, and this is what we found.

How Many Lux Does a TV Emit?

TV Size (in)	Room Lights On	Distance from Set (in)	Lux
27	No	48	40
27	Yes	48	250
27	No	12	120
27	Yes	12	300
55	No	48	60
55	Yes	48	260
55	No	12	200
55	Yes	12	320

Remember, light that exceeds the 200-lux threshold has been shown to impede melatonin secretion. In all but one of these situations, this amount was present when the room lights were on; in the other case, the light was measured 12 inches away from a big-screen TV. If melatonin suppression is the way in which television inhibits sleep, it probably has more to do with watching with the lights on than with television itself. But you can see that the distance from the set is also very important. Although 12 inches is closer than most people sit, sitting farther away is clearly protective (and how many parents have repeated conversations with their kids about sitting too close to the set?). Also, many kids watch television with the lights on, especially if what they're watching might be scary, and being excited in the setting of bright light suppresses melatonin secretion even more than bright light alone.[22] So, it seems to be the perfect setup: Stimulating TV watched at night, with the lights on, could easily cause a melatonin phase shift. In this sense, the *what* and *how* of viewing can interact to make the effects on sleep even stronger.

SCIENCE SHEDS SOME LIGHT ON TV AND SLEEP

The bottom line is that kids who watch a lot of TV have trouble sleeping. Judith Owens, MD, and her colleagues at Brown University surveyed the parents of almost 500 children ages 4 to 10. Compared to children who watched very little bedtime television, those who watched a lot were much more likely to resist going to bed, have trouble falling asleep and staying asleep, be afraid to sleep, and wake up during the night. In addition, their teachers said the children who watched more than 2 hours of TV per day on weekdays were more likely to be sleepy during the day (one of the signs of sleep problems discussed earlier). Interestingly, the parents in the study didn't identify daytime sleepiness to the same extent as the teachers did.[23] Of course, this could simply be because many parents don't see their school-age children during the day to observe just how drowsy they are. If you're concerned about how much sleep your children are getting, you may want to ask their teachers if they seem sleepy during the day.

To test the effects of television on preschool children, we conducted a study of 2,000 children under the age of 3. Parents were asked how many hours of television their children viewed on a typical day and whether they had consistent bedtimes and naptimes. We found that the more television children watched, the less likely they were to have regular sleep times. Toddlers who watched more than 3 hours per day were 20 percent more likely to have irregular bedtime schedules than those who watched none.[24] Keeping regular schedules ensures that children get an adequate amount of quality sleep, which is critical for their development and essential to help preserve parents' sanity.

Do these effects last? Quite possibly. Researchers from the New York State Psychiatric Institute interviewed 759 children and their mothers when the kids were 14, 16, and 22 years of age. Because of the way they collected their data, the researchers were able to adjust for the sleep problems that children had at age 14 and to assess their sleep problems at ages 16 and 22,[25] so we're certain that the sleep problems didn't lead to television viewing but rather that television viewing led to sleep problems. Their results are presented in the graph below.

Television Viewing at Age 14 and More Than Two Sleep Problems at Age 22

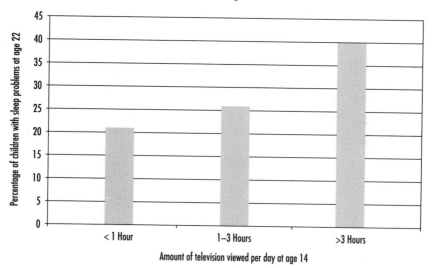

Amount of television viewed per day at age 14

Overall, 21 percent of children who watched less than 1 hour of television at age 14 had more than two sleep problems at age 22, compared to 26 percent of those who watched 1 to 3 hours and 40 percent of those who watched 3 hours or more. In other words, watching 3 or more hours of TV more than doubled the chances of these kids developing sleep problems that persisted into young adulthood. Considering how essential quality sleep is to overall health and happiness, those hours could perhaps be better spent elsewhere—probably in bed!

Television can be the cause of sleep problems in a variety of ways. What your children watch (content) is important because it can frighten them, lead to nightmares, and limit both the quantity and quality of their sleep. How they watch (context) is also important. Watching before bedtime, especially with the lights on, may make falling asleep more difficult. If your children have sleep problems of any kind, it's worth exploring television's role. Watching a program before bed may seem like a treat, but it can come at serious cost to good sleep. And it may surprise you to know that sleep deprivation has also been linked to overweight. Perhaps that's another one of the many ways in which TV can be accused of making our kids fat—the subject of our next chapter.

HOW TO MAKE TV WORK FOR YOUR CHILDREN'S SLEEP

ALL AGES

- If your children are having sleep problems, reduce television viewing, especially in the evening.
- If your children do watch television within 3 hours of bedtime, make sure that the room is dark and that they sit at least 5 feet from the screen.
- Take the TV out of your child's bedroom.
- Avoid televised news, especially local news, if your children are younger than 10.
- If your children do see scary news stories, talk to them about what's happening. Find out what they're thinking first, then provide honest

factual information in a way that they can understand. When possible, emphasize how "safe" they are from that threat.

- Avoid frightening programming. Here are some guidelines on what scares children, depending on their ages.[26]

2- TO 7-YEAR-OLDS

- Scary visual images: vicious animals, monsters, grotesque characters
- Character transformations, especially when a normal character becomes grotesque
- Stories involving the death of a parent
- Stories with vivid depictions of natural disasters

8- TO 12-YEAR-OLDS

- More realistic threats and dangers, especially things that can happen to the child
- Violence or the threat of violence
- Stories involving child victims

13–YEAR-OLDS AND UP

- Realistic physical harm or threats of intense harm
- Molestation or sexual assault
- Threats from aliens or occult forces

CHAPTER 6

DOES THE SCREEN ADD OR REMOVE 10 POUNDS? TELEVISION, BODY IMAGE, AND OBESITY

In general, my children refuse to eat anything that hasn't danced on television.
Erma Bombeck

If it weren't for the fact that the TV set and the refrigerator are so far apart,
some of us wouldn't get any exercise at all.
Joey Adams

After a typical school day, 13-year-old Laura Rhodes, who wore a size 24 dress, returned home and took a month's worth of her antidepressant medication. Described by her parents as a "happy, outgoing schoolgirl" and by her teacher as a "bright and hardworking pupil who had a close group of friends," she was bullied at school and suffered bouts of depression that ultimately overcame her. Her parents publicly decried the oppressive tyranny of weight consciousness and the mercilessness of her classmates. They released letters left behind by Laura that made it clear that the teasing she endured at school because of her weight became too much for her. Each morning as she thought about going to school, her heart beat faster and she felt a "gripping" sensation inside. Lying in bed, she hated every moment as she watched the seconds tick away until she had to get into the car to go to school. Taunts of "Oh, my God, look at the size of her" accompanied the efforts to trip her on her way from class to class.

Laura's tragedy was hardly an isolated incident. A Minnesota study found that adolescent girls are 60 percent more likely to try to commit suicide if they are teased by peers about their weight.[1] Self-inflicted injury is the starkest and most consequential effect of the obesity epidemic that is afflicting our children. But in addition to devastating peer persecution, the damage also includes health-threatening chronic conditions, such as type 2 diabetes (once called adult-onset diabetes), high blood pressure, and heart disease. For the first time in 200 years, the next generation of American children is projected to be the first to have shorter life expectancies than the previous one.[2]

In this chapter, we review two contrasting but equally damaging messages of television: the promotion of the "thin ideal" and the widespread celebration of an unhealthful diet. We will explore the ways in which television can affect children's body image by making them aspire to unrealistic, unnatural, and damaging standards for themselves and others and by promoting a societal weight consciousness that can marginalize, alienate, and ultimately victimize overweight children. We'll also address television's considerable role in making children obese.

NICE AND HEAVY

People on television—women in particular—are thin. They are much thinner than the U.S. population as a whole, to such an extent that fewer than one-quarter of women in the general population are as thin as the average female television character. The average woman on TV is 5 feet 7 inches and weighs 100 pounds. The average American woman is 5 feet 4 inches and weighs 140 pounds.[3] Not only are women on television thin, but they have become steadily thinner over time. In the 1960s, the average fashion model weighed 8 percent less than the average American woman. By the 1980s, she weighed 23 percent less.[4] By some estimates, up to one-third of female television and movie characters are thin enough to qualify as anorexic.

For men, the issues are somewhat different. Male television characters are also often thinner than the U.S. norm, although not by nearly the same margin as women. But men on television—whether as heroes of action-adventure shows or as state governors—are also much more muscled than normal men, and this creates its own image problem for boys. To be sure, there are several popular series that feature heavy men—*Drew Carey* and *The King of Queens*, for example—and it's unclear what effect (if any) the popularity of such shows will have on boys—or on girls, for that matter.

Children begin to acquire a sense of their own bodies around age 4, and by age 6 or 7 they have not only absorbed society's views of what constitutes attractive bodies but also adopted some social prejudices about moral qualities associated with body types. In one typical study, 6- to 9-year-olds were shown silhouettes of thin, normal, and heavy body shapes. The children liked the thin silhouettes best and described them as friendly, happy, and polite. They described the heavy silhouettes as lazy, lying, and cheating.[5]

Such prejudices do not originate with TV, but television viewing does sustain and nurture them. Kristen Harrison, PhD, of the University of Illinois showed 1st, 2nd, and 3rd graders simple drawings of either a heavy girl or a thin girl and asked whether they thought the child would be nice, smart, clean, unselfish, honest, and have lots of friends.[6] Boys who watched more television gave more negative assessments of the heavy girl's personality than of the thin girl's. While the type of TV the boys had been watching wasn't recorded, it's a fair bet that they hadn't just been curled up in front of the Discovery Channel.

Young boys seem ready to think the worst of heavy girls even before they meet them, and a great deal of commercial TV plays to this instinct. Thinner women get more compliments on TV, while heavier women get insults. Moreover, the effect appears to be cumulative, with each pound earning a couple of smart remarks, until the heaviest women serve no function at all except as objects of abuse. Certainly, TV did not invent the idea that thin is beautiful, but it may fairly be blamed for perpetuating the idea that both inner and outer beauty can be measured by looking at how a woman tips the scales rather than how she tips the waiter. Such so-called fat stereotyping can be very damaging to the ability of heavy children—especially heavy girls—to get along with others. It's very likely that the boys who tormented Laura Rhodes had their values reinforced via televised images.

THE ELASTIC BODY

Equally dramatic are the effects of television viewing on girls' and boys' self-images and self-esteem. The concern with body size starts early, with even some toddlers experiencing eating disorders.[7] By elementary school, up to 45 percent of children report wanting to be thinner, and 37 percent have tried some form of dieting.[8] Television teaches children about their bodies in subtle and not-so-subtle ways. Researchers at the State University of New York at Stonybrook were able to manipulate college students' assessments of their weight by showing them just 10 minutes of television advertising.[9] One group of students saw ads in which very sexy, attractive models were featured; the other group saw ads that were selected to be enjoyable but didn't feature especially attractive models.

After viewing the ads, participants were asked to identify as accurately as possible their own body types from a 10-picture assortment of different types. Women who saw the sexy ads rated themselves as significantly heavier than those who saw the nonsexy ads. But the results were different for men, reflecting the differing social values of ideal body type for each gender. Men who saw the sexy ads rated themselves as significantly skinnier than those who viewed the nonsexy ads. If watching just a handful of commercials can significantly change someone's estimate of their own body size, just think of the cumulative effect of watching *thousands* of commercials.

Given the remarkable effect of television on our ideas of our own weight, it's no surprise that both women and men who watch more television and movies—and especially music videos—are more dissatisfied with their weight, independent of how much they actually weigh.[10, 11] In the current controversy over the obesity epidemic, it's worth noting that 83 percent of girls who want to lose weight are actually of normal weight.[12] This observation provides an entrée for parents who want to discuss weight issues with their children. The bodies of TV actors aren't normal, and their thinness (for women) is often unhealthy. In fact, dieting isn't recommended for children and is advised only in extreme situations for adolescents. The best diet is a balanced one that includes regular meals, not reckless restriction or consumption.

As parents, you should have these issues on your radar screen because of the potential for real health consequences. Girls who watch a lot of television tend to diet more and are at increased risk for developing eating disorders such as anorexia and bulimia. Short of such tragic extremes, many women lose self-esteem and a sense of well-being after watching television.[13]

You might imagine that such effects are most common when watching "ideal-body" shows such as *America's Next Top Model*, *Models Inc.*, or *Extreme Makeover*. In fact, the effects are just as strong from all kinds of television.[14] One recent study looked at the effects of what might be called thin-ideal sports: gymnastics, ice skating, and cheerleading.[15] The researchers wanted to know how such television might affect "self-objectification," or the tendency to describe oneself in purely physically descriptive terms rather than in terms of abilities, talents, feelings, or thoughts. A group of teenage girls was divided into small groups who watched 8-minute video clips of either "thin-ideal" women's sports, other women's sports, or men's sports. Afterward, the girls were asked to complete the statement "I am . . ." in 20 different ways. Their answers were then grouped into five different categories, including:

- Body shape and size (e.g., "I am overweight"; "I am tall")
- Other physical attributes ("I am blonde")
- Physical abilities ("I am strong")
- Nonphysical abilities and traits ("I am friendly")
- Emotions ("I am sick of filling this out")

The girls who watched the thin-ideal women's sports wrote more responses that focused on body shape and size than girls who had seen other women's sports. Something as seemingly harmless as watching certain women's sports can have an important impact on how girls see themselves. In certain ways, TV can teach them to think of themselves more in terms of how their bodies look and less in terms of how they feel or what they can do.

Self-perception is directly related to self-esteem. The more likely girls are to describe themselves in terms of their bodies, the more likely they are to be depressed, to be dissatisfied with their bodies, and to have eating disorders.[16] But does body dissatisfaction caused by television actually lead to depression, or does depression alter the amount and kind of television people view? In fact, the evidence implies that television and movies truly do cause body image problems. When a group of college women viewed either 12 minutes of commercials with very thin, attractive female models or 12 minutes of commercials with "normal" women, those who saw the commercials with the thin models were more depressed, anxious, and angry, as well as significantly less satisfied with their bodies, than the other group.[17]

One of the most striking findings to emerge from this research is the very small amount of time it takes to significantly alter self-perception, self-esteem, and mood. In these studies, just 10 minutes of selected commercials was all it took for women and men to adversely change their estimates of how much they weighed. Just 12 minutes of commercials caused women to become dissatisfied with their bodies, depressed, and angry. Just 8 minutes of thin-ideal sports videos caused girls to think about what their bodies looked like rather than what they could do. This was true regardless of the women's weight—even if they had nothing at all to be concerned about.

A paradox of television is that it is blamed for promoting both body self-consciousness and obesity—divergent but equally damaging effects. But talking about the real and profound ways that TV can make children and adolescents want to be thin doesn't address the contribution of television to making children fat. Before we explore what science tells us about how television does (and does not) affect obesity, let's start by reviewing what we all already know: U.S. children are getting fatter.

THE METEORIC RISE OF OBESITY

The popular press inundates us with numbers confirming what we already know if we simply look around the playground: More and more children are overweight. The graph on page 130 shows a dramatic rise in obesity beginning in the late 1970s. In fact, the percentage of U.S. children who are overweight almost tripled between 1980 and 2000.

It is convenient and at times even fun to single out television as the sole culprit in the current obesity epidemic. The truth is, however, that the dramatic and startling rise in childhood obesity in this country and elsewhere is due to many factors.

Television viewing increased gradually at a steady pace from the 1960s to the 1980s, but it has remained largely unchanged over the past 20 years. By contrast, obesity rates also rose gradually from the 1960s to the 1980s, but they have skyrocketed since then. If TV viewing were *entirely* responsible for this increase, we would expect the amount of viewing time to also have risen during this period.

40 Years of Change in Children's Weight

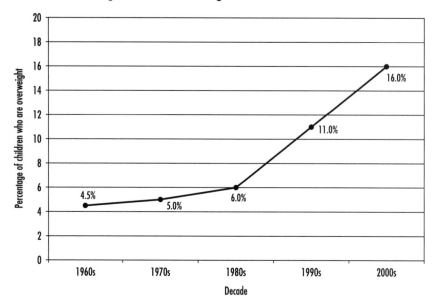

We do know that limiting television viewing can, at least partially, prevent excessive weight gain. Tom Robinson, MD, of Stanford University proved this for the first time in the best-done study to date. He selected two elementary schools and implemented a plan that used a variety of approaches to reduce television viewing among children at one of them.[18] Among other things, Dr. Robinson asked children to select activities other than watching television, he taught them about the problems of viewing, and he empowered them to resist viewing, and the students reduced their TV time by about 5 hours per week. At the end of the 6-month trial, those students were less overweight than students in the control school.

This study—the only one to date to employ this experimental approach—demonstrated a definitive relationship between television and obesity: Watching television *causes* obesity, and reducing viewing time *reduces* it. But Dr. Robinson's work doesn't answer the question of *how* decreasing television viewing decreases excessive weight gain. Is it what's on (content) that leads to weight gain because children eat what they see on commercials, or is it how it's watched (context), because watching is sedentary and burns fewer calories than being active? Before turning to these questions, a few words about weight and weight gain.

WEIGHT IS IN THE BALANCE

How do we gain weight? Fad diets notwithstanding, the simple answer is energy balance—calories in versus calories out. Gaining weight is strikingly easy—for an adult, 100 excess calories per day (the equivalent of one Girl Scout cookie) translates to an extra 10 pounds per year!

Weight gain in children is a bit more complicated since all healthy children gain weight as part of growing. For children, the issue is *excessive* weight gain. Television may be a double threat by affecting both factors in the energy balance equation: It could make us snack more and tempt us to eat unhealthy foods that we see in commercials, and it could reduce the number of calories we burn because we're passive while watching. Kids are by nature very active; if they weren't watching TV, the thinking goes that they would probably be doing something that would burn more calories.

It's also important to consider kids' basal metabolic rates (BMR). BMR is a measure of how fast your body burns calories while just existing—breathing, thinking, and circulating blood. This rate is different for everyone, but research has shown that as little as 20 minutes of vigorous physical activity per day raises BMR for 24 to 48 hours *after* exercise. So does television lower BMR? Does that effect linger even after the set is turned off? Researchers at Memphis State University sought to find out. A group of 31 children between the ages of 8 and 12 were brought into the lab and asked to lie on beds with their heads propped on several pillows.

Their BMRs were calculated in this sedentary position over a 25-minute period. Next, they watched television. The researchers chose *The Wonder Years*, a medium-paced, nonviolent, prosocial program that was very popular with this age group at the time. Their findings are summarized below.

Basal Metabolic Rate Before, During, and After TV Viewing

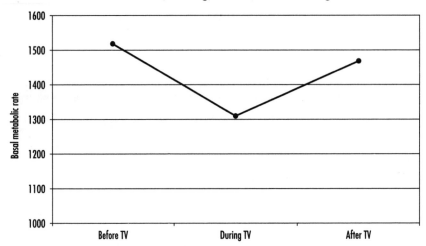

While the kids watched TV, their BMRs dropped by an average of 211 calories; after viewing, they increased by 150 calories but remained lower than before viewing. In other words, television (at least *The Wonder Years*) reduced their BMRs to the point where they were burning *fewer* calories than they would if they were lying down and doing nothing, and this reduction persisted to some extent for 25 minutes after the set was turned off.[19] How could this be? Is watching television somehow less active than doing *nothing*? And where does the energy saving come from? We still breathe while we watch; our hearts still beat. Are our brains (which consume a lot of metabolic energy) less active during viewing? Perhaps, but it would be pretty amazing if a program like *The Wonder Years* actually taxed the brain less than lying idly.

A second possible explanation for these findings is the "fidget factor." Metabolism expert Eric Ravussin, PhD, of Louisiana State University simultaneously measured calorie expenditure and motion in study subjects. He found that there were big differences in the way people performed an everyday activity like watching television. Some participants sat still without moving a muscle, others squirmed every now and then, and still others kept getting up and moving around the room. Dr. Ravussin estimated that the fidget factor burned 300 to 800 calories a day. In the case of the kids' BMR experiment, then, the choice of show may have actually been critical. A violent program that might excite them either physiologically (speeding up their heart rate) or physically (prompting them to squirm) might increase their BMRs, or at least not reduce them. *The Wonder Years* must have held their attention, riveting them to their beds and having the net effect of reducing fidgeting.

Indeed, another experiment had children lie in bed and either read, do nothing, or watch an episode of *The Cosby Show.* Researchers found the kids moved more while sitting and reading than while watching television.[20]

But screen time doesn't always mean less fidgeting. Young children are rarely inactive when they watch television, opting instead to play, jump, or act out what they are viewing (as when watching *The Wiggles*, which encourages toddlers to get up and exercise). This is particularly true of younger kids when they're not that interested in the content of the program.[21,22] Perhaps for this reason, although some researchers succeeded in reducing television viewing among preschoolers, they found no effects on their weight.[23] One recent study found that, among children who were playing a video game, their BMRs were actually increased relative to simply sitting. The researchers' estimate was that 7- to 10- year-old children would burn 20 to 40 more calories per day if they played 30 minutes of an interactive video game instead of simply lying on the couch.[24] Hardly a stay-fit strategy, but further evidence that not all viewing represses BMR. Clearly, BMR is not the whole picture, but parents who are concerned about their kids' level of activity can select programming that's more likely to increase the fidget factor. So, if BMR isn't the answer, what is?

MASHING THE COUCH POTATO THEORY

One of the most straightforward ways television may affect obesity rates is simply by making children more sedentary, thereby decreasing the number of calories they burn. The logic is simple, and it *seems* irrefutable. Over a 24-hour period, 16 of which are waking hours (excepting the bizarre sleep habits of teenagers), there is a finite amount of time for a variety of activities. The more television children watch, the less time they have for activities that burn more calories. But the linchpin of this theory is the assumption that television displaces activities that burn more calories rather than other sedentary ones, such as reading or playing with Legos. Figuring out just which activities television displaces is surprisingly difficult, but some evidence suggests that TV viewing *primarily displaces other sedentary activities.* (For example, although Dr. Robinson's students watched less TV, he found no evidence that they were more active.)

For example, the introduction of television in the 1950s led to a dramatic reduction in comic book reading among kids and in movie attendance among adults. (Remember, as discussed in Chapter 5, people often seek out television when they want to relax, not as an alternative to a game of touch football.) Just reducing TV time doesn't necessarily help kids lose weight or become more active. You should ask yourself whether your children are watching television during a time when they would otherwise be playing outside, or whether they're watching when the alternative would be gazing at a lava lamp. Our parents used to throw us out of the house when the weather was nice, in effect forcing us to find outdoor activities that were more calorically demanding. As Stanford's Dr. Tom

Robinson himself recently mused, "I wonder if the best approach might be to simply lock kids out of the house for 2 hours after school."

You must also consider that not all types of programs are equal. Children who play sports often like to watch them on television, and they frequently follow news of their favorite teams and players. As mentioned in Chapter 3, children's sports heroes inspire them to push themselves harder on the courts and fields. For this group of children, then, television viewing may even *increase* physical activity. A varsity basketball player who watches 12 hours of college games per week may have trouble finding time for homework, but she's unlikely to be obese as a result of viewing. If the Nike commercial that encouraged kids to strive to "be like Mike" made them play harder on the court and practice more often, TV may have helped them achieve a healthy weight rather than having the opposite effect. Once again, *content* and *context* drive the effects of television on children. It's not merely how many hours they watch (quantity), it's also what they watch (content and quality) and how they watch (context).

TV AND SNACKING

Alltvstuff.com sells TV snack trays that "are made of metal and give you that classic 'retro' look. You'll enjoy snacks and meals in comfort as you watch your favorite TV show." The retro look no doubt owes much to that American innovation, the TV dinner. Its roots lie in a time when Gerald Thomas, an executive at Swanson and Sons, was dealing with a turkey problem. After overestimating the demand for Thanksgiving turkey in 1953, the company had 270 tons left over and not enough room in its corporate refrigerators to store it. The interim solution was to have the turkey travel back and forth across the country in refrigerated trains (which must keep moving to stay cold).

Thomas's breakthrough idea occurred when he visited the food production site of Pan American Airways, where the food service trays gave him the idea of using something similar for his turkey. The trays were modified to tie into the nation's biggest craze at the time—television. The boxes were designed to look like televisions, but the intent was to capitalize on TV's popularity, not necessarily to encourage eating in front of the set. As Thomas said in an Associated Press interview on the 45th anniversary of TV dinners, "Television was the talk of the day. Television was something that if you had one, you were contemporary, you were cool. If it were today, we'd probably call it the 'digital dinner.'" Swanson gambled by making 5,000 dinners in the first production run, and more than 10 million were sold that year. The choice of packaging had an unintended effect however. A year later, more than 25 million TV dinners were served in front of television sets in living rooms across America.

Thanks to Thomas, eating in front of the television became popular right at the advent of the medium itself—and it's still a common practice. We recently found that 30 percent of children eat dinner in front of the TV,[25] a fact that may profoundly influence family relations. But perhaps more important to the relationship between television viewing and obesity is that an equal number of children regularly snack in front of the screen. Most viewers automatically connect TV time with snack time, and "TV snack" is part of everyday parlance. You can find hundreds of recipes for TV snacks on the Web. Here's an example.

1 cup plain Cheerios
½ cup Nestlé's semi-sweet chocolate chips

Mix Cheerios and chocolate chips in a bowl. Serves one. Enjoy!

The "chef" then adds, "I guarantee you will get hooked on it!"

Let's hope not. This single-serving TV snack has no fewer than 670 calories! You'll recall that eating as few as 100 extra calories per day is sufficient to result in a 10-pound weight gain over a year. Eating snacks like these while watching TV could have disastrous consequences to your midsection!

Could it be that eating in front of the television merely displaces eating elsewhere, much as watching television displaces other sedentary activities? There seems to be something more at work. We have to agree that there's something intensely gratifying about eating in front of the screen; why else would people pay such outrageous rates for popcorn at movie theaters?

Is eating while viewing so appealing that viewing leads to overindulgence? Nanette Stroebele, PhD, of Georgia State University was convinced this was the case and sought to test it.[26] The design of her study was quite clever. She and her colleagues had 78 undergraduate students keep diaries of precisely what they ate and when they ate it during a 7-day period. They also recorded when they watched television during the same period. On some days, students reported watching little or no television, and on others, they reported watching a great deal. Dr. Stroebele then looked at how many meals and how many calories the students consumed on days when they watched television compared to days when they didn't watch. She wasn't comparing food consumption by viewers versus nonviewers but rather how much food the students ate on days when they watched TV versus days when they didn't. Her results are impressive.

On days when the students watched television, they ate $3\frac{1}{2}$ meals on average, compared to $2\frac{3}{4}$ meals on non-TV days. And the additional meals were not small ones. Not only did they eat more meals, they also ate more calories. On TV days, the students consumed 1,900 calories on average, versus 1,737 on days when they didn't watch. What's more, the students recorded how hungry they were prior to eating a meal, based on a scale of 1 to 7 (1 for not hungry and 7 for extremely hungry). On TV days, as you might expect given the increased calorie intake, they reported being less hungry before eating (5.12 versus 5.42 on non-TV days). Thus, watching television caused the students to take in an average of 163 more calories per day, and they ate more even though they were less hungry before meals.

Eating while watching is a key contextual way in which television can lead to obesity. Try to avoid it, but if you feel compelled to satisfy your children's craving for snacks while viewing, choose nutritious options: Carrots or cut-up apples are good choices (and less messy than chips). Use the allure of the combination of viewing and snacking to increase your children's intake of fruits and vegetables.

TV AND FOOD CHOICES

When Ray Kroc, a Multimixer salesman, set out from Oak Park, Illinois, to visit a hamburger stand in San Bernardino, California, in 1954, he was interested in selling mixers, not in making U.S. children obese. Intrigued by the number of mixers Dick and Mac McDonald were buying, Kroc decided to visit their hamburger franchise personally to learn more about it. Quickly realizing that the growth of their enterprise would enhance sales of his product, he became very invested in their success—so much so that he took over the company himself in 1961.

Twenty-seven years later, *Fortune* magazine named McDonald's hamburgers among the 100 products America makes best. By all accounts, the rise of McDonald's from a small local hamburger stand to an international icon is a quintessential American success story. Although it's now frequently maligned as a major contributor to the rise in childhood obesity, until very recently, McDonald's success was heralded. U.S. Secretary of Agriculture Charles Murphy ate the 500 millionth McDonald's hamburger in a public ceremony in 1961. In 1963, the billionth hamburger was served by Ray Kroc on Art Linkletter's nationally televised show. And in 1990, *Life* magazine named Ray Kroc as one of the "100 most important Americans of the 20th century."

McDonald's meteoric rise in sales owes much to the success of its advertising campaigns, which remain the envy of many in the industry and a source of more than a few earworm jingles for the rest of us. In 2000, *Advertising Age* reviewed and ranked the most successful campaigns of all time. The 1971 McDonald's campaign, "You deserve a break today," was ranked number five. The jingle that accompanied the ads (can you hum it now?) was rated number one, ahead of the army's "Be all that you can be" and Campbell's soup's "M'm M'm good." Ronald McDonald was second only to the Marlboro man as an ad icon. He's credited with bringing fast food to children in the same way the rugged cowboy brought cigarettes to adults (and children).

These televised icons and advertisements and their accompanying jingles are problematic. People who watch a lot of television are more likely to rate unhealthy foods as "good for you."[27] More than half of 9- to 10-year-old Australian children believe that Ronald McDonald knows best what's good for children to eat, and television is where they grew to trust him. As much as 40 percent of McDonald's advertising—the overwhelming majority of which is televised—is directed at children. In 1965, the company's sales were $200 million; today, they exceed $37 billion. Sales began to take off in 1970 and have risen steadily ever since. Notably, that year was also when McDonaldland became the setting for a new series of advertisements directed at children, and in 1977, the Happy Meal was introduced. The meteoric rise in sales began when children became a major focus of the franchise business model. Coincidence?

THE POWER OF FOOD ADS

Food manufacturers spent $7 billion in advertising in 1997, the majority of which was focused on processed and packaged foods. As we'll discuss more thoroughly in Chapter 8, children are among the most aggressively targeted consumers: The average American child sees more than 20,000 television commercials per year.[28] During Saturday morning cartoons, children view an average of one food commercial every 5 minutes.[29] More than 90 percent of these advertisements are for high-sugar cereals and candy bars, salty canned foods, fast food, or other junk food.

In a recent lawsuit filed against Nickelodeon, Sherri Carlson, mother of three, claimed that her efforts to have her children eat healthy foods are being thwarted. "They turn on Nickelodeon and see all those enticing junk-food ads," Carlson said. "Adding insult to injury, we enter the grocery store and see our beloved Nick characters plastered on all those junky snacks and cereals."[30] Dan Mindus, spokesman for the Center for Consumer Freedom, counters, "Going out on a limb here, perhaps Carlson's kids want these foods not because of ads but because they're children."[31] In general, successful U.S. industries are nothing if not thoughtful and deliberate about how they spend their money. One can only imagine that they have conducted internal investigations to determine that their dollars are well spent and result in successful sales promotions. They are right.

Marvin Goldberg, PhD, and colleagues from McGill University in Canada went to three San Francisco–area schools in search of 1st graders for an experiment. They randomly assigned children to watch a 24-minute commercially produced cartoon, *Yogi's Gang,* replete with nine 30-second commercials for Mounds candy bars, LifeSavers lollipops, Cracker Jacks, Hershey's candy bars, Blow Pops, Milky Way candy bars, Kool-Aid, and Sugar Crisp and Fruity Pebbles cereals. The 4½ minutes of advertisements were inserted at five points during the program, as is typical in TV programming for children.[32] A control group wasn't exposed to any programming.

Afterward, both groups of children discussed their favorite television programs with a member of the study team. Then they were shown a series of posters, each containing pictures of six snack foods. Three of the six were considered wholesome (raisins, bananas, and peanuts), and the other three included an advertised snack (Mounds candy bars) and two unadvertised but equally unhealthy alternatives (chocolate stars and Jujubes). The researcher then told each child to pretend that Mommy and

Daddy were going out, and she was going to babysit for them. She said that because she didn't know what they liked to eat, she would give them three choices. They were also asked to choose their breakfasts from a selection that included sugary cereals, Kool-Aid, milk, oranges, and toast. In total, each child selected 18 foods. On average, children who saw commercials selected more than 12 sugary foods, while those in the control group selected 10.

While the difference between the two groups' choices isn't great—probably because, as Dan Mindus reminds us, "they're children"—one of the remarkable things about this experiment is that it demonstrated not only that commercials do affect children's food choices but also that kids don't necessarily choose the products advertised but pick other, equally unhealthy foods. There appears to be what psychologists call a priming effect at work. Priming occurs when the mind is preconditioned to react to a certain stimulus in a particular way. Being inundated with unhealthy food options may prime children's desire for nonnutritious food. Seeing Count Chocula may draw kids not only to his cereal but also to Cap'n Crunch and Tony the Tiger's Frosted Flakes.

As fascinating and compelling as these findings are, the fact is that children don't typically get to choose their snacks from a multitude of options—even if they're blessed with indulgent babysitters. But a real-world demonstration of advertising's effects on children's food choices was performed in Quebec, Canada, where a 1980 law eliminated advertising to children on all Quebec-based media. By design, this law had no bearing on American broadcasters, so the three major commercial networks (ABC, NBC, and CBS) continued to stream advertisements into the Quebec border towns that received their signals.

In 1990, Dr. Goldberg took advantage of this unique opportunity to see if children reacted differently to products marketed on television based on whether or not they were exposed to advertisements.[33] His first challenge was to reliably find a way of identifying children who would be likely to watch one type of programming more than another (American versus Canadian broadcasts). To accomplish this, he capitalized on the fact that Quebec is bilingual. As it turned out, both French- and English-speaking children in Montreal watched the same amount of television (22 hours per week), but presumably, the French-speaking children watched considerably less American television than the English-speaking children. He rounded up 9- to 12-year-old French- and English-speaking students from a variety of venues around Montreal. The children were given a comprehensive list of kid programs available on American TV and asked to circle the shows they watched regularly.

As expected, the English-speaking children watched almost three times as much American television as the French speakers (2 hours versus 45 minutes per day). Dr. Goldberg then gave his subjects a list of all commercially available high-sugar children's cereals (such as Cap'n Crunch, Fruity Pebbles, and Count Chocula) and asked them to check the ones that they currently had at home. On average, viewers of American television had more of these cereals in their homes (2½ boxes versus 2 boxes).

Dr. Goldberg then looked only at viewers of American television to see if more viewing was associated with more high-sugar cereals, and he found that there was a connection. In households where children watched 1 hour a day, the average was one box of sugary cereal; in households where kids watched 2 hours a day, it was more than two boxes; and in households where they watched 3 hours, the average was almost four boxes! The connection is straightforward: The more U.S. television Canadian children watched and the more commercials they saw, the more sugary cereals they had. Again, we see the tremendous power that the screen can exert on young children.

One important thing to remember is that high-sugar cereal ads may target children directly, but it's the parents who control the family pocketbook and do the shopping—the same parents who spend the Saturday morning cartoon time eking out some extra sleep, grateful to the TV gods for the respite. It is a Faustian bargain. Commercials aimed at children leverage what has been termed the nag factor. The nag factor, or pester power, is defined as "the degree to which parents' purchasing decisions are based on being nagged by their children." Most parents are familiar with the nag factor. According to a recent survey conducted by the Center for a New American Dream, a consumer and environmental group based near Washington, D.C., children between the ages of 12 and 17 typically ask nine times for an advertised product in the hope their parents will give in. More than half of the parents surveyed said that they ultimately buy the product.[34]

Priming the nag factor is standard operating procedure. The 1991 operations and training manual for McDonald's employees stated plainly that "children are often the key decision makers concerning where a family goes to eat. Although the parents decide when to go out, the children many times 'decide' where to go." It goes on: "Remember, children exert a phenomenal influence when it comes to restaurant selection. This means that you should do everything you can to appeal to children's love for Ronald and McDonald's."[35]

For years, Nancy Cotugna, DrPH, of the department of nutrition at the University of Delaware has done an odious task most of us could not stomach: She monitors ads on Saturday morning commercial children's television. She reported that 71 percent of commercials were for food, and of those, 80 percent were for foods of low nutritional value. This trend has been consistent since the 1970s and coincides with the increase in Saturday morning cartoons. Remember that the increase in obesity rates began in the late 1970s and continued to this day. Television viewing didn't dramatically increase during this period, but McDonald's sales did, as you've seen. So did sales of other low-nutrition foods among children. In fact, the more television people watch, the more likely they are to consume fewer fruits, vegetables, and whole grain cereals. Thus, it would appear that contrary to its reputation for inducing kids to be couch potatoes, television's actual role in the obesity epidemic is primarily that of conveyer of bad nutritional advice. Shown on page 144 is a summary of the kinds of "advice" children get from TV.

What General and Child Audience Food Ads Are Selling[36]

Food Type	All Ads (%)	Child Audience Ads (%)
Candy/sweets/soft drinks	36	43
Fast food	46	34
Cereals	9	14
Dairy	4	4
Fruits/vegetables	2	1

ELMO TO THE RESCUE!

Lest parents despair that they are helpless against the forces of aggressive and effective marketing (and their own inability to withstand the nag factor), the news isn't all bad . . . well, most of it is, but perhaps it needn't be. Pro-nutrition public service announcements (PSAs) have also been evaluated, and they do work. In the same study in which Dr. Goldberg showed children commercials for junk food and asked them to make snack and breakfast selections, he included a separate group that watched pro-nutrition ads. Those who watched these advertisements selected about 9 high-sugar snacks (remember that kids who saw commercials selected more than 12, and the control group selected 10).[37] So pro-nutrition advertisements can prime children to choose healthier snacks. Another study found that the benefits of PSAs in support of nutrition were considerably enhanced when a parent was present and reinforced the message.[38] Just as with prosocial programming, context is critical to make sure the appropriate message gets across.

To be sure, traditional PSAs have never been produced with the same flair as their commercial counterparts. This is partly because they are not as well financed—and it shows. Apart from the ads for the California singing raisins, campaigns for fruits and vegetables have traditionally been financed by the likes of the USDA. In 1997, these agencies spent $333 million; the food industry spent $7 billion.[39] (Or, to put it another way, the USDA could only spend $1 for every $21 the food industry spent.) Children have rated traditional PSAs as being worse than junk-food commercials, a fact that may not be surprising when it comes to how interesting the subject is to them, but they've also criticized the ads for lacking polish and being too preachy.[40] Marketing aimed at counteracting social trends and pressures can be effective. For example, recent commercials that were designed at considerable expense have been crediting with reducing smoking among teenagers.[41] Unfortunately, except for such high-impact advertisements—financed in large part with tobacco settlement money—there has been little on the airwaves to motivate more healthful eating. But help may be on the way.

Beginning with their 36th season in 2005, *Sesame Street*, which has never emphasized nutrition in their curriculum (think of Cookie Monster), introduced a "healthy habits for life" initiative. Every other day, health is the focus of the shows, which now include vegetable Muppets and feature Cookie Monster himself declaring that cookies are a "sometimes" food. Notably, there are product tie-ins here as well: Hain Celestial Group launched an organic, low-fat breakfast line called Earth's Best, which includes cereals, crackers, cookies, and oatmeal branded with Sesame Street characters. Let's hope that they're as successful in this venture as they have been in promoting literacy in school-age children.

Earlier in this chapter, we said that untangling television's effects on body image and obesity was awkward at best since, at first glance, the effects seem so divergent: TV is blamed for making children fat while making them want to be dangerously thin. Having now reviewed the evidence in support of both effects, it's clearer how TV can have such seemingly contradictory effects. Television sells being thin just as it sells unhealthful foods. In fact, thin people usually sell those foods in commercials! (The people in McDonald's ads look nothing like the people in

McDonald's restaurants, for example.) Some children are of course unaffected by these images, but some buy into the message of thinness, and some buy the junk food. Unfortunately and somewhat ironically, most children do both.

What's a parent to do? In Chapter 5, we stressed how important it is to talk with your children about the *action* on the screen. When it comes to body image, it's also important to talk about the *actors*. If they're unnaturally or unhealthily thin, point that out to your kids. As for the effects of advertising, we will explore them more fully in Chapter 8, but the good news for you as parents is that you do control what foods are brought into your house and what restaurants your children frequent (at least when they're young). With a bit of conscious planning (and a few of the tips in "Make TV Work for Your Children's Weight and Body Image"), you can eliminate the risks that television poses to your children's waistlines.

Sadly, though, obesity isn't the only risk faced by television-addicted children. In the next chapter, we will explore how TV sells even more frighteningly risky behaviors, including sex, alcohol, and dangerous stunts.

MAKE TV WORK FOR YOUR CHILDREN'S WEIGHT AND BODY IMAGE

ALL AGES

- Avoid snacking while watching TV, but if you must, have healthful food (real fruits and vegetables).
- Don't have meals in front of the television.
- Avoid commercial broadcasts as much as possible.
- Challenge the claims of junk-food commercials.
- Reinforce positive nutrition messages on television.
- Where possible, select programs that promote physical activity.

- Save allotted television time for periods when there are no other, more active alternatives available.
- Don't give in to pester power that goes against your sensibilities.

CHILDREN 8 AND OLDER

- Point out actors with unhealthy, too-thin bodies.
- Talk about what constitutes a healthy diet.

CHAPTER 7

RISKY BEHAVIOR AND RISKY BUSINESS: SEX, BOOZE, AND MTV

In this century, the mass media have come to rival parents, school, and religion as the most influential institution in children's lives.

Media & Values *magazine*

As parents and the home lose some of their hold on the imagination, senses, and emotions, children naturally turn elsewhere for spiritual and psychic sustenance. They find it in the media and its indomitable infantry, the peer group.

Kay S. Hymowitz, Ready or Not

On a Friday night in suburban Seattle, after a Skyline High School football game, 15-year-old Melvin Lee[1] marinated his shirt in rubbing alcohol in a zipper-lock bag, donned the shirt, and set himself on fire. His friends video-taped the experience in hopes of selling the video and making a lot of money. Lee wasn't depressed or even particularly odd—on the contrary, he was an A stu-dent and a well-adjusted, second-generation Chinese American from a solid family. He was simply imitating a stunt he'd seen on the popular television show Jackass. *Unlike the outcome of the* Jackass *version, though, Lee's shirt didn't quickly burn itself out, and he didn't escape injury. He didn't dance around gleefully afterward, and he and his friends didn't make a lot of money.*

Instead, he was rushed to the hospital with second-degree burns and grounded "for at least a year."

Lee chose his 15 minutes of fame poorly, and in this he is joined each year by dozens of teenagers around the country who imitate television and movie stunts by lighting themselves on fire, jumping from heights, running into each other with cars, shooting each other with guns, and even, in the case of one especially uninhibited 19-year-old, running through the streets of a Connecticut town manhandling a running chainsaw. The lucky ones, like Lee, are grounded. Some of the unlucky ones are seriously injured, and tragically, some are killed.

To be sure, teenagers have an endless ability to get themselves into trouble, and even without a show like *Jackass*, they're capable of coming up with plenty of ill-advised activities. But as you'll see, some television content does exert a significant influence on adolescent behavior and can increase the chance that teens will injure themselves, smoke, use drugs, or engage in risky sex.

In Chapter 4, we discussed how very young children directly imitate what they see on the screen.[2] Older children and adolescents do, too, although in different ways. Although parents are typically involved with selecting age-appropriate programs for younger children, teenagers have greater autonomy in choosing what they watch. All parents would like to believe that their teenagers have the same maturity, probity, and judgment that they, as parents, do, but many know otherwise. In fact, there are real physiological and neurological differences between teenagers and adults, and these differences mean that teens (especially young teens) are not yet neurologically capable of adult judgment. As a result, they tend to act from their gut, and their gut is strongly influenced by their peers, including those "peers" on TV with whom they strongly identify.

Not exclusive to the teen years, adolescence actually begins at age 6 to 8 with increasing skeletal growth, includes 4 to 5 years of puberty that begin at about 12, and continues with rapid changes in the brain that aren't complete until the early twenties.[3,4] During this period, adolescents must also negotiate the large and complicated task of making the transition socially and economically from childhood to adulthood. Most parents are aware of the physical and physiological changes that take place during adolescence, and most can at least feel the effects of the social changes, even if they don't always completely understand them. But the ongoing process of brain development, which is less obvious to outsiders and to the adolescents themselves, is an equally important part.

How the brain develops during this period crucially affects how television influences teen behavior. The risks of watching TV are real and can be significant. In short, some kinds of shows lead to dangerous behavior for some children and adolescents. In this chapter, we'll discuss what kinds of television *content* lead to the riskiest behavior—and why. The good news is that there is a lot that parents can do to foster mindful viewing by their tweens and teens and limit the effects of television on their actions. Let's start with a short description of the center of all such influences: the teenage brain.

THE TEENAGE BRAIN: STILL A WORK IN PROGRESS

We discussed early brain development in Chapter 2. Although the early years represent a critical period of structural development, the brain continues to develop during the teen years and isn't fully developed until the early twenties. The parts of the brain that control higher functioning, such as planning, impulse control, and judgment, are the last to be fully developed. These highly rational activities are what psychologists call executive functioning and are controlled by the frontal lobe, an area that some have called the CEO center of the brain. It goes through a period of massive development that peaks at age 11 to 12, and the development of executive functioning continues into the early twenties.

In one small experiment, 10 teenagers and 10 adults were asked to respond to an image of a face that presented a particular emotion while they were being monitored by a machine called a functional magnetic resonance image (fMRI) scanner. The scanner could determine which part of the brain participants were using in reaction to the faces. The results were surprising. The teenagers used a part of the brain associated with emotion, or gut reactions, while the adults used an area of the brain associated with judgment. Adults looked at the face dispassionately, thought about it, and answered the researcher's questions, while the teenagers reacted emotionally, almost as if the face's expression were directed at them individually. Even more surprising, while 100 percent of the adults correctly identified the emotion portrayed, only half of the teenagers did. So, unlike the adults, not only did the teens take the expression personally, they also couldn't accurately interpret it. No wonder the adolescent years are so volatile![5]

The wiring that occurs during the early years of brain development is the most fundamental and most important. It helps to develop a set of behavioral scripts that tell us what life is like and what we should do in a variety of situations. This period of development is a necessary precondition for developing socially appropriate behavior. In our view, this is yet another reason for parents to be aware of the influence television has on their children.

THE TASKS OF ADOLESCENCE

Socially, adolescents have a big job to do. Among other concerns, they must develop control over their own diets, cultivate satisfying relationships outside the family, refine their own moral codes, and begin to formulate a plan for economic independence. Accomplishing these goals depends on the development of what psychologists call mental schemas, or scripts, that guide behavior and attitudes in any given situation.

Mental scripts exist to help manage the tasks of adolescence and adulthood. As adults, we often take for granted our ease in negotiating social interactions and personal and professional decisions. We know the drill when we go to the grocery store, meet a stranger for the first time, go on a date, and so on. We don't have to think too much about how much to chat with the cashier, when and how to shake hands, or any of the other social niceties that make such interactions go smoothly. We're comfortable in these situations because we have already developed mental scripts based on models of normal behavior that we can rely on to guide our actions.

While for many parents, a lot of time has passed since their first date, if they had to go on a date tomorrow, they could do so with reasonable confidence because they know how the situation could unfold. For adolescents, though, the dating experience is so fraught with confusion and peril that they would probably reject the very concept of dating as too prosaic and dorky to be anything they would engage in. Adolescents have not yet developed the mental scripts to guide them safely through a large variety of social interactions and relationships.

When Fred was a teenager, he was surprised one day to see one of his sisters putting ketchup on her scrambled eggs. It was as strange a culinary move as if she'd reached out the window, grabbed a geranium, and wolfed it down. But the idea didn't emerge out of thin air. Both of Fred's sisters were avid gymnasts, and they had recently discovered that Olympic gold medalist Olga Korbut liked ketchup on her scrambled eggs. Who better to copy than the ideal role model for gymnast ambitions?

The process by which teens develop such short lists of behavior patterns is called social learning because it involves copying peers. Whether they're choosing their breakfasts or agonizing over what to say on a date, they are largely imitating what they think is normal or desirable behavior among their peers. Of course, they choose whom to copy and how to vary their scripts. They may decide to put ketchup on scrambled eggs because that's what Olga Korbut did or because they've taken the egg script and modified it to suit their own tastes. Either way, once they have that script—with or without the ketchup—they no longer have to think through it carefully each time.

At this developmental stage, the peer group is an essential guide. After all, when there are so many decisions to make, and when decision making is so difficult, simply imitating peers seems like a useful and highly effective strategy for making good decisions. This task of having to develop—in a few short years—an entire personal repertoire of mental scripts occurs at an age when television looms large. For many teens, the role of TV is to communicate and reinforce what their peers are interested in and how peers and adults respond to certain situations. Television, in short, represents a whole catalog of ready-made scripts for adolescents to selectively copy.

TELEVISION SCRIPTS

When children watch television, they learn how to dress and how to behave. With its intimate portrayals of adults and cool kids, television provides unique access to the lives of the in-crowd. Of course, teens could certainly learn how to behave from their parents and how to dress from their friends, but teenagers want to look just like everybody else—only a little better—and they want to behave like adults but not like their parents. What better way to meet these needs than to flip on the tube and check out *The Bachelor, Survivor, The O.C., Dawson's Creek,* or *General Hospital*? The information that teens get from these popular shows and from movies like *Titanic* or *Mr. and Mrs. Smith* is often perceived as crucial in discovering how the adult world works.

Television provides an abundance of ready-made scripts for how to behave as an adult. Getting breakfast? Come downstairs in a hurry and grab some orange juice from the fridge, like Claire on *Six Feet Under,* before running out the door. Going on a date? No worries; Marissa, Kaitlin, Ryan, and Seth have been there before you. Going to a party? Dawson and Pacey can tell you what to drink.

In the areas of sex and drugs in particular, television's scripts provide, for the most part, the exact opposite of the messages that parents would like to send. For some kids, this difference is not significant because they can understand that those scripts are fictional. Others, however, take what they see on television as a faithful representation of what life is like—or could be like. Half of all 10- to 13-year-olds say that the situations in alcohol ads reflect what happens in real life.[6] We'd like to show you how to keep your children in the other half—the portion of teens that views television with a critical eye.

When you watch TV, you unconsciously label the situations depicted as either true or false. A scene in which a working mother drops her child off at school and waves goodbye registers as true, or realistic. A scene in which a student sits in class and has a pizza while learning about Cuba registers as false, or unrealistic, and (the director hopes) funny. But trouble can arise when viewers set the default label as "true." How real are reality TV shows that carefully select competitors for survival? How real are talent shows for which contestants are selected precisely because they're laughably poor performers? These so-called reality shows are presented as true renditions, and many adults—let alone children and adolescents—believe them to be true.

It takes much more mental effort to remember a situation model as false than to remember it as true. When we watch television passively, we don't actively think about what we're viewing, and behavior in certain situations can come to seem normal; we're simply too inattentive or lazy to mentally label the situation as false. Women humiliating themselves to compete for a man on *The Bachelor* can come to seem like normal behavior if we see it often enough and don't invest the mental effort necessary to label the situation as unrealistic. Simply put, mindful viewing can help children apply the correct true or false label to what they see on TV.

For unmindful viewers, television subtly but profoundly transforms what we consider to be normal behavior. Several studies have shown that people overestimate the probability of unlikely events that they've frequently seen on television. As you saw in Chapter 5, children (and adults) who often watch local news can come to view the world as scary and unsafe. Moreover, the magnitude of their overestimation increases with the amount of television they watch. For example, soap opera viewers estimated that there are more divorces, illegitimate children, and abortions in the United States than did nonviewers. These results were the same when the researchers compared groups of viewers with nonviewers of the same age, gender, and education level.[7]

These effects are notable, particularly given the patent unreality of many soap opera setups. But much of television purports to be realistic, or even portray reality itself. How real is it, actually? *The Real World: Austin* offered all the tawdriness of a soap opera with none of the escapism. Several college-age men and women were provided with a house and budget in Austin, Texas, and told to produce a documentary about a local music festival. Their approach to filmmaking involved fighting, sex, and very little shooting of film. In the first episode, one of the participants was punched in the head and sustained a broken jaw. The injury set the stage for the rest of the series. Prompted by the short temper and bad behavior of one of the roommates, who perceived any slight as a personal affront, one roommate tried to beat the daylights out of another. Because he was drunk at the time, no one was hurt. A typical question on the show wasn't about camera angles or framing but "How did I end up in jail again?" One character claimed, "There is a lot of partying to be done, and that takes priority over this documentary." So much for the real world!

In this chapter, we'll discuss how television provides scripts for normal behavior in two areas that, as parents, you would probably rather script yourselves: drinking and sex. We'll also discuss how and why music videos exercise a particularly salient influence in these areas. First, though, we'll look at something you may never have considered a risk: the role of television in modeling behavior that can lead to injuries.

SUPERHEROES IN TRAINING

The potential of television examples to affect children's behavior is cap-
tured in an anecdote published in the online magazine *Stay Free!*

*When I was about 5 or 6, I was totally infatuated with Underdog—a
cartoon canine with a secret identity. Especially intriguing to me was the
"super energy pill" hidden in Underdog's ring. When he found himself in
trouble or when the apple of his eye, Sweet Polly Purebred, called for help,
U-dog would open his ring and pop a pill. Accompanied by a triumphant
chorus, he would transform from a wimpy pup into a muscle-bound,
albeit clumsy, hero complete with a cape and the ability to fly. As an
aspiring hero myself—already hopped up on many a Saturday morning
episode of* Batman, The Lone Ranger, *and* Zorro—*I thought the pill
option was the quickest route to public adulation. And I knew of many
pills hidden in the house. One afternoon, I climbed the counter and took
a bottle of the orange-flavored St. Joseph's Aspirin for Children. Over
the next several hours, I flew through the living room, jumping on and off
the sofa, battling bad guys up and down the stairs, and downing the
orange tabs as crime-fighting circumstances dictated. By dinnertime I
was barely able to rise from the sofa. After repeated questioning from my
mom, I showed her the empty bottle. She gave me a glass of milk, and,
upon finishing it, I upchucked my fantasy onto the basement floor.* [8]
     —Dan Cook, Chicago (now a professor of consumer studies)

Unintentional injury is the leading cause of death among grade school
children. At all ages, children watch a lot of television that depicts dangerous acts in both animated and live-action form. Dangerous activities
shown on television include jumping from heights, confronting wild animals or fierce dogs, pill popping, and of course, the ubiquitous gunplay. In
1997, after a television commercial in Great Britain depicted two rugby
stars jumping off a waterfall, 14 children were killed imitating the stunt.[9]

And these are just the events that are intended to be compelling, though fictional. Reality TV, or so-called game-docs, inverts this situation, presenting events that are highly contrived, though nonfictional.

In 2006, *Variety* reported that a contestant on *Fear Factor South Africa* "lost half the hair on her head, suffered a concussion, and was badly bruised during [a] stunt, in which contestants were dragged behind a 4×4 over sand dunes."[10] One interesting study of 6- to 9-year-olds showed that just 7 minutes of exposure to television depictions of dangerous activities significantly increased the likelihood that the kids would take risks.[11] Using a test that had been shown to accurately predict children's real behavior, researchers found that, compared with kids who'd seen 7 minutes of nonrisky activities, those who watched high-risk activities stated they were more likely to jump off a porch from greater heights, go closer to a flaming barbecue, or run in front of a car.

We can't know for sure how long these effects might have lasted. In order to protect the kids, they were all given careful instruction on avoiding risk in general and in the specific situations presented in the films and the risk-attitude inventory. After being retrained, all of the children returned to a normal level of risk taking.

For a brief period before the retraining, however, just 7 minutes of watching risky behaviors performed on TV in patently unrealistic situations—by supernatural characters and in cartoons—was enough to change these children's attitudes about what constitutes safe behavior. The implications are clear—television viewing has the capacity to be a major influence on how children assess risk and what they perceive as appropriate behavior in real-world situations.

While many of the most dangerous acts on TV are in cartoons targeting younger children, there's plenty of foolish risk taking on television targeted at teenagers and adults, much of it directed at a particularly sensitive area of adolescent activity—driving. While most of the four or five driving scenes per hour on primetime television involve normal driving, 20 percent include excess speed, 25 percent involve squealing tires, 8 percent depict changing drivers at full throttle or forcing another car off the road, and 5 percent include weaving in and out of traffic.[12] The "car chase" is a mainstay of movies and is featured in all genres, from romantic comedies to thrillers. In fact, VaRaces sponsors the "People's Chase" contest, in which the Internet "public" votes for the year's best car chase in fictional TV and movies. Voters are encouraged to use their own criteria based on "amount of destruction, expert driving, car choice, or stunt work." What may be worse, real car chases are often covered live by TV news cameras and by all accounts are immensely popular.

Although viewing even a small amount of television that portrays risky behavior does affect children's attitudes in ways that can change their behavior and put them at risk, parents can take heart. Talking to your children about what constitutes safe, appropriate behavior can restore their attitudes to a more cautious level. When they see risky behavior on TV, make sure they know it isn't real and that they understand what safe behavior is. Doing so will not only change their risk attitudes but also help over time to engender mindful viewing when they're exposed to similar scenes in the future.

WATCHING UNDER THE INFLUENCE

In an article published in 2006, medical researchers at Dartmouth verified the link between drinking in movies and teenagers' own drinking. They surveyed more than 4,000 adolescents ages 10 to 14 and found that the typical child had been exposed to more than 8 hours of drinking scenes in the movies they could recall seeing. More than 90 percent of the movies seen by these adolescents contained drinking scenes, such as the drunken revelry in *Wedding Crashers* and other films. When the researchers talked to the teens again 18 months later, they discovered that those who had seen more depictions of drinking in movies were more likely to have started drinking than those who had seen fewer such scenes; among those who had already started drinking, the amount of movie drinking they'd seen was a powerful predictor of how much they subsequently drank.[13]

The impact of what is watched (content) is crucial to the effect of television on drinking behavior. You can modify the effects of movies on your child's drinking behavior by starting early to select films that contain few scenes involving alcohol.

On television, alcohol is the most frequently portrayed food, drink, or drug. Recent research has revealed some interesting facts.[14] One hundred percent of all made-for-TV movies and 75 percent of dramas contain some mention of alcohol. On average, there is one drinking scene on TV every 22 minutes. Movies portray alcohol use even more frequently: Of the 16 most popular R-rated films among teenagers in 1996, every one contained scenes of alcohol use, with an average of 16 episodes per film.[15] When teenagers see this, they get the sense that people drink a lot more alcohol than they really do.

When we think about teenagers learning from their peers, these depictions of alcohol use are particularly worrisome because the people shown drinking tend to be familiar, high-status characters, the ones whom teen viewers naturally like and want to emulate. Moreover, any bad consequences of drinking are nowhere to be seen.[15] While drinking is typically unnecessary to the plot, scenes of casual, incidental drinking are probably all the more likely to create the sense that drinking in social situations is normal. In Chapter 4, we discussed how seeing frequent violent scenes give kids the sense that the world is less safe than it is. In the same way, frequent portrayals of drinking make alcohol use seem more common and safe than it is.

Recent research on drinking among college students has shown the direct link between the students' beliefs about other people's drinking habits and how much they drink themselves. When something happens to change their beliefs about how much typical students drink, the students change their own drinking behavior.[16-18] Using this finding, researchers have identified an effective and relatively inexpensive way to reduce drinking among college students: give them accurate information about how much other students are drinking.[19, 20] This information deflates their inflated notions of what's normal and decreases their drinking. The bad news for parents is that this finding implies that television can increase children's drinking by making it seem normal for teens to drink a lot and at young ages. The good news is that you can turn this around by teaching your child that underage drinking and excessive drinking are not the norm.

Alcohol is marketed on TV and elsewhere as a means of relaxing, having fun, and socializing. It's also portrayed as a useful companion to romance and sex. While it's true that alcohol reduces inhibition and judgment, try to let your older kids know (in a subtle, fun way, perhaps) that there is no physiological basis for the idea that alcohol is an aphrodisiac. Rather, alcohol tends to adversely affect sexual—as opposed to romantic—interest. Portrayals on TV and in movies are a different matter: They provide people with scripts instructing them on how to behave when drinking. When young adults start drinking, they remember these scripts, and they start to relax, have more fun, and become chatty and more interested in sex.

In a series of fascinating experiments, researchers have been able to isolate the effects of believing one has had something to drink from those of actually having consumed alcohol.[21] They showed that people who have had nothing to drink but think they did act out their scripts of how people behave when drinking.

In a typical experiment, researchers divide college students into two groups one evening. One group is given mixed drinks and told to relax and have a good time. The other group is given sham mixed drinks, with minute amounts of alcohol on the rims of the glasses, and told that they're drinking gin and tonic, rum and coke, and other mixed drinks. This ruse is always successful—the smell of the alcohol on the rim of the glass is sufficient to persuade people that they are actually drinking.

Those who drink the sham alcohol typically become markedly louder, less inhibited, and more interested in the opposite sex, despite not having drunk anything alcoholic. Watching people in alcohol ads can therefore help create a self-fulfilling prophecy as the scripts become lodged in teens' minds and influence their behavior.

The part of this that should be reassuring to parents is that despite your fears, you can have a profound influence on how your teens form their beliefs. You can step in to break the link between television portrayals of alcohol use and your children's beliefs about drinking. This will go a long way toward limiting any adverse effects of drinking scenes on television and in movies.[22–26] To do so, you must maintain open communication with your child. We'll discuss this in more detail later on, but first, let's look at another area of concern to parents—one that often goes along with alcohol use.

SEX AND THE SUPER-PEER

While we're on the subject of things that drive parents of teens crazy, let's talk about sex on TV. Whenever we look at the research on this subject, we're reminded of something actor Keenan Ivory Wayans once said: "Society as a whole has moved into a taboo-free zone."

A study in 1999 looked at where teens got their information about sex.[27] Twenty-nine percent cited television as their principal source (up from 11 percent in 1986). An additional 45 percent mentioned friends as their primary source—and presumably, the friends were highly influenced by TV. (Heartbreakingly but perhaps not surprisingly, only 7 percent mentioned parents, and only 3 percent mentioned formal sex education.) Because of its profound influence on the entire peer network, television has been called a super-peer: the beautiful, all-knowing, ultra-cool friend who is, at the same time, always inviting and always available. No wonder it can be hard to resist its influence!

To understand how these influences come into play, imagine what happens when two high school seniors, Patrick and Tiffany, meet for the first time at a friend's party. Suppose Patrick is new to the school and just starting to know his way around. At first, the two exchange the usual chatter, with Tiffany asking Patrick about where he used to live, and Patrick asking Tiffany about the football team at this school. After a while, he says quite earnestly that Tiffany is wearing a nice sweater. She giggles. He gives her a few more compliments. The conversation returns to neutral topics, and they talk about other students. Before long, though, they return to a teasing, increasingly touchy-feely discussion of each other's hair and physical appearance. Eventually, Patrick remarks, "You know, I live just a few blocks from here, and my parents are out of town tonight."

What happens next will emerge from a complicated brew of psychology, adolescent hormones, and opportunity. Keep in mind that a major determinant of what happens—and how—is the teenagers' beliefs about what's normal in this situation. They have acted out the situational norm of two teens meeting at a party, and it went smoothly because both were on the same page in terms of what to say and do. The next part is trickier, and undoubtedly many parents wouldn't want it to unfold unsupervised— but they are largely out of the picture by this time. These two kids are attracted to each other, and what that means for their behavior will depend on their ideas about what normal teenagers do when they're attracted to each other. If they believe it's normal to have sex, they will. If they think it's normal to shake hands and agree to go to Starbuck's next week, they will do that. So where do these ideas of normal behavior come from?

Clearly, parents have a big role in defining what is normal. But by the time kids turn into teens, they are usually convinced of their parents' love and support (notwithstanding occasional complaints to the contrary).[28] Now, their main interest is in gaining the acceptance of their peer group— and directly and indirectly, TV plays a major role in defining for them what their peer group believes. It teaches them when it's normal to start acting romantic and being sexual—along with how, when, and with whom that behavior should happen.[29]

WHAT DOES TELEVISION TEACH ABOUT SEX?

Today's parents are faced with a TV environment that is much more sexually charged than the one in which they grew up. In one episode of *General Hospital*, Sonny and Carly are romantically engaged on a couch, kissing and fondling. "Sonny," she whispers, "I don't want to think. We're no good when we think." As the music swells, the couple is shown discreetly but in considerable detail, silently undressing, embracing, and making love.[30]

In his book *The Other Parent*, Jim Steyer points out that sex came into its own on TV following a wave of deregulation during the Reagan administration.[31] In the words of a recent *Entertainment Weekly* article, "TV has sex on the brain ... There's more deflowering going on than in a badly managed greenhouse."[32]

In 2005, 77 percent of shows broadcast in the so-called family hours (7:00 to 9:00 p.m.) had some sort of sexual innuendo or activity, up from just 43 percent of shows with some sexual content in 1976.[33, 34] Moreover, the type of sexual content is much more explicit than it once was.[35-37] Among shows favored by teens, there are 6.7 sexual scenes per hour.[38] (Talk about an overestimation of reality!) Of these, more than half include talk about sex, and one-third include sexual behavior (passionate kissing, physical flirting, and intimate touching). Moreover, among shows for teens, there is an average of one instance of sexual intercourse for every 9 hours of programming, or about three intercourse scenes per week for a typical viewer.[39, 40] Only 20 percent are shown on-screen, with the other 80 percent implied, but still, one on-screen depiction of teen sex every 2 weeks would strike many parents as quite a lot for adolescents. Even the implied sexual acts can be fairly racy, whether they're erection jokes on *Everybody Loves Raymond* or seduction scenes on *Jack and Bobby* or *The O.C.*

Movies are no different. The typical R-rated film includes 18 instances of sexual behavior and 10 instances of nudity. The most frequent involve sexual intercourse between unmarried characters. Commercials (which we discuss further in the next chapter) are another source of sexually themed content. Bratz dolls are hipper and sexier versions of Barbie dolls—which are arguably already highly sexualized—that are marketed to children as young as 5 on shows such as *Rugrats*.[41]

Sadly, your ability to restrict your children's exposure to these influences is surprisingly limited. A large majority of programs that contain sexual behavior are not appropriately labeled as such by the television industry, so the V-chip—to the very limited extent that it's understood and used by parents—is largely ineffective. When teens go to the movies, they can buy tickets at a multiplex for a PG-rated film and then go to any R-rated film in the place. In the many homes that subscribe to cable television, R-rated and even X-rated films are readily available, and viewing them is all too common. Sixty-three percent of high schoolers report that they frequently view R-rated films, and 92 percent of 13- to 15-year-olds have seen an X-rated film at least once.[42] Think this doesn't or won't pertain to your children? There's the third-person effect at work again.

Parents hold a variety of opinions about sexual attitudes and what is appropriate for teens in terms of romantic activity and physical intimacy. Almost all parents would agree, however, that depictions of sex and romantic relationships for teenagers should be sensitive and thoughtful. Ideally, they should emphasize care in choosing partners (whether for dates or for some extent of physical affection), a level of physical involvement that's appropriate for the parents' values and the children's emotional maturity, and safe sex for those who are already involved in some level of physical intimacy. The sad truth? The typical television presentation has none of these elements.

The vast majority of on-screen sex and sexual references involve unmarried partners, and half involve people who aren't in committed relationships.[43–45] Mentions of sexual risk or responsibility are rare, although they are increasing—perhaps the one sliver of good news in this area. Now, about 15 percent of shows with any sexual content include some reference to safe sex, up from almost zero a decade ago. Yet the number of safe-sex messages on TV is still comparatively small, and of course, endorsements of abstinence are almost nonexistent.[46]

Nitty-gritty sex isn't the only subject being taught on TV; also on the syllabus are the cultural norms about sexual attractiveness, how to be sexual, why to have sex, with whom to have it, and the appropriate sequence of activities during it. These messages are conveyed through themes, storylines, characterizations, dialogue, and action. In 1993, a researcher at UCLA carefully analyzed the 10 most popular shows among adolescents to extract the messages they convey to children.[47] Psychologist L. Monique Ward, PhD, began by noting that people can think about sex and romance in three different, overlapping ways: as recreation, as the means of procreation, or as a component of a rich interpersonal relationship. Television, she found, places primary emphasis on the purely recreational aspect of sex, with the relationship aspect second. As might be imagined, sex for procreation figures almost not at all on television.

The most common message from teen shows on television is that sex is a competitive sport. The thrill of the chase, which frequently involves complicated strategies and subtle manipulations, creates the excitement. On the show *Martin*, one man gives some advice to another man about an attractive co-worker: "It's all part of being a man. It's your job to conquer that territory. You climb that mountain and plant that flag. It's the call of the wild."

Interestingly, while this message is conveyed primarily to and about men, the message for women isn't all that different. Instead of reinforcement of the old stereotypes about women being either passive and/or elusive, researchers have found that television portrays women as participating equally in the game of sex. In an episode of *Two and a Half Men*, Evelyn, a real-estate agent, explains to her adult son why he found a bra in the car: "Well, if you must know . . . I sold a $12 million house and I wanted to celebrate . . . I was with the seller's realtor. Splitting that juicy commission made us both so hot we barely made it off the lawn!"[48]

TELEVISION'S EFFECTS ON ATTITUDES TOWARD SEX

The research on risk taking helps us understand the very real potential for children's behavior to be influenced by what they see on the screen. For preadolescent children, TV changes beliefs about the danger of certain activities. For adolescents, who are confronting choices about sex and drinking, it changes views about what's normal as well as about the consequences of particular actions.

Views of what's normal are both shaped by television and reinforced by it. Many teens can see their peers drinking at a party once or twice—whether in real life or on TV—and write it off as abnormal behavior. But when they see the same thing many times—indeed, many times a week—it begins to seem normal.

In one experiment, researchers assembled 13- and 14-year-old boys and girls and divided them into three groups.[49] For a week, one group watched typical TV shows that portrayed and referenced sexual activity between unmarried partners. A second group watched similar shows but with no sexual references, while the third group watched no television. At the end of the week, the teens in all three groups were presented with TV portrayals of marital infidelity and asked to rate on a 10-point scale how bad the transgression was and how much the victim had been wronged. Those who had seen the TV-with-sex were less likely to see the victim as having been wronged and rated the transgressions less severely than those who had seen either no-sex TV or no TV. At least in the short term, television portrayals of premarital and extramarital sex do make teens more accepting of them as normal behavior.

While researchers can test the capacity of television to alter attitudes and norms, ethics makes it trickier to study the effects on actual behavior. Yet a few clever and carefully done studies have verified that there is at least some effect of television on sexual behavior. One study, done by

Rebecca Collins and her colleagues at the Rand Corporation, followed teens who began at the same level of sexual behavior and found that those who watched the most sex-related television were twice as likely to begin having sex by the following year as those who watched the least amount of sex-related television. This change happened even when they didn't see overt depictions of sex or even physical intimacy. Exposure to television that involved only dialogue about sex had the same effect as television with depictions of sex.[50, 51]

SEX, VIOLENCE, AND ROCK 'N' ROLL

If fictional and reality television programming is the super-peer that speaks so forcefully to the peer group, music television sings to it, and frequently cacophonously. Most popular music is perfectly innocuous; sometimes beautiful, sometimes inane. But most parents would find at least some of it objectionable, and the objectionable subset has genuine adverse effects on those who listen to it.

Music Television (MTV) started in 1981 and has since been joined by several other channels that show music videos, including Video Hits 1 (VH1), Black Entertainment Television (BET), and Country Music Television (CMT). All are very popular: About 80 percent of high schoolers watch music videos on a regular basis. Viewing time varies, but a reasonable estimate of the average is 15 to 30 minutes per day, with some children watching 2 hours or more per day.

The effects of music videos on attitudes and behavior are similar to those of "regular" television, but the response is more pronounced for two reasons: first because of the role music plays in kids' lives and second because the content is different.

Music can have powerful emotional effects on the listener. In fact, one of the main gratifications of music for teenagers is to give expression to their powerful emotions. As music researcher James Lull has written, "Music promotes experiences of the extreme for its makers and listeners, turning the perilous emotional edges, vulnerabilities, triumphs, celebrations, and antagonisms of life into hypnotic, reflective tempos."[52]

Sometimes these emotions are negative, and adults are sometimes frightened by explicit, graphic, violent or degrading lyrics. For the past 50 years, from the protests about the evils of rock and roll to the efforts of Tipper Gore to create a ratings system for lyrics, much attention has been focused on lyrics and the potential danger they present to young people. Yet, careful psychological research has failed to provide consistent evidence that lyrics themselves present any real danger to listeners.

Music videos are an entirely different matter. In fusing lyrics, music, and screen images, videos have considerable emotional power. Strong emotion makes it difficult for kids to think critically about what they're watching, yet, as you saw earlier, critical processing of content is vital for limiting the adverse effects of viewing on attitudes and behavior. If kids are either having a great time watching a video or getting really pumped up by it, it's difficult for them to think about the values the video is expressing and whether, in a calmer moment, they would endorse or reject them. The effects of music videos on mental scripts are accordingly more dramatic than the effects of just watching television.

The emotional power of music paired with video images might not matter if the images were as innocent as many of the lyrics. But many music videos contain violent and sexual material, as well as images of drinking, smoking, and illicit drug use.

Approximately one-quarter of all music videos show drinking or smoking, usually by the lead singer. Typical viewers of music videos can expect to see alcohol use every 14 minutes, smoking every 15 minutes, and illicit drug use every 40 minutes.[53] This is considerably more exposure than from regular television, as shown in the graph on page 170.

Nearly two-thirds of music videos feature sexual content, and among those that do, there are 4.8 instances of sexual behavior per video.[54] About 15 percent of videos portray interpersonal violence, with an average of 6 violent acts per video.[55] MTV shows the most violent videos—22 per-cent—compared with 12 percent each for VH1, BET, and CMT.[56] In vid-eos with violence, the main character—usually the band leader, a sympathetic character and a likely role model for viewers—is the aggres-sor in 80 percent of the instances. Much of the violence is also arbitrary: Unlike violence in movies or TV shows, the violence in music videos often arrives suddenly, without any warning or dramatic rationale. In a particu-larly dangerous combination, music videos often pair sex and violence. Of videos that feature violence, 80 percent also feature sex. The presence of sex glorifies the violence, and the presence of violence debases the sex.

Frequency of Sex, Alcohol Use, Smoking, and Drug Use on Television and in Music Videos

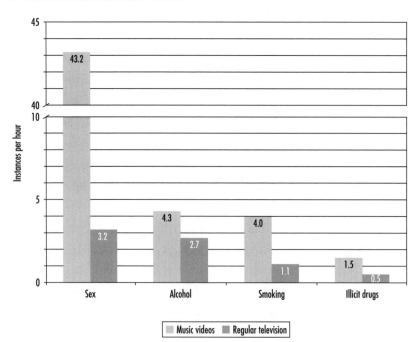

Research on the effects of viewing music videos largely parallels that on the effects of watching television, but because of differences in content, it has focused on somewhat different themes. One provocative study examined the effects of music videos on career ambitions.[57] A group of African American high-school boys was randomly divided into three groups. The first group saw violent rap videos, the second watched non-violent rap videos, and the third saw no videos. Later, as part of a supposedly different experiment, the boys were shown images of a boy struggling to attend college and of another boy the same age who was driving a BMW, had lots of "bling," and ostensibly was not working. Those who had watched either violent or nonviolent rap videos were less likely than those in the control group to want to be like the young man attending college. Here, viewing rap videos seemed to change the boys' impressions of normal career options in a way that was notably unhealthy.

The bottom line is that for most kids, most of the time, music is a perfectly innocent source of pleasure. It isn't something that parents should be overly concerned about. However, listening to a heavy diet of music with excessive violence may be an indication that all is not right, and it may exacerbate whatever emotions or beliefs drive teenagers toward violent music in the first place. Such emotions may be signs of depression or anxiety, and too much of this kind of music can make a bad situation worse. Music videos are a particular problem given that so many of them have explicitly sexual and/or violent themes in which the sex and violence are both glamorized and paired with music that has a powerful influence on mood. Parents whose children listen to large amounts of depressive or violent music (heavy metal or some kinds of violent rap music) should consider limiting the music videos viewed at home, discussing their objections to such content with their children, or encouraging alternative activities. Measures such as these may provoke a teen's anger (or even ridicule), but their long-term impact may outweigh the short-term annoyance of intrafamilial power struggles.

GIRLS: SECONDING SEX

For reasons that are poorly understood, girls tend to be more susceptible to the sexual messages on television and in movies than boys are. To some extent, this difference may be a result of taste. Research has revealed that girls, especially younger ones, are hungry for romantic plots and actively seek out content that includes sexual themes or subtexts.[58] Soap operas are perennial favorites of girls, with *General Hospital* and *All My Children* drawing the largest audiences.[59] There is some evidence that the most sexually advanced girls seek out the most sexual content on television and that the content contributes to the development of their sexual behavior, forming a self-reinforcing cycle.

Another possibility is that because girls tend to be highly invested in and attuned to peer relationships, it may be that TV's role as a super-peer is more salient for them. Given the existing research, parents of teen girls may wish to handle their daughters' television viewing differently than do parents of boys. Since more girls are drawn to romantic and sexual television content than boys are, it's even more important for parents to discuss such content with their daughters and encourage them to view it mindfully. They should also pay attention to the particularly weighty influence that television seems to have upon girls. They can help offset this influence by discussing it directly with their daughters or by proposing reasonable alternatives.

THE PEER GROUP: AN ECHO CHAMBER OF TELEVISION VALUES

By adolescence, teens have largely shifted their need for approval away from their parents and toward their peers, and they report that parents have only a minimal influence on their behavior. This is not to suggest that parents are either unimportant or helpless. On the contrary, their past parenting is a very important part of how teenagers will choose their friends and how they will react to television. Teens whose parents maintained good channels of communication with them in the preadolescent years and have told them that television should be viewed both critically and with mental alertness are much less susceptible to the messages of television than teens whose parents have had greater trouble communicating or who have sent the message that television is pure entertainment to be enjoyed passively. Active communication and active viewing are vaccines that inoculate children against the negative effects of television on their values.

But what of peers? Teenagers are indeed profoundly influenced by their peers. Melvin Lee might never have set himself on fire had he not had the encouragement of his buddies. But the influence of peers doesn't appear out of nowhere. Friendships and patterns of influence occur against a background of heavy television viewing among most adolescents. So when a 15-year-old says to his friends, "I know! I'm going to light myself on fire!" The response from his pals is not "What a dumb idea!"—it's "Just like on *Jackass!*" When a 17-year-old talks to his friends about wanting to have sex with the housecleaner, as he saw on *Seinfeld,* the response from his clique isn't "Whoa, dude . . ."—it's "Giddyup!"

Peers at this age function as a kind of echo chamber, in which ideas and values are tried out and amplified. And one of the most important sources of these ideas and values at this age—the one big speaker going into the echo chamber—is television. Where, after all, do teens get the idea that drinking is sexy, cool, and athletic, when alcohol in fact reduces sexual interest, sex appeal, and coordination? How do kids learn that teen sex is a necessary part of adolescence? Television and movies are a huge part of the answer.

As mentioned earlier, one out of four kids say that TV has a major influence on their sexual behavior, and three out of four say that it has a major influence on their peers' behavior.[60] Adolescents report that television is their greatest source of pressure to become sexually active, and three-quarters say that the reason young people have sex is that television makes it seem normal for teenagers.[61, 62]

The direct effect of television may be modest, but when amplified by the peer echo chamber, the influence is enormous.

THE BRIGHT SIDE OF THE BRIGHT SCREEN

It may seem from the preceding that television is fraught with peril for teenagers, and that's true. But TV also has great potential to promote communication between you and your children and to model good behavior as well as bad behavior.

Not all television shows have an effect on attitudes about sexual norms; only those that contain sexual content do. And research has shown that portrayals of sex between married people have no effect on viewers' attitudes about premarital sex. As with the other effects of television, the content—what is watched—plays an important role in defining the effects of viewing.

Good content can have a positive effect—when given a chance, that is. Half of adolescents report that TV helps them know how to talk with a partner about safe sex or gives them ideas about how to say no. One-third say a sexual situation they saw on TV encouraged them to talk about the issue with their parents.[63] For example, one episode of *Friends* involved a pregnancy resulting from the failure of a condom and communicated messages about both the importance and the potential pitfalls of condom use. A study done shortly after the episode aired found that 10 percent of its teen viewers spoke to their parents about condom efficacy after watching the episode. The majority of these teens watched the episode with their parents, which again underscores the advantages of watching with your kids.[64]

Because most of primetime television shows relate to sex, parents who want to limit the effect of television on their children's attitudes and behavior may find that they have few options. Yet *how* television is watched—its context—also plays a major role. The Rand Corporation's Dr. Collins and her group wondered whether the effect of television would be as strong among those teens who reported good relationships with their parents as among those who didn't. They asked the teens to complete a survey about their family communication styles. Some families had an open communication style, in which parents listened carefully to their children's point of view. These parents tended to defend their rules with a discussion of possible consequences if a rule were violated. In a family with this communication style, a parent might say, "I know you want to take your five friends to the game in our car because you want to save gas, because not everyone can get a car that night, and because it's more fun. But our rule is only three teenagers in the car at a time because too many kids in the car can lead to distractions while driving, and that can lead to accidents." By contrast, a parent with a closed communication style would say, "You can't take your friends to the game with you because that's the rule."

Dr. Collins found that in families with an open communication style, the effect of television on attitudes toward sex was nonexistent! All of the increases in sexual practices were seen in kids from families where a more closed, or authoritarian, style prevailed. Clearly, open communication has powerful applications. In Chapter 8, we'll discuss how it's also useful with younger children in putting a stop to nagging requests for toys advertised on TV.

Open communication may be helpful in inoculating children against the effects of television in part because it gives them practice in thinking critically about what they see. If you stress the rationale for the rules you give your children, they will come to see the world as a rational place in which thinking about something may have a payoff for them. Open communication between parents and children promotes mindful viewing. Teens who invest the most mental effort while viewing—who actively and critically think about what they're seeing—are also immune from the effects of television on their attitudes. Unless viewers actively attach a mental "false" or "inappropriate" tag to what they see, the examples of behavior shown on television can, by default, come to seem normal and appropriate.

Teaching your kids to actively question what's on TV and using an open communication style to do it will help them develop greater control over their own attitudes. Even though it takes active mental effort, mindful viewing will limit the effects of television on your child's beliefs and behavior, so you should do all you can to encourage it.

TEEN TELEVISION: A QUALITY-OF-LIFE ISSUE

This is not news: there is a lot of sex, a lot of violence, and a lot of drinking and smoking on television. With regard to these behaviors, television both reflects current societal attitudes while at the same time pushing them a little further. What's more, as yesterday's television portrayals become today's realities, the medium must push even more to retain its edgy quality.

For many children, television does have some effect on drinking and sexual attitudes and behavior. Even small doses of TV, movies, or music videos can have a meaningful impact in the short run, though to what extent these influences persist in the long run is less certain. Television exercises its effects by:

- Changing teens' views of what is considered normal and appropriate in any particular situation
- Giving teens new ideas of what to do
- Reinforcing examples of how to do things

Girls may be more susceptible than boys to the effects of on-screen sexual content on sexual behavior, and boys are more susceptible than girls to the normalizing of aggression and force in sexual situations. Both boys and girls seem to be susceptible to the effects of television portrayals of drinking and dangerous behavior. Parents can mitigate or even eliminate these effects by maintaining open communication with their children and by encouraging them to adopt a thinking, critical approach to television viewing.

Beyond the direct effects of television viewing on attitudes and behavior, however, the greater effects may lie in how it changes the social environment in which children live. For example, a recent study indicated that most sexually experienced teens wish they had waited longer to begin sexual activity.[65] Television is a super-peer that speaks loudly to many peer groups, and as parents, we can't help but wonder about its effects on the environment in which our children grow up. While there's little that can be done in the short term to change the toxic effects of television on peer groups, parents can and should intervene to keep TV's influence on risky behaviors to a minimum.

So, you've seen that television has a profound effect on teenagers' beliefs and views of what's normal. For the most part, this process occurs through regular programming, and it's a result of producers and directors trying on the one hand to be realistic and on the other to push the limits of what truly is normal by presenting salacious scenes and dialogue to hold viewers' interest. On the whole, this is all very innocent, if not innocuous.

But of course, there are those who have a vested interest in manipulating teenagers—the advertisers. We address the subject of television advertising, including alcohol advertising, in greater detail in the next chapter.

HOW TO MAKE TV WORK TO SUPPORT YOUR FAMILY'S VALUES

ALL AGES

- Use an open communication style with regard to rules for television and movies.
  - Listen to your children's points of view. Acknowledge their need to feel grown up and to be current with popular culture.

- Be firm with your rules, but recognize that occasional flexibility is a virtue. As your children change and mature, so can the rules.
- Justify your rules with a rationale that makes sense to your children. Couch the rules in terms of your genuine concern for them, and be realistic about risks.
- Recognize that often, open communication is a one-way street. Your attempts to promote communication may not always be reciprocated, but it's still worth the effort.
- Encourage mindful viewing by discussing whether on-screen behaviors and actions are realistic and what consequences they might entail in the real world.
  - Tell your children how stunts are filmed and created on television and in movies. Explain why they can't be replicated at home.

TEENAGERS

- Take seriously the potential for risks associated with portrayals of sex and drinking on TV. Focus on what you can do to limit this risk.
- Consider the underlying messages of sexual content on TV when helping children make viewing decisions.
- Encourage mindful viewing by discussing the consequences of unsafe behaviors portrayed on television and in movies, even if you're not there to watch with them.
  - Explain the importance of safe driving and emphasize that driving as portrayed on television isn't like driving in real life.
  - Use portrayals of sex on TV as opportunities to discuss any questions your children might have about safe sex and abstinence.
  - Use portrayals of drinking to discuss the risks of alcohol use.

CHAPTER 8

THE CAPTIVE WALLET: CHILDREN AND THE TV MARKETING JUGGERNAUT

Television's message has always been that the need for truth, wisdom, and world peace pales by comparison with the need for a toothpaste that offers whiter teeth and fresher breath.

Dave Barry

In 1965, children's television host Soupy Sales had a few extra minutes to fill at the end of one of his live shows. He was used to filling time—having hosted many variety shows in his long career. He was used to almost every adventure and misadventure in television. In fact, Soupy Sales (born Milton Supman) was a pioneer in children's television, having hosted the first noncartoon Saturday morning program on the ABC-TV network. He went on to tremendous success and is known for his favorite gag—throwing pies in the faces of celebrity guests. He became known as the pie-throwing champion of the world, targeting Frank Sinatra, Sammy Davis Jr., and some 19,000 others with his pastry projectiles.

On this episode, though, the pies were gone, so he ad-libbed a few jokes. "Kids," he's reported to have said, "your mom and dad are probably still sleeping. I want you to tiptoe into their bedroom and find your mom's pocketbook and your dad's wallet, which are probably on the floor. You'll see a lot of funny little green pieces of paper with pictures of guys in beards. Put them in an envelope and send them to me. And you know what I'm going to send you? A postcard from Puerto Rico!"[1]

The ploy was a gag: Although he told the children to send him their parents' money, he didn't provide an address. By contrast, modern marketers have become both more forthright and more subtle. They don't directly ask children to send them their parents' money, but they've become adept at making sure that children follow their materialistic commands.

Advertising serves two purposes: to inform and to persuade. To achieve these goals, it must also entertain. A Careerbuilder.com commercial showing monkeys partying in front of a company chart showing improved sales was a great example of a commercial that amused and entertained us, but it also emphasized the possibility of finding a more gratifying job when the graph was turned to show that sales were actually on a downward trend. Some advertising can be useful when viewers are able to parse true information from false information and information from persuasion.

Consider the case of Jaime Gonzalez, whose story was told on NPR. Jaime was flipping channels one evening a couple of years ago and came upon a commercial that grabbed his attention. It wasn't for sex or beer—it was for school. Jaime was 17 and had left school after 8th grade because the village in Mexico where he lived didn't have a high school. He immigrated to the United States and lived with a family in Houston. Jaime was likable and hardworking, and despite his limited English, he soon found work washing trucks to help support his family. He liked the work and assumed he'd be washing trucks for a long time. The commercial changed that assumption: It told him about a free high school for newcomers that the Houston school district had initiated. He could attend high school in the evenings and on weekends to accommodate his work schedule, and the teachers—many of whom were also immigrants—would understand his situation. Soon he would have a high school degree, a better command of English, and some crucial new job skills, all of which would open new doors for him. Jaime jotted down the number shown on the screen and resolved to call them the next day.[2]

As with so much of television, children are exposed to both opportunities and dangers from advertising. Jaime Gonzalez's experience is an exception rather than the rule. Unlike many adults, children aren't generally able to capitalize on the good aspects of advertising while waving away the bad parts.

Even teenagers are easily swayed by the siren song of a good pitch. As we saw in Chapter 6, advertising is effective in getting children to change their preferences and habits. Much more than adults, children are easily swayed by marketers' dulcet messages. Young children believe what advertisers say and follow their advice. Older children, too, are susceptible to these exhortations.

Soupy's gag brought a lot of angry letters from parents and a week's suspension from the show. Today, there is considerably less outrage about trying to separate parents from their money by advertising to children—even to children as young as 2. On the other hand, many children watch a considerable amount of television without being unduly influenced by the ads. What factors are at work here? The reasons for these kids' apparent immunity have a lot to do with how their parents have taught them to watch television. Our goal in this chapter is to give parents enough knowledge to minimize the dangers of marketing and advertising and help them transform those marketing messages into learning opportunities for their children.

KIDPOWER = $$$

Parents may recall their own years of watching TV and think they know firsthand about the potential pitfalls and dangers of advertising to children. Yet in the past few decades, the entire landscape of marketing to children has changed. For starters, there is the sex. Images of women—scantily clad, in suggestive poses, and giving knowing looks—have always been used to sell to adults, but they are now being used to hawk wares to children, even those as young as 4. This tactic is part of what marketers call age compression—the practice of treating children of every age as older than they really are. Age compression has become one of the principal means of appealing to children.

Not only has the emphasis in children's advertising changed, the intensity has as well. Spending on advertising to children has soared from $600 million in 1989 to $15 billion today, a 25-fold increase in 17 years. Commercials are not only more slickly produced than they once were, they're also more plentiful. The average primetime show is now beset with more than 16 minutes per hour of commercials, promotions, credits, and so on. But the amount for daytime TV now reaches 21 minutes per hour—almost 30 percent more than during primetime and more than one-third of children's total viewing time.[3] Indeed, children now see 40,000 commercials a year.[4]

In the influential book *Kids as Customers*, a strategy manifesto that's treated as a bible by marketers, James McNeal outlines the development of the child consumer beginning at age 1, when the child first sees "the wonderland of marketing." "By age 2," McNeal notes, "a few connections between TV advertising and store contents are probably being made by the child," and he observes that starting "around age 2, the youngsters begin to make requests while shopping with Mom and Dad." By the time they are about 7 years old, children begin to go out on their own "to a supermarket for a candy bar, to a fast-food restaurant for a soft drink." As McNeal writes, these children "sense that they have opened the door not just to a store but to a world of want-satisfying things."[5]

The role of the marketer is to channel this development to create maximum loyalty to a life of shopping. McNeal says the marketer must sow the seeds early to "begin an alliance with these new customers that can last a lifetime." His description highlights the three distinct profit opportunities offered to those who market to children.

- Children as a **primary market**, in which they have $8 billion of their own money to spend
- Children as an **influence market**, in which they directly or indirectly influence $300 billion of their parents' spending
- Children as a **future market**, in which they have the potential for an immeasurable amount of future spending

This tale of the developing child consumer illustrates four concerns we have about the ways in which advertising targets children.

- Marketing in general, and television advertising in particular, targets children who are too young to understand or defend themselves against the persuasive purpose of advertising.
- As a result, children are induced to directly buy or to nag their parents for products that are not healthy for them, such as candy bars and soft drinks.
- Children are used in marketing wars among products, such as cars, that are meant for adults.
- Excessively materialistic values that have adverse long-term consequences for children's well-being are promoted at an age when children are highly susceptible and when parents find them difficult to counteract.

We agree with McNeal and other marketers that children represent a large market. Advertising *can* be effective in influencing children's attitudes and loyalties. Spending habits for and by children can be changed by advertising, and subtle, long-term effects of advertising persist into adulthood. We also agree that the scientific method offers the best way to understand these issues. The difference is that we believe marketing to children represents a potential danger to them.

STARTING AT THE VERY BEGINNING

The most eager television marketers are arguably the cereal manufacturers, who are right there chomping at the bit as children reach the age of 2. Cereal boxes are a veritable who's who of children's characters, a rotating television hall of fame. Whether with Dora, Spiderman, or Robots, cereal manufacturers are determined to get your children's attention, and television commercials make sure that these tie-ins are reinforced. Often it's the tie-in rather than the cereal itself that becomes the most attractive feature for children. Some "stars" on the cereal shelf include Flintstones Fruity Pebbles, Toy Story Sugar Fruit Snacks, and Lucky Charms with Narnia displayed on the box, as if the cereal were a hidden portal itself.[6] Even Elmo now has his own fruit snacks. (In Dimitri's house, Kix was known as Bob-the-Builder cereal, and when the character's face no longer graced the box, it was hard to convince the children that it was the same brand.) By the time children reach the age of 4, a host of advertisers struggle to capture their attention and win their loyalty, and this attention continues through the tween and teen years.[7]

The growth of children's awareness of and responses to advertisements may surprise you. By 18 months of age, children recognize logos. Before they are 2, they begin to ask for products by name, with Burger King and McDonald's being perennial favorites. Sometime in their third year, many children begin to believe that what you consume is who you are—in other words, that the brands your parents buy can make you cool or smart.[8]

It isn't until about age 4 that children begin to be able to distinguish commercials from regular programming, usually because commercials are funnier or shorter or louder. Of course, knowing what a commercial *is* isn't the same as knowing what it's *for*. When do young children understand the true purpose of advertising, with its persuasive intent? The standard answer among researchers is that there is a "magic age" of 8, because several studies have shown that after that age, most children choose "to persuade" from a list of four or five possible purposes of advertising. For this reason, the American Academy of Pediatrics has declared that advertising directed at children younger than 8 is "inherently deceptive" and exploitative, and the American Psychological Association has deemed it "inherently unfair."[9]

Thorough research, however, reveals a more nuanced story involving a gradual transition toward understanding ads as children age. The best research on this question was conducted by Dr. Caroline Oates of the University of Sheffield in England, who asked almost 100 children an open-ended question: "Why are commercials on television?" She then coded the children's responses into four categories, giving each child generous credit for partially understanding alternative uses. The results, shown in the graph on page 186, show that although by age 8 many children say that advertising exists to persuade us to buy or to do something, even by age 10, only about one-third identify persuasion as advertising's main function. At 10, more children believe that advertising's primary purpose is to inform rather than to persuade, and a small but meaningful portion of kids continue to believe that advertising is there only to amuse us.[10, 11]

While children are naive about the true aims of advertising until a fairly advanced age—well past the time when they start to influence their parents' spending decisions—advertisers are anything but innocent of children's desires, hopes, fears, preferences, and habits. Just as in the Christmas carol that celebrates the big, fat, jolly bringer of toys who "sees you when you're sleeping, [and] knows when you're awake," there is no privacy from the marketing juggernaut. Marketers employ a phalanx of psychologists to report on children's dreams and desires at all ages; armies of anthropologists to do careful in-home assessments of how children play, work, dress, sleep, and bathe; numerous neuroscientists to perform brain scans of children as they watch TV and look at toys; and of course, enough musicians, artists, actors, and writers to keep the whole nation in community theater for a decade of summers.[12, 13] Many television commercials are directed by A-list Hollywood types, such as Ridley Scott, either to get a start, to practice their art, or to earn a quick buck.[14]

The Development of Children's Understanding of the Purposes of Advertising, Ages 6 to 10[15]

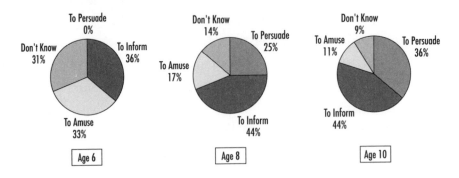

THOSE JOLLY JINGLES

Many parents and most children believe they are immune to the effects of advertising. Yet ample research and commercial experience has demonstrated that the majority of people are quite susceptible to its influence. First, there's the oft-observed fact that if advertising to children didn't work, marketers wouldn't spend $15 billion per year on it. A host of careful research studies have also documented the ability of advertising to influence children's tastes and behaviors.

Parents and adolescents may think that advertising doesn't affect them because they are skeptical of it. Yet on closer examination, children—like adults—are skeptical of advertising in general but not of advertising for their favorite items or brands. Most children are sympathetic to toy and game commercials, and recent research has demonstrated that children are influenced by ads even when they are skeptical of them.[16]

In 1974, in an upper-middle-class suburb of Montréal, researchers conducted a revealing experiment.[17] They divided 133 boys, 8 to 10 years old, into two groups, each of which saw a half-hour episode of *The Flintstones*. For one group, the episode was interspersed with one or three commercials for a new toy called Cool Cast, which allowed the boys to mold plastic into the shapes of football or basketball players. The other group saw unrelated commercials. After viewing *The Flintstones*, the boys were asked to solve a puzzle consisting of a set of iron rings and a rope that had to be disentangled and were told that the first boys to untangle the rings would get the advertised toy, while the remainder would get a Hot Wheels car.

Unbeknownst to the boys, however, the puzzle was unsolvable, so the length of time they worked on it could be seen as an indication of how much they wanted the advertised toy. Those who hadn't seen the Cool Cast commercial tried to solve the puzzle for about 14 minutes, while those who had seen either one or three commercials worked on it for an average of about 20 minutes. (One brave lad soldiered on for $2\frac{1}{2}$ hours before throwing in the towel, no doubt to the surprise of the researchers and the pride of his parents.) Evidently, viewing just one commercial for a new toy was sufficient to induce 9-year-old boys to work almost 50 percent longer on a frustrating puzzle. Too bad there aren't more ads for homework!

ADVERTISING ALCOHOL

In Chapter 6, we talked about the role of television advertising in fostering the nation's obesity epidemic. You saw that the well-known effects of TV on obesity are due primarily to advertising unhealthy foods and not, as many people believe, to the sedentary nature of TV viewing. Obesity is hardly the only effect of television food ads targeted for children. A diet heavily weighted toward the junk foods and sodas frequently advertised on television has been shown to be associated with more cavities and bone fractures.[18, 19] While real damage can be done—to teeth, bones, and waistlines—by the effects of TV commercials for sugary foods and beverages, these dangers pale in comparison to those of alcohol advertising.

Marianne had a shock when she took her 3-year-old son Scott to the grocery store one day. Scott watches a lot of sports with his dad, and it had never occurred to Marianne that there could be anything objectionable about it. Scott seemed to enjoy the time with his dad, and she could often hear enthusiastic howls or groans of disappointment coming from the two of them in the basement on weekend afternoons. When Marianne and Scott turned into the beer aisle in the store, Scott surprised his mother by singing the advertising jingle for the national beer brand that was right on the corner. As they passed the next brand, Scott broke into that jingle as well. And so it went all the way down the aisle, with Scott singing and chanting a new jingle for every beer brand they passed.

Scott may have been precocious, but he isn't alone. One recent study found that 60 percent of 5th and 6th graders—who are about 8 years shy of legal drinking age—could match a still photo from a beer commercial to the correct brand of beer, and a 1990 study found that 88 percent of 5th and 6th graders could match the Spuds Mackenzie character to Bud Light.[20]

Alcohol is or should be an important concern to all parents of teenagers. For teens, beer is the alcohol of choice. In 2003, approximately 11 million underage children reported having a drink in the previous month, and about 7 million reported binge drinking.[21] To put these numbers in context, think back over the past 2 weeks. What have you done? Rented a movie? Gone to a dinner party? Read a good book? In those 2 weeks, one-third of America's high school seniors have gotten drunk.[22] More will get drunk within the next 2 weeks.

Some drinking by teens is responsible and moderate and can represent the kind of experimentation that's inevitable in adolescence, but the long-term implications of early initiation of drinking can be severe. Those who start drinking early are at greater risk of adult alcoholism and all its attendant ills: cirrhosis of the liver, poor sleep, obesity, depression, divorce, and so on. And some of the short-term implications can be tragic. Every day in the United States, nine teens die of alcohol-related causes, including drinking and driving, which is among the most common causes of death for teenagers.

Children and teenagers are exposed to 1,000 to 2,000 alcohol ads on TV each year. During primetime, there is one alcohol commercial every 4 hours; the average teenager would be targeted by about seven alcohol ads each week if he watched just primetime shows.[23] During sports events, the intensity is much greater, with 2.4 ads *per hour*, so teens with an interest in sports have much greater exposure.[24] In addition, segment sponsorships (such as the Miller Lite Rookie of the Race in NASCAR races) have proliferated in recent years, to a rate of about three per hour.[25]

What role does alcohol advertising play in the development of teen drinking? In 1977, the National Science Foundation concluded, "There is a preponderance of evidence that cigarette advertising and alcohol advertising are a significant factor in adolescents' use of these two drugs." Since those words were written, 90,000 teens have died of alcohol-related causes. Far more have become hooked on alcohol and face a host of ill effects in adulthood.

Researchers have estimated the magnitude of the effect of alcohol advertising to be modest but meaningful.[26-32] Just as with fictional portrayals of drinking in regular programming, advertising influences children's beliefs about the effects of alcohol (and of course, downplays its dangers) and normalizes social drinking as an integral part of young Americans' experiences. The association between drinking alcohol and having fun, promoted by television advertising, can be exceptionally strong. Some 12- to 13-year-olds have reported to researchers that they wished that they could drink so they could have that level of fun.[33]

Half of teenagers and one-quarter of preteens report that some of their favorite ads on TV are for alcohol. It's no wonder. These ads are slickly produced and carefully designed, making use of every arrow in the psychologist's quiver to be effective. The cost to produce a 30-second beer ad can exceed the cost of producing an entire half hour of regular programming.[34]

As you've seen in the research on risk taking, from beliefs and norms there is a direct link to behavior. One study found that 39 percent of adolescents exposed to a lot of alcohol ads on TV reported driving "while I was really too drunk to drive," as opposed to 29 percent among those exposed to the smallest number of ads.[35] While 29 percent is still a large proportion of teens to be drinking and driving, the effect of raising this number to 39 percent is enormous. Another study examined the correlation between the density of alcohol advertising and fatality rates and concluded that a total ban on alcohol advertising could save 5,000 to 10,000 lives *per year*.[36] According to another study, a total ban on alcohol advertising would result in reducing adolescent drinking by 24 percent and adolescent binge drinking by 42 percent.[37] Partly on the strength of research such as this, Sweden banned all beer and wine ads on TV in the mid-1970s and has seen a 20 percent decline in alcohol consumption, with the biggest decline among the young.[38]

The adverse effects of alcohol advertising could be at least partly offset by public service announcements (PSAs), including responsible drinking campaigns mounted by the beer companies. PSAs can be effective, but their impact depends on reaching a large audience at the right time.[39] In practice, many PSA campaigns are generally too small and too ambiguous to do much good. A tiny fraction of PSAs air during primetime, and half are on between 1:00 a.m. and 7:00 a.m., when they are guaranteed to have almost no impact.[40, 41]

PSAs may actually be part of the problem. More of these ads have been developed on the use of designated drivers than on any other subject,[42] and a survey of 16- to 19-year-olds found that 80 percent thought that drinking is acceptable as long as there is a designated driver. The mixed message that teens seem to be taking away may be due in part to the participation of alcohol companies, which have developed the designated driver PSAs. Many of the spots use themes and images that seem to celebrate drinking, just as regular alcohol advertising does, which may significantly dilute the message.[43] In general, media campaigns against drunk driving have little effect on adolescents. What effect they do have comes indirectly and has to do with the context, or how the spots are viewed: Parents who see the ads are motivated to talk to their children about the issues.[44] This underscores the important role parents can play in helping their children interpret mixed messages from television. In this case, they can encourage their kids to put off starting to drink and to drink responsibly when they do begin.

TV, TOTS, AND TOYS

While parents of teens may be particularly concerned about the messages from alcohol advertising, the vast majority of ads directed at children are for things not nearly as dangerous as alcohol. Food is the biggest category of children's television commercials, followed by toys. Increasingly, promotions for toys aren't limited to advertising but have also been designed into the programs themselves.

Researchers at Stanford University used an experimental television reduction approach to test how watching less television might affect the extent to which 9-year-olds badger their parents for toys. After an intensive 6-month program aimed at getting kids to watch less TV, the results were impressive. As a result of watching less, the children made only *one-third* as many toy requests compared with similar children who hadn't been exposed to the TV-reduction program.[45]

Product placement is now a staple of both television and movies. Adults can hardly watch any contemporary film or program without seeing a bottle of Pepsi, a bag of Doritos, or the latest sports car, cell phone, or other shiny toy. But in children's shows, the true product placement is often the characters themselves, as the line between commercials and content has blurred almost to invisibility in recent years.

In the late 1960s, *Sesame Street* was developed with a large budget from private foundations and the U.S. Congress. The writers used this initial investment to produce wonderful episodes based on a solid conceptual model and then to follow up with careful research to ensure that the show's educational standards were maintained. Unfortunately, this business model is no longer feasible for children's shows—even high-quality educational shows.

Today, merchandising opportunities are an essential part of the planning and vetting of a new show. The *Financial Times* of London reported in 2004 about the fate of a clever new animated children's show called *Porter and Daughter,* about a girl mechanic and a father who can cook.[46] The show had several things going for it, including clever, likable characters, an interesting twist, and high production values. But it had one flaw: too few merchandising opportunities. For this reason, it failed to get a distribution deal and was abandoned. The show's producer was stoic but disappointed: "My brief is to make a great show. But you have to take these things into account because you can't 'just' make a great show these days because you can't finance 'just' a great show."

So instead she took a commercial for Milky Bar candy that featured a boy mechanic, targeted it for very young children, added lollipops growing in fields, turned it into a 30-minute show called *Engie Benjy,* and had no trouble raising money and getting a distributor. The show is reportedly now a mainstay merchandising hit for the ITV network in the UK, and parents are able to buy Engie Benjy toys, lunchboxes, and duvet sets for their kids.

Typically, only 20 to 40 percent of the cost of a new kids' show is provided by advance sales and the show's intended network. The rest comes from merchandising deals.[47] Even Sesame Workshop, which produces *Sesame Street,* now gets 68 percent of its ongoing financing—$66 million a year—from merchandising. The sale of everything from Elmo sheets to Big Bird wet wipes keeps the show on the air.

How did children's shows get to this point? How did a major public commitment to producing an innovative, new children's show in the late 1960s deteriorate to the point where up to 80 percent of the cost of some shows is provided by those who want to sell children toothbrushes, toys, clothes, and candy?

In 1969, Mattel produced a program known as *Hot Wheels* and at the same time released the Hot Wheels line of toy cars. A complaint was made to the Federal Communications Commission (FCC)—the government agency that regulates TV—to the effect that the *Hot Wheels* show was in essence a 30-minute commercial for Hot Wheels cars. The FCC concurred with this view, and the show was pulled. At that time, there was a limit on children's advertising of no more than 16 minutes per hour.

As recounted in Jim Steyer's fascinating book *The Other Parent,* television advertisers then struck gold with the election of Ronald Reagan and his free-market policies. His FCC chair, Mark Fowler, eliminated the restriction on TV advertising to children. The marketers responded ebulliently, flooding the airwaves with thinly veiled program-length commercials for their products, such as *Rambo, He-Man, Go-Bots, Transformers,* and *G.I. Joe.* There were also plenty of shows for girls, such as *My Little Pony.* And of course, the value of the younger child market wasn't lost on marketers, who offered *The Smurfs* and *Strawberry Shortcake.*[48, 49] These half-hour commercials swamped programming originally designed without explicit commercial intentions, which largely disappeared from the airwaves. The made-to-be-marketed era was in full swing.

By 1987, there were more than 75 such program-commercials on the broadcast stations. The quality of these program-commercials—sometimes called kiddie-mercials—was almost always poor because the marketing companies that produced them spent no more on the half-hour show than on their 30-second spot for the product associated with it. Despite the shows' poor quality, the manufacturers had little trouble getting them on the air. When necessary, they promised kickbacks in the form of additional advertising if stations aired their programs. Some manufacturers even granted television stations a cut of the profits from toy sales.[50]

At one point, 11 of the 20 top-selling toys had program-commercials promoting them. Most were designed for boys and centered on violence.

This process reached its peak with *Teenage Mutant Ninja Turtles*, which spawned more than 70 products, a movie, and a breakfast cereal. The success of the Turtles is ironic only when you learn that they were developed originally as a parody. Apparently, it wasn't possible to exaggerate the worst aspects of the genre to the point where children—and their parents—would see the perversity of it all.[51]

Parents have had reason to believe that the much-beloved PBS is above this commercialism. After all, it's a nonprofit organization with a mandate to serve the public and with a yearly Congressional allowance. But that allowance has been shrinking in real terms each year, to the point where now less than 15 percent of PBS's budget comes from Congress—just over $1 per citizen per year. And serving the public is expensive, even for a venerated nonprofit. So what did the network do? It turned to merchandising opportunities. PBS itself makes a relatively small amount from merchandising, but it fills broadcast hours with shows that have lucrative merchandising opportunities of their own. In some cases, its educational mission is compromised. For example, *Teletubbies* has never been shown to have any educational value—and in fact, a recent study showed that it inhibits language development among the young children for whom it's targeted.[52] But the show continues to be aired on PBS, and its global merchandising profits to date have been estimated to exceed $1.5 billion,[53] some portion of which is returned to PBS. Norway considered the show so predatory that it banned it.[54] In conjunction with Comcast, PBS has now launched a new commercial digital network that pairs the PBS children's lineup with advertisements.

And lest you think this merchandising is a ploy directed solely at unwitting younger children, note that teenagers are also not safe. The critically acclaimed 2001 skater "documentary" *Dogtown and Z-Boys* was paid for by a company with a large vested interest in teens' buying habits: Vans sneakers.[55]

HOW MARKETERS GET BETWEEN PARENTS AND KIDS

If children are, because of their age and intellectual development, natural, easy targets for marketers, the biggest impediment to reaching this market is parents, who in most cases are more mature, more experienced, and more wary of marketers' claims. And since it's usually the parents' money that's on the line, they have an added incentive to resist TV consumerism. Marketers' biggest challenge, therefore, is sidestepping the parents and reaching the kids directly. To achieve this goal, they have employed three major techniques.

- Undermine parents as authority figures by making it clear to children that parents are nerdy non-necessities.
- Treat children as young consumers, encouraging them to weigh in on everything from the family vacation to the family car.
- Encourage children to think of themselves as older than they really are. As mentioned earlier, this phenomenon is called age compression by researchers. Marketers call it "kids are getting older younger" (KAGOY).

A father is bent over a computer, helping his grade school daughter with her homework. She's looking up anatomy in an online encyclopedia and is clearly losing patience with her bumbling father. Even the family dog is disgusted. Finally, the mother appears in the doorway and tells the father, "leave her alone."

So much for the helpful father. This scene isn't reality; it's a commercial for a wireless phone company. After many protests, the commercial was pulled, but many more like it survive. While fathers are particular targets, no parent—or even grandparent—is safe from the withering glares of children observing fantastical portrayals of adult incompetence.

Ads have carefully and deliberately cast parents as idiots—ineffectual nerds, prudes, and generally the most irrelevant people on the planet. These antiparent messages usually take the form of portrayals of parents as uncool bumblers, as in the ad for a CD player in which parents are depicted singing dorky songs on a road trip. One marketer summed it up aptly: "Advertisers have kicked parents out. They make fun of the parents."

In her book *Born to Buy*, economist and sociologist Juliet Schor, PhD, illustrates how marketers deliberately create "utopian" spaces that are free of parents. She quotes an unnamed media critic who points out, "It's part of the official advertising world view that your parents are creeps, teachers are nerds and idiots, authority figures are laughable, and nobody can really understand kids except the corporate sponsor." As Dr. Schor observes, "The lesson to kids is that it's the product, not your parent, who's really on your side."

As authority figures, teachers fare no better. Nickelodeon's back-to-school campaign featured a "slime the teacher" segment and a contest sponsored by a tobacco company for which the prize was a slime shower for the principal and the chance to have Nickelodeon take over the school.[56] All of this antiparent and antiteacher rhetoric can take a heavy toll on family relations. It's highly successful at promoting the "street cred" advertisers need to influence children's own spending decisions and—even more lucratively—their nagging.

Kid marketer James McNeal estimates that children ages 4 to 12 influence about $300 billion in purchases annually. These include 67 percent of car purchases, including 30 percent of car purchases by parents whose kids are half a decade or more away from driving age.

Much of this influence is exercised through nagging, (the "pester power" mentioned in Chapter 6). Children nag their parents for weeks, asking up to dozens of times for a particular toy or food item, and many are ultimately successful. Parents spend an average of $10 more when grocery shopping with children than when shopping without them.[57]

Most parents are intuitively aware of the power of commercials to generate wants. What parent has not been incessantly nagged at least once for some bauble or toy, some doll or gizmo that "all the other kids have," as seen on TV? The ubiquitous nagging is one reason that children in the United States buy 45 percent of the toys produced in the world despite constituting only 4.5 percent of the world's population of children.[58] Despite their voracious consumption of toys, children are always encouraged by marketers to think of themselves as ever more grown up.

The KAGOY phenomenon can be startling to those who have been out of touch with marketing to kids for a while. In the 1980s, G.I. Joe was for 11- to 14 year-olds; now he's rejected by 8-year-olds as too babyish.[59] Sex is used to sell everything from magazines to dolls to an audience of girls who are not yet into their teens, and some of the juxtapositions can be jarring. Teddy bears and candy mingle in ads with high heels and push-up bras. Why? Girls and boys like to be thought of as 3 or 4 years older (and more experienced) than they really are. No self-respecting 17-year-old would buy *Seventeen* magazine anymore: It's now pitched to younger teens and even preteens. It is now possible for girls to buy "boy-crazy fashion fiend" dolls with skimpy clothes and heavy makeup. The targets: 4- to 6-year-olds.[60]

These central messages of marketing—questioning parents' legitimacy in children's eyes, inducing kids to nag parents for certain "must-have" items, and making them think of themselves as older than they really are—are echoed by the content of television shows. Even when the shows aren't explicitly influenced by promotional deals and merchandising tie-ins, they reflect and reinforce the cultural messages that kids see in the commercials, creating a fertile ground for marketing.

TOTALLY UNREAL LIFESTYLES OF THE RICH AND FAMOUS

The image of the American economic landscape painted by typical shows popular among children is a luxurious one. As an economist, Fred has always been struck by the laughable contrast between TV characters' standards of living and their professed occupations. *Seinfeld*'s Kramer—ever the self-parodist—represented an extreme of this tendency. He had no visible means of support but lived in a large, comfortable apartment in a nice neighborhood in Manhattan. Or consider shows like *Friends*, in which a waitress, a massage therapist, an aspiring writer, an aspiring actor, and a chef—all intermittently employed—had fabulous apartments in Manhattan. More realistically, all six of them would have been crammed together in a cramped flat in Queens.

Added to the unreality of average TV characters' living standards is the fact that a large number of shows revolve around those with an inordinate income. The ZIP code 90210, for example, is the 24th richest in the United States.[61] Because children and adolescents are drawn more to sitcoms and glamour dramas like *Models, Inc.* and *The O.C.* and less to social-realist series like *NYPD Blue* and *Law and Order,* they are subjected even more often to stratospheric lifestyles than are adults.

Part of the allure of TV has always been escapism, and we want to escape into visions of wealth, not visions of people slogging it out at home with two jobs and two kids and one car that's always in the shop. We don't take TV living standards seriously. Anyone who goes to New York, gets a job as a waitress, and tries to live like the characters on *Friends* should have her wallet examined. But the affluent images do sink in. One study asked people to estimate how prevalent some products and services are in American society. The list included items associated with affluent lifestyles, such as maids, hot tubs, diamond necklaces, charity balls, and convertibles. Those who watched more TV estimated that such items were much more prevalent than did those who watched less.[62]

Such a result is hardly surprising. How are most of us supposed to know what percentage of Americans have diamond necklaces? Unless we're in the habit of going to charity balls, we can only gauge from TV—which is exactly how to get a highly inaccurate view of what kinds of lifestyles our neighbors have.

Hence the appeal of the so-called reality shows: Everyone wants to know "what's normal." These shows are pitched as the equivalent of peeking over the back fence to spy on the Joneses. But reality shows are in fact highly contrived and unreal—unless we're interested in the lifestyles of those who manage to get themselves stranded in Outer Mongolia with nothing to help them find their way home but a matchstick and a ball of cotton and 10 equally good-looking bumblers.

The typical lifestyles portrayed on TV are on the whole much more luxurious than any of us can afford. The danger comes when we start to feel deprived and frustrated in our aspirations to an otherworldly TV standard.

Of course, children who digest this cornucopia of consumerism could be inspired to do better—to strive to earn more so they can spend more and have more. Television has been shown in several studies to significantly affect the value children and adults place on material things. As television critic Neil Postman has written, TV's foremost commandment is "Thou shalt have no other gods than consumption."

Dr. Schor developed an index of materialism for adolescents, which includes materialism-oriented statements that teens are asked to agree or disagree with. They tap several distinct domains of consumerism with statements such as, "I wish my family could afford to buy me more of what I want," "I care a lot about my games, toys, and other possessions," and "I like clothes with popular labels." Dr. Schor surveyed preteens in the Boston area and found that the more television they watched, the more materialistic they were. Her statistical technique enabled her to tell whether the TV viewing was leading to the materialism or vice versa, and she found that the causality was entirely one-way: TV was causing the increase in materialism. She writes, "Television induces discontent with what one has, it creates an orientation to possessions and money, and it causes children to care more about brands, products, and consumer values."

Watching all those images of fast cars and fancy clothes really makes kids value such things more. Or maybe it's because of all the nasty remarks on TV about those who don't have such things. Most parents won't be surprised by these results, since they deal daily with a host of requests for clothing, gear, and games—even apart from those things that are frequently advertised.

No doubt because of television's effect on the value people place on material possessions, those who watch a lot of television spend more money, even independent of income. A recent poll found that more than half of those who are heavily in debt also watch a lot of TV. Economic research has found that if one compares two families, with the same income and the same number of children, who live in the same community and differ only in the amount of television they watch, the family in which the adults watch more television spends more of its income and saves less. On average, each hour per week that an adult watches TV corresponds to $208 less in savings each year.[63] Given how much TV adults typically watch, the average family watches enough to set it back $2,200 a year in savings. So much for network television being free!

The effects of television on materialism go beyond a few annoying toy requests. In her study of Boston preteens, Dr. Schor found that the increase in materialistic values that results from television viewing leads directly to depression, anxiety, and lower self-esteem.[64] Other studies have confirmed this circular relationship between materialism and depression. Those who are depressed withdraw from friends and hobbies into a world in which things have disproportionately large importance. In turn, the emphasis on things rather than on experiences, socializing, and hobbies leads to more depression.[65]

Perhaps in response to the dangers of just such a negative feedback cycle, many religious traditions try to reduce the emphasis on materialism for young people. Yet we are all too familiar with the co-opting of religious celebrations for the opposite aim. One study quantified the effect of television on Christmas, comparing Sweden, where there is no toy advertising on TV, to England, where such advertising is permitted. Kindergarten children in both countries were asked to write letters to Father Christmas

(Santa Claus). The letters then were analyzed to see how many toy requests the children made and how many of the requests were for specific, branded products as opposed to generic requests for "a doll" or "a model airplane." The English children on average made 28 percent more toy requests and 37 percent more branded requests than the Swedish children.[66]

When it comes to toy requests at Christmas or the ramping up of bar mitzvah expectations, we have all endured our share of the commercial hailstorm. But when it becomes clear that securing the newest doll or video game can have an effect exactly opposite to the one parents hope for—when instead of joy and glee, these consumerist attitudes cause depression and damaged self-esteem—perhaps it's time to take the issue a bit more seriously.

THE BELEAGUERED PARENT

Where do beleaguered parents fit into all this? Actually, the parents' role is central, despite assaults from several sides. One strategy is to reduce how much advertising kids see. Our friend Avi likes to watch sports on TV with his children, but he has developed a good strategy to deal with the commercials. He mutes the sound when commercials come on and uses the time to talk about the game. Avi's strategy to avoid commercials gradually evolved into fun and useful sports "chalk talks." Our friend John has a similar strategy with his two sons. One of them is designated as "mute boy." If a commercial is allowed to run more than 2 seconds before the mute boy mutes it or changes the channel, anyone can call out "mute boy!" and that person gets control of the remote.

Please know that you have a profound influence on how your children view the commercials on TV. We have consistently emphasized mindful viewing, and the realm of advertising is one in which mindful viewing is most important. It starts with teaching children about responsible spending and about how advertisers benefit from our purchases. By default, many families delegate this important teaching responsibility to television. The jargon of shopping—*good deals; buy now, pay later; bargain-basement prices*—all comes to children via the small screen, which is probably not the medium parents would choose to teach their children about value. Yet how many parents proactively discuss with their 3-year-olds what these words mean? If you don't talk about it, and you let kids watch television alone, you implicitly cede control to marketers.

Always remember that you are in control. Children whose parents actively teach them about making careful expenditures are less likely to spend recklessly or needlessly. Research has shown that children who have strong home support and open communication with their parents are less affected by advertisements. Such communication doesn't have to be elaborate or sophisticated; it helps to simply tell kids early on that things cost money and that money is limited.

Part of this communication should be specifically about personal finances. A recent study cited by The Mint (www.themint.org), an excellent Web site with personal finance information for kids and parents, found that only 10 percent of high school seniors could adequately answer basic questions about financial issues, such as how paying the monthly minimum on a credit card affects the total interest paid on a purchase and so on. (The quiz is available at www.pueblo.gsa.gov/quiz.htm). Talk with your kids about what it takes to run a household and how much things cost, such as groceries and gas. As they show more interest, talk to them about how prices fluctuate, how compound interest works, and other financial information. Most kids are fascinated by money since it seems like such an adult issue and such a taboo subject. Break the taboos—teach them, with hard numbers, that wanting and buying things aren't just emotional issues but mathematical (and ethical) ones as well.

You can also consider directly commenting on ads when you watch TV with your children. A sarcastic comment like "Yeah, right!" can be effective with adolescents, who are used to dealing in skepticism. Younger children may respond to comments like "Our family doesn't buy that stuff" or "They want us to believe that their cereal will make us strong, but that's not true—it won't." Teaching children about the deceptions and distortions so common in ads can be helpful in defusing their impact and helping to develop healthy skepticism toward advertisements in general.

One common distortion that you can point out to kids, and beware of yourself, is the use of what marketers call a wholesome halo. This trick uses a wholesome attribute to promote a product that in fact is not whole-some. The classic example was the addition of "8 essential vitamins and minerals" to sugary cereals. Yes, vitamins are healthful, but children in the United States get plenty of vitamins and minerals from other foods. The cereals marketed this way are so laden with sugar that they are cer-tainly one of the negatives, as opposed to the positives, in children's diets. The wholesome halo now includes "whole grain," "low fat," "cholesterol free," and other nutritional claims that are entirely beside the point in promoting truly healthful fare. Disney now markets Film Star Classics cookies that are high in sugar but have a Mickey Mouse thumbs-up proudly displayed on the front of the package because they are a "good source of calcium." Don't be fooled by the wholesome halo—make up your own mind about what your children's nutritional needs are and be thoughtful about how to meet those needs.

Most important, you should be firm and authoritative but consistent and reasonable about purchases, including everything from sugary cereals and soft drinks to advanced game systems and CDs. Marketing research has shown that when subjected to repeated nagging, 70 percent of parents typically cave in. The main reasons for caving in are that the parents want to be the child's friend or simply want to indulge her. Yet when the child's health is at stake, as with food purchases, being a "friend" and being a good parent may be two different things. In Fred's house, when he was growing up, there was a rule that only cereals with less than 10 percent sugar content were allowed—no exceptions. This rule permitted Cheer-ios, Kix, Total, and a few others, but the vast majority of cereals adver-tised on TV were off-limits. There was no negotiation over this rule, and it was presented in a friendly, reasonable, and absolute way. This is an example of how straightforward it can be to be consistent (the rule was in place for many years and is in effect in Fred's own house to this day), authoritative (the rule was explained in terms of the ill effects of sugary cereals on teeth), and firm (no exceptions and no negotiations were allowed).

One study found that a mother's style in dealing with pestering is crucial in determining her child's reaction. Some toys are so alluring that the child will continue pestering no matter how the parent responds. In many cases, though, using a calm, warm, and reasonable tone of voice will induce the child to desist from further requests. By contrast, if the parent is harsh, authoritarian, or controlling, the child will continue to nag or will escalate the requests into a tantrum. Note the very important difference between *authoritative*, in which parents communicate that a rule comes from their knowledge of health effects, and *authoritarian*, in which parents insist that children follow rules just because the parents made them.

You should decide what foods, toys, games, or clothes are appropriate and permissible for your children, then stick to those decisions. Both parents should agree on the rules, agree about any possible exceptions beforehand, and agree to enforce the rules. Marketers call the 30 percent of parents who aren't susceptible to persistent nagging the bare-essentials parents. A better name would be stick-to-reasonable-limits parents, or simply good parents. Soda or an extra toy can be seen as an occasional treat, not as a bargaining chip or as something to be given out of exasperation.

You can also reduce the intensity of nagging and the other effects of advertising by limiting your children's exposure to it. To some degree, changing what TV children watch can affect exposure to advertising. There is, after all, less advertising on PBS than on commercial channels. As you've seen, though, even PBS features a subtle form of merchandising that some parents may not be comfortable with. An alternative strategy is to rent DVDs of high-quality programs, skip past the inevitable ads at the beginning, and let children watch the rest essentially ad free.

Advertising matters. Children of all ages who are exposed to ads are influenced by them, and they make spending decisions with ads very much in mind. Whether it's a 4-year-old looking at a commercial for a sugary cereal, a 10-year-old looking at an ad for a video game, or a teenager looking at a beer ad, TV commercials have a profound effect on children's behavior.

By now, you have a thorough sense of what the latest and best science has identified about the effects of television on your children. You know that television affects everything from kids' sleep to hyperactivity. You have tools to help you manage the three determining factors of TV's impact—*what* your children watch, *how much* they watch, and *how* they watch it. In the next chapter, we put these suggestions together and help you build a comprehensive strategy to make television work for you and your children.

HOW TO MAKE TV WORK FOR YOUR WALLET AND YOUR KIDS' SELF-ESTEEM

ALL AGES

- Shield all children—especially preschoolers—from commercials. Muting the ads helps, but try to skip them altogether by using TiVo, ReplayTV, or DVDs.
- Be firm about purchases—don't allow yourself to be unduly influenced by pester power. Set firm, reasonable limits and stick to them consistently. Have a budget for kids' purchases, and tell them what it is. For example, "Each child may choose one food item from the grocery store" or "Our family eats fast food only on Saturdays."

GRADE-SCHOOLERS

- Talk to children about commercials, explaining why they're on TV and who benefits from them. Start by asking what the kids think of the commercials—are they cool, boring, funny? Then ask what they think the commercials want them to do.
- Talk about the purpose of commercials. Explain that they are expensive to make and that it costs money to put them in a show. Discuss how the only way to make money with commercials is to sell *more* of whatever is advertised, and the only way to sell more of something is to change the behavior of the people who watch the ads.

GRADE-SCHOOLERS AND TEENAGERS

- Watch TV with your children and point out distortions and deceptiveness. Watch with a critical eye yourself. When you start to pay careful attention, you'll be amazed at how often you find yourself saying "As if!"

CHAPTER 9

GETTING TO MINDFUL VIEWING: RETHINKING, RESTRUCTURING, AND REDUCING TELEVISION

We can put television in its proper perspective by supposing that Gutenberg's great invention had been directed at printing only comic books.

Robert M. Hutchins, News Summaries, *December 1977*

I hate television. I hate it as much as peanuts. But I can't stop eating peanuts.

Orson Welles

It's not a question if it's human beings or not; it is a question of whether it's a good story. You don't need to have special effects or a naked woman or violence to make a good movie.

Emmanuel Priou, producer of March of the Penguins

In the late 1970s, researcher Charles Winick, PsyD, became curious about how people might cope without television. Over 6 years, he visited police stations in New York City to find people whose apartments had recently been robbed. He went to TV repair shops and collected the names of those whose sets were being repaired. Then he contacted more than 1,600 of these people and interviewed them about how it was going.

Universally, the first 3 or 4 days without a set were the worst. Even among families who didn't feel that they watched a lot of TV, family members had difficulties adjusting to life without it. They became anxious, depressed, and aggressive. By the 5th to 8th day, most people were beginning to cope much better. By the end of the second week, they had adjusted to life without television, and the initial stress and boredom had been replaced by new activities.

Whether you watch TV a little or a lot, if you own a set, it figures into your family routine in some way. How much may become obvious only when you try to change your habits. Changing TV habits disturbs routines that are comforting and useful. If your family watches a lot, it may seem impossible to imagine life without it. If you're confident that your family currently uses television appropriately, you may be reluctant to examine your use of it. Whatever your television habits are, however, we believe that you must become a mindful viewer. As we've said, the unexamined television is not worth watching—be it for 10 minutes or 10 hours.

In the previous chapters, you've learned about many of the ways that television can affect your child's cognitive, social, and behavioral development—both positively and negatively. We said at the outset of this book that there is no proper amount or type of television for every child and every family. Changing television habits—whether by reducing overall viewing, watching different kinds of shows, or adopting new ways of interacting while viewing—should be undertaken thoughtfully and deliberately. Now that you are well-informed, it's time to take control of your family's television viewing and make it work for all of you.

In this chapter, we challenge you to *rethink* television, to view it as more than just a relaxation tool or a babysitter or a necessary evil. We will suggest that you *restructure* your television habits—and those of your family—in a way that you can feel good about. Finally, if you've decided that your family watches too much TV, we'll discuss strategies to *reduce* the amount of time you spend in front of the screen. Rethinking, restructuring, and reducing are the 3 R's of making television work for your family.

DEVELOP A STRATEGIC PLAN

In the 1960s, researchers conducted an international comparison of television content and viewing habits.[1] They found that the percentage of households with televisions varied widely from country to country (from 25 percent of households in Bulgaria to almost 100 percent in the United States), but the amount of viewing among families with TVs was almost exactly the same in all countries: about 2 hours per day. Moreover, there was no relationship between the kinds of programming offered and the amount watched: Poles, Peruvians, and Americans all watched the same amount despite different programming content. And while content was similar in France and Belgium—with considerable overlap—among all countries surveyed, the French watched the least television, and the Belgians watched the most. Programming content was not—and still isn't—a major determinant of how much time people devoted to television.

In Chapter 1, we likened television to a power saw, a tool that while dangerous, also has useful potential. Yet unlike television, there is always *intention* involved in using a power saw. Seldom does anyone casually walk over to a saw; flick on the thundering, spinning blade; and idly saw wood. When you approach a power saw, you have a mission. This isn't true of television. People of all ages routinely click it on with no purpose. When asked why they watched television last night, few people say that they picked a specific program. Most say they just *watched,* as an end in itself. As many as one-third of viewers don't select a program but watch whatever someone else in the room chooses. And this is true not only for adults; older children and adolescents routinely channel surf. Younger children ask their parents, "Can I watch TV?" or "Can I watch a video?" without requesting a particular program. This is evidence of a fundamental and pervasive problem in families' approach to television: They lack a strategic plan. As Yogi Berra once said, "If you don't know where you're going, you might end up somewhere else."

By a strategic plan, we mean more than a set of rules regulating television; many households already have those. We mean that each rule should serve some preconceived purpose. Many families' rules are well-intentioned and good but are haphazardly conceived. Rules typically seek to avoid inappropriate content or minimize overall viewing time. Both of these are desirable goals, but neither addresses the ways in which television can figure *positively* into your children's lives. Very few parents actually think about how to optimize television viewing so that it's ultimately a *good* thing, not a neutral or bad thing, for their families.

To begin, consider what you would like to get out of television and what you want to avoid getting from it. The previous chapters can give you some ideas. What are your goals for television viewing? TV can serve many purposes if used correctly. It is entertaining—itself a worthy goal—but that's the least that it can do. It can also be a source of enrichment. Preschoolers can learn reading and prosocial behaviors from educational shows; they can engage in music and dancing with other kinds of shows and practice problem-solving abilities with still others. Grade-schoolers can expand their horizons by watching programs about science, nature, and other cultures. Adolescents can pursue their own specialized interests through selected documentaries. Television can be used as an opportunity for parents to maintain open communication with children and teenagers about difficult topics. You may find it easier to start a conversation with your teen about drinking, sex, or money by referencing a television character rather than by plunging into such touchy subjects by talking about your child's behavior.

Using television purely recreationally, without a mindful approach, sells your children—and television—short. If your preschooler watches both prosocial television and violent cartoons, you are sabotaging your own efforts to teach her to be kind. If your teenage athlete stays up past midnight to watch his favorite West Coast team and is too tired to get up the next morning, he is jeopardizing both his school and athletic performance. Using the table below, identify what you want yourself and your children to get from television and what you want to avoid getting.

What You Want	What You Don't Want
Entertainment	Shorter attention spans
New horizons	Poor nutritional choices
Educational programming	Risky behaviors
Early literacy	Aggression
Social values	Consumerist attitudes
Positive role models	Sleep problems

Whatever goals you establish for television, it's critically important that it serves *you* and not the other way around. It is a tool, and as such, it should meet your needs, not dictate them. Once you and your family have agreed on what you want from television, you must ask yourselves to examine its current role in your family's life—how it figures into your day-to-day routine. Knowing both what you want from television and what you're currently getting from it will help you set goals.

To begin, consider the following questions.

1. How much television do your children watch (quantity)?
2. What programs do they watch (content and quality)?
3. How do they watch (context)?

HOW MUCH TELEVISION DO YOUR CHILDREN WATCH?

One of our research assistants once conducted a telephone interview with the mother of a boy named Sanjay, who was participating in one of our studies. Both of Sanjay's parents are wealthy and well-educated and work for a Seattle-area software company. The interview started off easily enough with questions about her child's age (7), hobbies (Lego Bionicals, snakes, computers), and other activities (swimming lessons). But when the research assistant asked about television viewing, there was confusion. The research assistant heard the phone being placed on the countertop and then heard an increasingly excited conversation in a foreign language in the background. After quite some time, the mother returned to the phone and answered, "1.3 hours per day on average. But that's just a guess."

Knowing how much TV your children watch may seem like an easy starting place, but in fact, many parents don't actually know. They rely on their own recollections, which are frequently biased. Sometimes they think their children watch more than they actually do, sometimes less, and sometimes they don't have any idea. But even the best estimates are based only on the viewing parents are aware of. For older children, parental estimates typically don't include viewing that occurs at friends' houses, at night after parents are asleep, or while in the relative privacy of their own rooms. For young children who are cared for outside the home, estimates typically don't include viewing that occurs in daycare settings.

In a recent study we did of more than 2,000 daycare centers across the United States, we found that children in home-based daycare watch more than 1 hour of television per day, effectively doubling, on average, their daily viewing time. Children in institutional daycare watch less, typically on the order of 20 minutes per day. On the opposite page is a graph of our results.

Almost 90 percent of home-based daycares and 35 percent of daycare centers allow children to watch some TV. Many parents are surprised by these findings and dismayed that there is a significant source of additional screen time in their children's daily life, over whose content and quantity they exert no direct control. Keep in mind that many centers, especially home-based ones, care for children in a wide range of ages, so it's highly likely that TV content (using a one format fits all approach) won't serve all of the children present. You should ask about television policies when choosing a child care provider.

Total Television Viewing in Daycare Settings, by Program Type

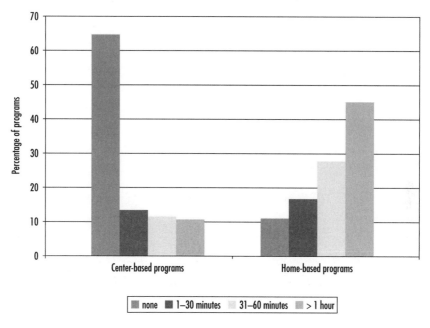

KEEPING A DIARY

In our research, we have developed an elaborate and successful set of materials that we use to help parents optimize their children's television viewing. Our program is based on the latest techniques to help motivate people to change their behavior. It includes educational materials, motivational counseling, and pragmatic strategies tailored to each family's needs. In order to figure out those needs, we must first examine how families actually use television, which we do by having parents track their children's viewing for a period of time. Invariably, we hear from parents that this is the most helpful aspect of our approach.

In developing your strategic plan, we suggest that you keep a detailed television diary for 2 weeks. Record the amount of time that your children watch, the specific programs, and anything else they're doing while watching. Try to include viewing outside your home. Ask your children's friends' parents and daycare providers how much television your children watch on the days for which you're collecting data. It's also helpful to record how it was being viewed (on DVD, television, TiVo, and so on) because that will give a sense of the flexibility of your viewing across time. You can create a simple diary form such as the one we use in our studies. Below are 3 days' worth of actual data for a 5-year-old Seattle boy whom we'll call Conrad.

Monday, February 19					
Start Time/ Stop Time	What Was Your Child Watching?	Was It on TV, Video/ DVD, TiVo?	Where Was It Watched?	Who Else Was Present?	What Else Was Your Child Doing at the Same Time?
8:00– 8:30 a.m.	Sesame Street	TV	Kitchen	Younger sister	—
8:30– 8:45 a.m.	Clifford	TV	Kitchen	Younger sister	—
5:00– 6:30 p.m.	Aladdin	DVD	Family room	Younger sister	Hitting sister
7:00– 7:30 p.m.	CBS News	TV	Dinner table	Mother, father, younger sister	Eating dinner, talking
Tuesday, February 20					
8:00– 8:30 a.m.	Sesame Street	TV	Kitchen	Younger sister	—
5:30– 6:30 p.m.	SpongeBob	TV	Family room	Younger sister	Playing with blocks

Tuesday, February 20 (cont.)					
7:00– 7:30 p.m.	CBS News	TV	Dinner table	Mother, father, younger sister	Eating dinner, talking
Wednesday, February 21					
8:00– 8:30 a.m.	Sesame Street	TV	Kitchen	Younger sister	—
8:30– 8:55 a.m.	Clifford	TV	Kitchen	Younger sister	—
5:15– 6:45 p.m.	Aladdin	DVD	Family room	Younger sister	Playing with sister
7:00– 7:30 p.m.	CBS News	TV	Dinner table	Mother, father, younger sister	Eating dinner, talking

After completing the 2-week diary, calculate how many hours your child watches on an average weekday and weekend. Calculate the hours separately because children typically watch different amounts on weekdays and weekends. Once you have your totals, you may want to know how they compare to national averages.

Data on how much children watch comes from a variety of sources. Frequently, it's based on parents' estimates, which, as mentioned, aren't very accurate. These figures also come from companies (such as Nielsen) that collect them for advertisers, but these aren't reliable for children and don't include any video/DVD viewing, a major part of children's screen time today.[2] The best data comes from diaries of activities that parents keep, much like the one above. The Panel Survey of Income Dynamics, an ongoing national study of how children spend their time, collects these diaries and has produced the calculations that we feel are most reliable.

Daily Average Television/Video/DVD Viewing in a National Sample of U.S. Children

Age (years)	Weekday (per day)	Weekend (per day)
0–2	1 hour 9 minutes	1 hour 11 minutes
3–5	2 hours 1 minute	2 hours 25 minutes
6–8	1 hour 45 minutes	3 hours 3 minutes
9–12	1 hour 56 minutes	3 hours 19 minutes

How does your children's total viewing time (on weekdays and weekends) compare to the national estimates? Is it more or less? Is the difference a cause of concern for you? Do you feel your children watch too much? We'll focus on how to reduce viewing later in this chapter, but before considering a change in how much they watch, you'll want to develop a thorough understanding of what they watch. Here again, you may turn up some surprises.

WHAT DO THEY REALLY WATCH?

An occupational hazard of doing television research is that parents seek us out for absolution. A colleague of ours recently told us that his 3-year-old son, Jacob, watches only *Sesame Street* and *Mister Rogers' Neighborhood,* for a total of about 7 hours per week, and he wanted to know if that was okay. Of course, we were very encouraging and reassuring. But at the office Halloween party, Jacob ran over to a 7-year-old in a SpongeBob costume and sang, "Who lives in a pineapple under the sea?" (the beginning of the show's opening ditty).

As we have repeatedly stressed, *content* and *context* are as important as *quantity.* Our colleague didn't consider that Jacob was watching what his older brother was. This oversight is very common. For example, in the example cited above, Conrad's family watched television during dinner, a practice they shared with one-third of U.S. families. But when asked about what he watched, his parents might easily have overlooked dinnertime viewing. After all, the whole family watched the news during dinner; it wasn't intended for Conrad. While the set was on, he talked, ate, and interacted with his family and hardly paid attention to the TV.

Likewise, Maggie, Conrad's younger sister, almost 3 years old, followed her brother around constantly. Her viewing was largely driven by his tastes, and her diary should include the time she spent in the room when the television was on. Given her young age, the amount and content of what she watched may not fit with her parents' goals for her viewing.

HOW DO THEY WATCH?

Conrad's diary is similar to most children's in that there are discernible patterns to his viewing. Some shows were regulars and others varied, but the *times* during the day that he watched were fairly consistent, as were the reasons he watched during those times. This is true for most children. After breakfast, Conrad watched *Sesame Street* from 8:00 to 8:30 a.m. while his parents cleaned up and got ready to leave the house. Some days, he started watching *Clifford* (which comes on right after *Sesame Street* on their local PBS station) before they rushed out the door to drop him and Maggie off at preschool. Both of these morning selections served an educational and prosocial purpose, which was important to Conrad's parents. But if that were truly the sole motivation for having him watch, other activities might be as good or better. When asked, Conrad's parents said that they would prefer to read and play with him, but they conceded, "There just isn't time in the morning. It's too hectic."

Twice in a 3-day period, Conrad watched *Aladdin* on a DVD in the evening while his parents got dinner ready. In all likelihood, Conrad's parents spent less time deciding what he should watch on video that evening than they did deciding what to make for dinner. "Conrad loves *Aladdin* so much, we bought the DVD," his father reported. In fact, it's remarkably common for children these days to regard a movie with the same level of affection that was once reserved for a favorite toy. Treating videos as if they were toys has its downside. Ask yourself what purpose is served by watching the same video repeatedly: Is it beneficial for your child? Is he still entertained by it? Or is he watching simply for your convenience?

Later in the evening, watching the news during dinner provided Conrad's busy working parents with a way to catch up on the day's events. "None of us really watch it," Conrad's mother conceded. "It's more like background noise with pictures. We really focus on the kids during mealtime, but if there is something of interest, I watch out of the corner of my eye." While Conrad's mom was saying this, she realized that she actually didn't like this idea. She learned that her children are also distracted by the screen and that they do watch the news, something we don't believe is wise for children Conrad's and Maggie's age.

RETHINKING VIEWING

You now have two elements of your strategic plan in place: your goals and your assessment of where you are. Before moving on, you should examine these carefully together. Do the reasons for your children's viewing correspond to the goals? If not, you'll want to modify either the goals or the viewing, and either approach is acceptable.

When we do studies of television, we have parents complete the diaries, and then a member of our research team reviews them with families. Together, they discuss these issues and rethink their viewing habits. Over 3 days, Conrad's parents learned that he watches about 2½ hours per day. Of this time, about one-quarter was intended to serve his educational needs, just over half was for entertainment only, and one-quarter wasn't intended for him at all. Before completing and reflecting on the diary, Conrad's parents said that they felt television was "at worst" neutral and actually mostly positive in his life. "He watches educational television mainly," his father said. "Sometimes we use it during meal preparation, but he doesn't watch very much overall." Once their diary was completed, Conrad's parents could see that their perception of his TV viewing and the reality didn't match. So they decided to *rethink* his viewing.

First of all, they thought that they used TV primarily for educational purposes, but they found out they were relying on it just as much for babysitting. Their use of it during meal preparation (and their own desire to watch the nightly news, a fixed, primetime, live program) tripled his total viewing time and dwarfed its educational component. Conrad's parents were surprised by the small percentage of his viewing that was entirely educational. By tracking his viewing and comparing it with their goals for TV, they immediately saw that they could better achieve their original goal of education (as well as their previously unacknowledged goal of keeping him occupied during dinner preparations) just by changing what he watched in the evening.

Also, Conrad's parents had the news on during dinner but confessed they didn't really watch it. Background television is quite common: 30 percent of households report having the TV on all the time even when they say no one is watching! Conrad's parents' use of background television during dinner suggests casualness about viewing. The news was on as a contingency in case something interesting occurred or the conversation and demands of dinner hit a lull. It was primarily a distraction and wasn't being watched mindfully.

Mindful viewing is an important skill to model for your children. It involves watching selectively and thoughtfully and then being savvy about what you're actually seeing. Let your children see you think critically about what you and they watch. Let them detect intention in your use of television and sense that you use it with the same care and planning as you would that power saw. Don't channel surf any more than you would idly cut wood, and don't let them do it, either. Take control of your own viewing as well as theirs. Control is the cornerstone of your strategic plan.

RESTRUCTURING VIEWING

Once they had rethought what role television should play in Conrad's life, his parents *restructured* his viewing. He now watches only 30 minutes of television in the evening (the amount of time his parents actually need to be free to make dinner), and they select programming that's appropriate for him and that they feel good about. This strategy involves more work on their part. They have to find a variety of sources for quality content. They have to spend time planning his viewing, something they never did before. Indeed, TV was previously thought of as a time-sparing activity. It still is, but now watching requires more of an investment than Conrad's parents previously made. Technology has proven very helpful with this. TiVo enables them to maintain a compilation of programs from PBS that Conrad likes, so he can watch them when they want him to. They now record the news, too, and watch it after the children are asleep. Getting DVDs by mail makes it possible to have alternatives to *Aladdin* for Conrad's recreational viewing without necessitating stops at the video store.

But restructuring your child's viewing is not only about changing *content*, it's also about changing *context*. How families watch television is yet another way in which its use has changed significantly over time. As you know, at the time of its creation, TV was very much a medium that brought families together. Primetime programming was full of family-friendly shows, and parents and children assembled in the living room after dinner to watch *Kukla, Fran, and Ollie* or similar programs. (In fact, *Kukla, Fran, and Ollie*, which aired between 1947 and 1957, was watched by more adults than children and counted Orson Welles, John Steinbeck, and Adlai Stevenson among its many adult fans.)

Today, television routinely pulls families apart. Children often watch alone while their parents watch somewhere else. This practice sends exactly the wrong message about TV, but that needn't be the case. Dimitri's family has a weekly ritual—family movie night. Every Friday, he or his wife chooses a movie to watch with their 8-year-old son, Alexi, and 5-year-old daughter, Ariana. The movies include some classics that the parents enjoyed as children, such as *The Wizard of Oz, Chitty Chitty Bang Bang, Mary Poppins, The Sound of Music, Benji,* and some newer ones, such as *Honey I Shrunk the Kids, The Polar Express,* and *March of the Penguins.* More recently, family movie night has expanded to include Discovery Channel nature specials, since both children have become obsessed with snakes and insects.

But even when used for educational purposes, television should be treated as a means and not an end in itself. You should use television to engage and develop your children's inherent interests, not to *satisfy* them. Are your children learning letters on *Sesame Street?* Reinforce the lessons with a book. Are they interested in lions? Find a high-quality nature show about the big cats, but keep the interest alive when the show is over by segueing into other activities. Talk about lions, get books about lions, Google lions, go to the zoo to see lions. Most of all, be involved in your children's viewing. Know what they watch, talk about what they watch, and watch with them. Conrad's parents now cook dinner while he watches *Clifford* in the adjoining family room. They keep track of the show enough to talk about it with him over dinner, something no one had any interest in doing after the 50th viewing of *Aladdin.*

REDUCING VIEWING

If you're like the majority of parents, you would like to reduce your child's screen time but are concerned or unsure about how to do it. If you do plan a reduction, use your strategic plan. Be sure to selectively reduce television that doesn't serve your child's needs or yours. We have found in the course of our research that parents are often not thoughtful about what programs they eliminate, and they sometimes reduce high-quality programs in favor of low-quality ones. Conrad's parents reduced his viewing by 1 hour a day simply by letting Conrad watch a 30-minute program (and an educational one to boot) rather than a feature movie while they prepared dinner.

TIPS FOR REDUCING VIEWING

1. **Experiment with no TV for a week or two.** We are often asked by parents how they can possibly cook dinner for their families without putting their toddlers in front of the tube. Despite the fact that dinners have been cooked for millennia and television has graced us for only 50 years or so, many people are convinced it's impossible to make dinner without a video babysitter for the kids. Now, we recognize that times have changed, there are more families in which both parents work and more single-parent households, and life is generally more stressful, but toddlers themselves haven't changed all that much. Their needs are the same; their wiring is the same. Their capacity for self-entertainment, for helping in the kitchen, and so on, has remained biologically stable.

What has changed is *our* reliance—and hence theirs—on certain strategies for entertainment and on certain expectations for gratification. "I'm bored" can be a parent's problem, or it can be a child's incentive to be creative. There's no question that plopping children in front of the screen is convenient, but convenience can lead to overindulgence. There are times when a brief break from TV is crucial to help regain perspective and recalibrate expectations. Sometimes ending dependence on television, as with dependence on other addictive substances and activities, requires a cold turkey approach. Fortunately, unlike other substances, television can be safely reintroduced. A good time to do this is when you actually feel that you don't need it. Think of your break as a time to separate the wheat from the chaff. Your goal should be to discover what aspects of TV you miss and want to reintroduce and what aspects you can continue to avoid. For example, you may find alternatives to having your children idly watch television in the afternoon, but not for a specific show that you and they really like.

If you do decide to take a break, plan ahead. Set a start date for a turn-off period at least 2 weeks in advance. Use your diaries to determine when and why you *need* or simply *use* the television. Come up with potential alternative activities that will meet your needs at times you typically rely on television. If you use it to keep the kids occupied while you make dinner, have some craft projects ready or plan meals that they can help with during this time. Or let them play with blocks on the kitchen floor (something new will hold younger children's interest better than something old). If you use television for relaxation, come up with alternatives for yourself. Some take more effort, but as you saw in Chapter 3, they are in fact more relaxing. Plan to take a warm bath in the evening, buy some of your favorite teas for the pantry, or get some good books or even some trashy magazines! If you use television for family entertainment, plan alternative activities. Playing family board games (either ones you have and like but don't play often enough or a new one that the whole family can enjoy) is a great way to spend some time with your children while doing something fun.

If giving up weekend viewing seems as if it will be a problem, line up some events in advance. In our studies, we send families calendars culled from newspapers and Web sites that list low-cost or free activities around town. Sometimes they're seasonal (pumpkin-patch trips), and sometimes they're merely timely (free concerts at the zoo). We also send them suggestions for home activities, cooking, and craft projects. Parents unanimously reported that these were the best parts of our intervention. As one said, "Thanks for the newsletters. I realized when I got them that there was so much more I could do with my child, and too often it was my own laziness that had me resort to the screen." You can find many of these on the Internet; we suggest some useful sites to visit in Appendix 2.

As you plan your break, make your children part of the team. Explain what you're planning and have them come up with a list of alternative activities. Tell them that it will be a fun experiment. Let them know that the whole family is giving up television, including you, and that you're nervous but excited about it. It may take a while to adjust to life without TV, but be patient and confident: You can do it!

2. **Severely restrict or eliminate television on school nights.** Having a rule stating "no TV on school nights" reduces viewing by almost 75 percent, and it's one that's easy to explain, sends the right message regarding priorities, and is easily enforceable. As with any rule that is important to you—whether it's about when to eat dessert, how to treat other children, or using caution when crossing the street—it's easiest for you to start with this rule early, be consistent in enforcing it, and have a solid rationale. For favorite shows that air during the week, use TiVo or a VCR to record them and have your children watch them as part of their weekend viewing. Better yet, watch them as a family on Friday or Saturday nights.

3. **Out of sight, out of mind: Deemphasize TV's presence in your house.** A television set looms large in most living rooms today. It's a dominating presence that is frequently central to the room itself. If possible, move the set. Put it in the basement or some other dedicated TV room. Reduce the overall number of sets in your home so TVs aren't constantly in sight. In particular, get it away from the family dining table and use dinnertime for conversation. This can be remarkably beneficial: Studies have shown that children from families who eat dinner together are less likely to engage in aggressive behavior or risky sex or use drugs and alcohol.[3, 4]

4. **Get it out of your child's bedroom.** Thirty percent of children and 70 percent of teenagers have televisions in their bedrooms. As we've shown, there are lots of documented reasons to avoid this: It can interfere with sleep, lead to watching inappropriate content, and encourage excess viewing. In our study, we found that having a television in a child's bedroom increased viewing by more than 1 hour per day.[5] If your children currently don't have a TV in their bedrooms, let them know that they never will. If they do have it, take it out. Model good behavior as well: If you have a set in your bedroom, get rid of it.

TAMING THE ELEPHANT IN THE LIVING ROOM

Once you've established your goals and developed your strategic plan, come up with rules of viewing that will implement your plan. You can do this when your children are at any age, but it's best to start when they're as young as possible. Studies show that television habits that are developed at an early age persist through adolescence. Moreover, rules that are established and maintained early in children's lives are easier to enforce.

Don't believe it? Consider the sequencing of dinner and dessert. All of us have to tell our very young children on numerous occasions that dinner comes before dessert (if dessert is to be had at all). We have this conversation early on as children develop the capacity to prefer and request certain foods, but we seldom have it with children past the age of 5. By that time, they simply know that dessert cannot precede dinner. In fact, given how accustomed they become to the sequence, it would strike them as very odd if we ever served dessert first.

Rules about watching TV that are set and enforced consistently will function the same way. Fight and win your television battles early in your children's life. The key in this struggle is to be consistent and firm while maintaining a sense of humor. Remember that you are the parents, and you have the right to enforce your rules, provided they are well thought out, reasonably conveyed, and gently enforced.

Whatever your rules are, feel proud of them, not resigned to them. As parents, you convey a host of opinions and attitudes to your children, both consciously and unconsciously. Things that you feel particularly strongly about are typically conveyed the most strongly. These could be religious or moral or political convictions, or they could be philosophical approaches to life. Elevate television viewing to this level. After all, it is an enormous influence on your children's lives. Determine your feelings about its place in your family's life, develop your strategic plan, implement your rules, and be proud of them. What's more, make your children proud of them.

Dimitri's children boast about their TV rules at school, and their teachers use their TV habits as an example of good behavior!

If nothing else, we hope you will see this book as an exhortation to take a hard look at the elephant in your living room. We urge you not to be defensive or defeatist as you do so. Don't let the elephant stomp all over your family. With what you know now, you can feel confident that you have the skills to tame the elephant and make television work for your family.

EPILOGUE:

MAKING TELEVISION WORK FOR ALL CHILDREN

Children will watch anything, and when a broadcaster uses crime and violence and other shoddy devices to monopolize a child's attention, it's worse than taking candy from a baby. It is taking precious time from the process of growing up.

Newton Minow, chairman of the Federal Communications Commission, to a Senate subcommittee on juvenile delinquency in 1961

Throughout this book, we have emphasized the very real opportunities to make television work for your children. We have highlighted the good and bad aspects of this medium, but fundamentally, we have operated on the assumption that television is here to stay and that it is what it is. Despite this pragmatic approach, we believe that we can do better. If we all dare to dream a little bigger, television need not remain what it currently is. TV's potential is underrecognized and underutilized. Notwithstanding some bright spots, the TV landscape is far too desolate for children.

As parents and as experts in child development, we are saddened by a view of childhood that sees it only as preparation for adulthood. We see no need for television and movies to rush children into adult roles. We would rather see these media used to give children experiences that will enhance what's best about childhood. We say this because children are not little adults. Their needs are completely different, although their interests can at times be hammered into adult forms—and unfortunately, that's how most media treat those interests. The vast majority of children's shows and movies are essentially adult fare simplified and put into child-friendly format, with animation, children's voices, simpler dialogue, and more physical humor.

Examples of children's television shows and movies mimicking adult shows and movies abound, and in a few instances, the children's shows are direct rip-offs of adult fare. *The Flintstones*—a cartoon comedy involving two sets of married friends, dominated by a large, well-meaning bloviator—was conceived as a satirical version of *The Honeymooners*. While less explicit, it isn't hard to find similar copies elsewhere. *Scooby-Doo* is a reinterpretation of just about any adult crime drama of the same era. (Think of Scooby as Rockford, for example). *Speed Racer* isn't so different from *Starsky and Hutch*. And early cartoon characters—such as Bugs Bunny, Wile E. Coyote, and Sylvester and Tweety—seem to be taken directly from the early slapstick creations of Charlie Chaplin, Laurel and Hardy, the Keystone Kops, and Buster Keaton, sometimes with sight gags and pratfalls unaltered.

The same is true of modern movies. Consider *Toy Story*, a movie in which the Tom Hanks character (Woody) teams up with a motley bunch of irregulars, each with his own personality quirks and special skills, to rescue one of their own trapped behind enemy lines. Doesn't this sound a lot like *Saving Private Ryan?*

In *The Little Mermaid*, a buxom and frequently underclothed female leading character from the depths of the sea falls in love with her social superior and gets into trouble, albeit with a happy ending. Doesn't this sound rather like a million other Hollywood offerings, among them *Maid in Manhattan?*

HAPPY ENDINGS

Children deserve their own movies and programs, designed for them, that appeal to their interest in participating in the adult world and to their curiosity about their own world. What's needed are shows that have been designed from the ground up with children in mind. Some excellent examples for young children include *Mister Rogers' Neighborhood*, *Sesame Street*, *Barney & Friends*, and *Blue's Clues*. All have been thoroughly researched and were designed entirely to meet the developmental and entertainment needs of children. As a result, they are nothing like adult shows, and children like that. However, such shows are expensive to research, produce, and test. It takes real commitment to make them.

For this reason, we deplore the steady public defunding of PBS, which now gets only 11 percent of its support from Congress, compared with 70 percent in 1970. Today, the United States spends only about $1 per person on public broadcasting, while Japan spends $17 and Great Britain about $40 per person. We believe that a great nation is measured by the care it takes with its children. With television being such an important and integral part of our children's lives, we believe that their future is worth more than $1 a year from each of us. PBS is now developing a commercial channel to air its award-winning educational programming for children, and despite assurances to the contrary, we fear it won't be long before commercials compromise or overwhelm the educational value of the shows themselves.

Our culture expects parents to raise their children well. Of course, parents should bear the primary responsibility for this task, but today's harried parents have little control over either their children's social and peer environment or the values of their classmates. Parents have little knowledge or information to help them navigate a difficult and increasingly complex media environment, filled as it is with many risks and opportunities. Over the past generation, the cost of living, commute times, and work hours have all increased, leaving less time for parent-child interactions and adult supervision of children's activities. In this environment, television, movies, music, electronic games, and the Internet have become profound sources of influence on children's developing personalities and intellects.

This book has examined the effects of the most powerful of these media on a variety of health, intellectual, and developmental issues. As academic researchers, we have tried to stay as close to the science as possible, but as parents, we worry about effects that can't be evaluated by careful scientific research. We have looked separately at the effects of television viewing on teens' consumer attitudes and on their sexual behavior, and in doing so we have been careful to isolate the effects of television and to abstract from other social influences (such as children's peers or parents' own level of knowledge). In fact, though, we believe that television is part and parcel of those other social influences. When a teenage girl turns to television for advice on romance, she finds that it's vital to be cool, that part of being cool is defined by boys' interest in her, and that physical attractiveness is the primary means of attracting boys' attention. When she turns to TV for advice on how to make herself attractive, she learns she must dress in just such a way, which includes wearing all the right clothes. When all the girls in school do the same thing, school becomes a sexualized, consumerist environment in ways that would be unrecognizable to many parents. Yet the direct effects of television in this phenomenon may be small and difficult to measure. Girls may report that they are just trying to fit in and are imitating their friends. But each year, the boundaries are pushed a little further—and a little more aggressively—by new products and clever marketing campaigns largely waged through TV.

Earlier, we spoke of television as a super-peer. At times, it also functions as a super-parent, preempting the choices and influences most of us would like to see defined and made in the home by us. Our choices about television are also choices about our own roles—as parents, as adults, and as citizens. Our challenge is not to deny or to live without television but rather to find ways to live sensibly with it. And it isn't a challenge only for us. The ones with the most at stake are the children—our own and our neighbors'.

We believe that the way to improve television's impact lies in a greater societal, community, and parental commitment to use TV in the best interests of children. This will be a difficult task, but we hope this book has offered some constructive ways to move forward.

APPENDIX 1

SELECTED EMPHASIS AREAS OF TELEVISION PROGRAMS BY AGE GROUP

Educational television programs are not all the same. There are big differences between the ages at which they are targeted and the kinds of skills and learning objectives they focus on. The tables below will help you assess which shows are good for what kinds of learning. Most of the offerings are for preschool children, with considerably less for older kids. Of course, many elementary-age children and middle-schoolers can certainly enjoy and learn from adult documentaries and science and nature shows.

Literacy Skills		
Preschool	**Grade School**	**Middle School**
Arthur	Arthur	—
Between the Lions	Between the Lions	
Sesame Street		

Math Skills		
Preschool	**Grade School**	**Middle School**
Sesame Street	Cyberchase	Cyberchase

Problem-Solving Skills		
Preschool	**Grade School**	**Middle School**
Arthur	Arthur	—
Dragon Tales		
Blue's Clues		
Dora the Explorer		
Go Diego Go		

Imagination/Creativity		
Preschool	**Grade School**	**Middle School**
Barney & Friends	—	—
Dragon Tales		
Mister Rogers' Neighborhood		

Music/Dance		
Preschool	**Grade School**	**Middle School**
Boohbah	—	—
The Backyardigans		
Jack's Big Music Show		
Little Einsteins		
The Wiggles		
Animal Jam		

Nutrition/Health & Safety		
Preschool	**Grade School**	**Middle School**
Barney & Friends	—	—
Sesame Street		

Science/Nature		
Preschool	**Grade School**	**Middle School**
It's a Big Big World	Zoboomafoo	Dragonfly TV
Zoboomafoo	Zoom	Croc Files
Go Diego Go	The Magic School Bus	Nova
The Magic School Bus	Croc Files	Science
Peep in the Big Wide World	Nature (preview content)	Nature
	Nova (preview content)	Beakman's World
	Bill Nye the Science Guy	Bill Nye the Science Guy
	Beakman's World	

Prosocial Behavior		
Preschool	**Grade School**	**Middle School**
Arthur	Arthur	Maya & Miguel
Barney & Friends	The Berenstain Bears	
The Berenstain Bears	Clifford the Big Red Dog	
Caillou	Maya & Miguel	
Clifford the Big Red Dog	Sagwa	
Clifford's Puppy Days	Hey Arnold	
Dragon Tales	All Grown Up	
Mister Rogers' Neighborhood		
Sesame Street		
Franklin		
Miss Spider		
Max & Ruby		
Timothy Goes to School		
The Koala Brothers		
Higglytown Heroes		

Geography Skills		
Preschool	**Grade School**	**Middle School**
It's a Big Big World	Postcards from Buster	—

Cultural Diversity		
Preschool	**Grade School**	**Middle School**
Sesame Street	Maya & Miguel	Maya & Miguel
Dora the Explorer	Postcards from Buster	
Go Diego Go	Sagwa	

APPENDIX 2

INTERNET RESOURCES FOR PARENTS

One of parents' most important jobs is to assess the quality of what their children are watching. With so many different TV programs and movies out there, this can be a daunting task. The following Web sites are some that we have found helpful in separating the wheat from the chaff when it comes to children's media.

Television Rating Sites	
Organization	**Web Site**
Common Sense Media	www.commonsensemedia.org
Parents Television Council	www.parentstv.org

High-Quality Toys	
Organization	**Web Site**
Dr. Toy	www.drtoy.com
Children's Technology Review	www.childrenssoftware.com

Minimizing the Effects of Advertising	
Organization	**Web Site**
Campaign for a Commercial-Free Childhood	www.commercialfreechildhood.org
The Mint	www.themint.org
National Endowment for Financial Education Teen Resource Bureau	www.ntrbonline.org

Media Literacy	
Organization	**Web Site**
Action Coalition for Media Education (ACME)	acmecoalition.org
New Mexico Media Literacy Project	www.nmmlp.org
Center for Media Literacy	www.medialit.org
National PTA	www.pta.org/archive_article_details_1117641429406.html
Children Now	www.childrennow.org/issues/media

Alternative Activities to Television	
Organization	**Web Site**
TV Turnoff Network	www.tvturnoff.org/action.htm
LimiTV, Inc.	www.limitv.org/alternat.htm

NOTES

Chapter 1

1. Except as noted in the text, the anecdotes in this book, including this one, are the stories experienced by our friends, relatives, or study participants. Names and some identifying details have been changed to protect privacy.

Chapter 2

1. Letters to the Editor, *Pediatrics Post Publication Peer Review,* January 12, 2005.

2. J. M. Healy, *Endangered Minds: Why Children Don't Think—And What We Can Do about It* (New York: Simon & Schuster, 1990).

3. J. Richards and T. Gibson, "Extended Visual Fixation in Young Infants: Look Distributions, Heart Rate Changes, and Attention," *Child Development* 68 (December 1997): 1041–56.

4. Ibid.

5. U.S. Department of Health and Human Services, *Mental Health: A Report of the Surgeon General* (Rockville, MD: U.S. Department of Health and Human Services, Substance Abuse and Mental Health Services Administration, National Institute of Mental Health, 1999).

6. G. S. Lesser, *Children and Television: Lessons from Sesame Street* (New York: Random House, 1974).

7. M. L. Hooper and P. Chang, "Comparison of Demands of Sustained Attentional Events between Public and Private Children's Television Programming," *Perceptual & Motor Skills* 86 (1998): 431–34.

8. J. Baird, J. C. Stevenson, and D. C. Williams, "The Evolution of ADHD: A Disorder of Communication?" *Quarterly Review of Biology* 75, no. 1 (2000): 17–35.

9. D. L. Linebarger and D. Walker, "Infants' and Toddlers' Television Viewing and Language Outcomes," *American Behavioral Scientist* 46, no. 10 (2004): 1–22.

10. F. J. Zimmerman and D. A. Christakis, "Children's Television Viewing and Cognitive Outcomes: A Longitudinal Analysis of National Data," *Archives of Pediatric Adolescent Medicine* 159 (2005): 619.

11. P. K. Kuhl, F. M. Tsao, and H. M. Liu, "Foreign-Language Experience in Infancy: Effects of Short-Term Exposure and Social Interaction on Phonetic Learning," *Proceedings of the National Academy of Sciences USA* 100 (July 22, 2003): 9096–9101.

12. Ibid.

13. L. K. Friedrich and A. H. Stein, "Aggressive and Prosocial Television Programs and the Natural Behavior of Preschool Children," *Monographs of the Society for Research in Child Development* 38, no. 151 (1973).

14. E. A. Geist and M. Gibson, "The Effect of Network and Public Television Programs on

Four- and Five-Year-Olds' Ability to Attend to Educational Tasks," *Journal of Instructional Psychology* 27, no. 4 (2000): 250–61.

15. It isn't pacing alone that accounts for these differences. See D. R. Anderson, S. R. Levin, and E. P. Lorch, "The Effects of TV Program Pacing on the Behavior of Preschool Children," *AV Communication Review* 25 (1977): 159–66.

16. D. A. Christakis et al., "Early Television Exposure and Subsequent Attentional Problems in Children," *Pediatrics* 113 (April 2004): 708–13.

17. American Academy of Pediatrics Committee on Public Education, "Children, Adolescents, and Television," *Pediatrics* 107, no. 2 (2001): 423–26.

Chapter 3

1. D. R. Anderson, "Educational Television Is Not an Oxymoron," *Annals of the American Academy of Political and Social Science* 557 (May 1998): 24–38.

2. Ibid.

3. D. R. Anderson and S. R. Levin, "Young Children's Attention to *Sesame Street*," *Child Development* 47 (1976): 806–11.

4. E. P. Lorch and V. J. Castle, "Preschool Children's Attention to Television: Visual Attention and Probe Response Times," *Journal of Experimental Child Psychology* 66, no. 1 (1997): 111–27.

5. D. R. Anderson, "The Effects of TV Program Comprehensibility on Preschool Children's Visual Attention to Television," *Child Development* 52 (1981): 151–57.

6. A. Jonsson, "TV—A Threat or a Complement to School?" *Gazette* 37 (1986): 51–61.

7. A. Jordan, "The Role of Media in Children's Development: An Ecological Perspective," *Journal of Developmental Behavioral Pediatrics* 25 (June 2004): 196–206.

8. J. W. J. Beentjes, "Televised Stories vs. Audio Stories and Printed Stories," *Comenius* (Fall 1991): 290–301.

9. J. W. J. Beentjes, "Television Viewing vs. Reading: Mental Effort, Retention, and Inferential Learning," *Communication Education* 42 (July 1993): 191–205.

10. W. A. Collins, "Children's Processing of Television Content: Implications for Prevention of Negative Effects," *Prevention in Human Services* (Fall/Winter 1982): 53–66.

11. G. Salomon, "Television Watching and Mental Effort: A Social Psychological View," in J. Bryant and D. R. Anderson, eds., *Children's Understanding of Television: Research on Attention and Comprehension* (New York: Academic Press, 1983): 181–98.

12. Jordan, "The Role of Media."

13. E. H. Woodard, *Media in the Home 2000: The Fifth Annual Survey of Parents and Children* (Philadelphia: Annenberg Public Policy Center of the University of Pennsylvania, 2000).

14. D. L. Linebarger and D. Walker, "Infants' and Toddlers' Television Viewing and Language Outcomes," *American Behavioral Scientist* 46, no. 10 (2004): 1–22.

15. A. B. Jordan, *The 1998 State of Children's Television Report* (Philadelphia: Annenberg Public Policy Center of the University of Pennsylvania, 1998).

16. Ibid.

17. V. C. Strasburger and E. Donnerstein, "Children, Adolescents, and the Media: Issues and Solutions," *Pediatrics* 103 (January 1999): 129–39.

18. G. S. Lesser, *Children and Television: Lessons from Sesame Street* (New York: Random House, 1974).

19. Ibid.

20. B. Gunter and J. L. McAleer, *Children and Television*, 2nd ed. (London and New York: Routledge, 1997).

21. Jordan, *1998 State of Children's Television Report*.

22. Anderson, "Educational Television."

23. Lorch and Castle, "Preschool Children's Attention to Television."

24. Lesser, *Children and Television*.

25. M. L. Rice et al., "Words from *Sesame Street:* Learning Vocabulary while Viewing," *Developmental Psychology* 26, no. 3 (1990): 421–38.

26. J. Culhane. "Report Card on *Sesame Street*," *New York Times Magazine,* May 24, 1970.

27. V. Lovelace. "*Sesame Street* as a Continuing Experiment," *Educational Technology Research and Development* 38 (1990): 17–24.

28. R. Diaz-Guerrero and W. H. Holtzman, "Learning by Televised *Plaza Sésamo* in Mexico," *Journal of Educational Psychology* 66, no. 5 (1974): 632–43.

29. Lesser, *Children and Television*.

30. Ibid.

31. Ibid.

32. A. M. Crawley et al., "Effects of Repeated Exposures to a Single Episode of the Television Program *Blue's Clues* on the Viewing Behaviors and Comprehension of Preschool Children," *Journal of Educational Psychology* 91, no. 4 (1999): 630–38.

33. A. M. Crawley, "Do Children Learn How to Watch Television? The Impact of Extensive Experience with *Blue's Clues* on Preschool Children's Television Viewing Behavior," *Journal of Communication* 52 (June 2002): 264–80.

34. Crawley et al., "Effects of Repeated Exposures."

35. Linebarger and Walker, "Infants' and Toddlers' Television Viewing."

36. Woodard, *Media in the Home 2000*.

37. A. C. Huston et al., "How Young Children Spend Their Time: Television and Other Activities," *Developmental Psychology* 35, no. 4 (1999): 912–25.

38. M. Valerio et al., "The Use of Television in 2- to 8-Year-Old Children and the Attitude of Parents about Such Use," *Archives of Pediatrics & Adolescent Medicine* 151, no. 1 (1997): 22–26.

39. D. A. Christakis et al., "Television, Video, and Computer Game Usage in Children under 11 Years of Age," *Journal of Pediatrics* 145 (November 2004): 652–56.

40. S. S. Yalcin et al., "Factors That Affect Television Viewing Time in Preschool and Primary Schoolchildren," *Pediatrics International* 44 (2002): 622–27.

41. T. Gorely, S. J. Marshall, and S. J. Biddle, "Couch Kids: Correlates of Television Viewing among Youth," *International Journal of Behavioral Medicine* 11, no. 3 (2004): 152–63.

42. L. K. Certain and R. S. Kahn, "Prevalence, Correlates, and Trajectory of Television Viewing among Infants and Toddlers," *Pediatrics* 109, no. 4 (2002): 634–42.

43. Linebarger and Walker, "Infants' and Toddlers' Television Viewing."

44. D. R. Anderson et al., "Early Childhood Television Viewing and Adolescent Behavior," *Monographs of the Society for Research in Child Development*, 66, no. 1 (2001).

45. F. J. Zimmerman and D. A. Christakis, "Children's Television Viewing and Cognitive Outcomes: A Longitudinal Analysis of National Data," *Archives of Pediatric Adolescent Medicine* 159 (2005): 619.

46. R. J. Hancox, B. J. Milne, and R. Poulton, "Association of Television Viewing during Childhood with Poor Educational Achievement," *Archives of Pediatric Adolescent Medicine* 159 (July 2005): 614–18.

47. Jordan, "The Role of Media."

48. T. Koppel, "And Now, a Word for Our Demographic," *New York Times,* January 29, 2006.

49. R. Gibson, J. C. Hudson, and L. Watts, "Low Recall of Local Television Health Care News Segment Topics, Sponsors, and Program Names," *Health Marketing Quarterly* 17, no. 2 (1999): 55–65.

50. K. L. Slattery and E. A. Hakanen, "Sensationalism vs. Public Affairs Content of Local TV News: Pennsylvania Revisited," *Journal of Broadcasting and Electronic Media* 38 (Spring 1994): 205–16.

51. J. Hamilton, *All the News That's Fit to Sell: How the Market Transforms Information into News* (Princeton, NJ: Princeton University Press, 2004).

52. A. B. Krueger, "A Study Looks at What the Public Knows or Doesn't Know about Economics, and Why," *New York Times,* April 1, 2004: C2.

53. K. L. Schmitt, *Public Policy, Family Rules, and Children's Media Use in the Home* (Philadelphia: Annenberg Public Policy Center of the University of Pennsylvania, 2000): 35.

Chapter 4

1. A. N. Meltzoff, "Imitation of Televised Models by Infants," *Child Development* 59 (October 1988): 1221–29.

2. H. C. Paik and G. A. Comstock, "The Effects of Television Violence on Antisocial Behavior: A Meta-Analysis," *Communication Research* 21 (August 1994): 516–46.

3. B. J. Bushman and C. A. Anderson, "Media Violence and the American Public: Scientific Facts vs. Media Misinformation," *American Psychologist* 56, no. 6/7 (2001): 477–89.

4. R. Starch, *America's Watching: Public Attitudes toward Television* (New York: Roper Starch Worldwide, 1995).

5. W. S. Rubin, "Sex and Violence on Television," *Journal of Advertising Research* 21, no. 6 (1981): 13–20.

6. A. Jordan and E. Woodard, *Parents' Use of the V-Chip to Supervise Children's Television Use* (Philadelphia: Annenberg Public Policy Center of the University of Pennsylvania, 2003).

7. F. Yokota and K. M. Thompson, "Violence in G-Rated Animated Films," *Journal of the American Medical Association* 283 (May 24–31, 2000): 2716–20.

8. F. Rich, "The Great Indecency Hoax," *New York Times,* November 28, 2004.

9. A. J. Weiss and B. J. Wilson, "Emotional Portrayals in Family Television Series That Are Popular among Children," *Journal of Broadcasting & Electronic Media* 40 (Winter 1996): 1–29.

10. Ibid.

11. L. Berkowitz and P. C. Powers, "Effects of Timing and Justification of Witnessed Aggression on the Observers' Punitiveness," *Journal of Research in Personality* 13 (1979): 71–80.

12. V. B. Cline, R. G. Croft, and S. Courrier, "Desensitization of Children to Television Violence," *Journal of Personality and Social Psychology* 27, no. 3 (1973): 360–65.

13. C. Atkin, "Effects of Realistic TV Violence vs. Fictional Violence on Aggression," *Journalism Quarterly* 60 (Winter 1983): 615–21.

14. R. A. Baron, "The Influence of Hostile and Nonhostile Humor upon Physical Aggression," *Personality and Social Psychology Bulletin* 4, no. 1 (1978): 77–80.

15. G. A. Comstock and H. C. Paik, *Television and the American Child* (San Diego: Academic Press, 1991).

16. R. W. Poulos, E. A. Rubinstein, and R. M. Liebert, "The Effects of Television on Children and Adolescents: Positive Social Learning," *Journal of Communication* 25 (1976): 90–97.

17. L. K. Friedrich and A. H. Stein, "Aggressive and Prosocial Television Programs and the Natural Behavior of Preschool Children," *Monographs of the Society for Research in Child Development* 38, no. 151 (1973).

18. L. K. Friedrich and A. H. Stein, "Prosocial Television and Young Children: The Effects of Verbal Labeling and Role Playing on Learning and Behavior," *Child Development* 46 (1975): 27–38.

19. L. K. Friedrich-Cofer et al., "Environmental Enhancement of Prosocial Television Content: Effects on Interpersonal Behavior, Imaginative Play, and Self-Regulation in a Natural Setting," *Developmental Psychology* 15, no. 6 (1979): 637–46.

20. M. E. Goldberg and G. J. Gorn, "Television's Impact on Preferences for Nonwhite Playmates: Canadian *Sesame Street* Inserts," *Journal of Broadcasting* 23 (1979):27–32.

21. F. J. Zimmerman et al., "Early Cognitive Stimulation, Emotional Support, and Television Watching as Predictors of Subsequent Bullying among Grade-School Children," *Archives of Pediatrics and Adolescent Medicine* 159, no. 4 (April 2005): 384–88.

Chapter 5

1. "Brain Basics: Understanding Sleep," National Institute of Neurological Disorders and Stroke (www.ninds.nih.gov/disorders/brain_basics/understanding_sleep.htm), February 2006.

2. National Sleep Foundation, *2004 Sleep in America Poll* (Washington, DC: National Sleep Foundation 2004).

3. Ibid.

4. H. Aok et al., "Minimum Light Intensity Required to Suppress Nocturnal Melatonin Concentration in Human Saliva," *Neuroscience Letters* 252, no. 2 (1998): 91–94.

5. J. A. Owens and V. Dalzell, "Use of the 'BEARS' Sleep Screening Tool in a Pediatric Residents' Continuity Clinic: A Pilot Study," *Sleep Medicine* 6, no. 1 (January 2005): 63–69.

6. J. Owens et al., "Television-Viewing Habits and Sleep Disturbance in School Children," *Pediatrics* 104, no. 3 (1999): e27.

7. K. Harrison and J. Cantor, "Tales from the Screen: Enduring Fright Reactions to Scary Media," *Media Psychology* 1, no. 2 (1999): 97–116.

8. J. Van den Bulck, "Media Use and Dreaming: The Relationship among Television Viewing, Computer Game Play, and Nightmares and Pleasant Dreams," *Dreaming* 14, no. 1 (2004): 43–49.

9. C. Hoffner and J. Cantor, "Developmental Differences in Responses to Television Characters' Appearance and Behavior," *Developmental Psychology* 21 (1985): 1065–74.

10. P. Messaris, "Mothers' Comments to Their Children about the Relationship between Television and Reality," in T. R. Lindlof, ed. *Natural Audiences: Qualitative Research of Media Uses and Effects* (Norwood, N.J.: Ablex Pub. Corp., 1987): 95–108.

11. K. L. S. Forge and S. Phemister, "The Effect of Prosocial Cartoons on Preschool Children," *Child Study Journal* 17, no. 2 (1987) 83–88 .

12. F. Yokota and K. M. Thompson, "Violence in G-Rated Animated Films," *Journal of the American Medical Association* 283 (May 24–31, 2000): 2716–20.

13. D. Rajecki et al., "Violence, Conflict, Trickery, and Other Story Themes in TV Ads for Food for Children," *Journal of Applied Social Psychology* 24, no. 19 (1994): 1685–1700.

14. J. Cantor and S. Reilly, "Adolescents' Fright Reactions to Television and Films," *Journal of Communication* 32, no. 1 (1982): 87–99.

15. B. Bettelheim, *The Uses of Enchantment* (New York: Random House, 1989).

16. J. Cantor, B. J. Wilson, and C. Hoffner, "Emotional Responses to a Televised Nuclear Holocaust Film," *Communication Research* 13 (1986): 257–77.

17. K. Harrison and J. Cantor, "Tales from the Screen: Enduring Fright Reactions to Scary Media," *Media Psychology* 1, no. 2 (1999): 97–116.

18. J. Cantor and B. L. Omdahl. "Effects of Fictional Media Depictions of Realistic Threats on Children's Emotional Responses, Expectations, Worries, and Liking for Related Activities," *Communication Monographs* 58 (December 1991): 384–401.

19. G. Fairbrother et al., "Posttraumatic Stress Reactions in New York City Children after the September 11, 2001, Terrorist Attacks," *Ambulatory Pediatrics* 3, no. 6 (2003): 304–11.

20. K. L. Slattery and E. A. Hakanen, "Sensationalism vs. Public Affairs Content of Local TV News: Pennsylvania Revisited," *Journal of Broadcasting & Electronic Media* 38 (Spring 1994): 205–16.

21. V. J. Rideout, E. A. Vandewater, and E. A. Wartella, *Zero to Six: Electronic Media in the Lives of Infants, Toddlers, and Preschoolers* (Menlo Park, CA: Kaiser Family Foundation, 2003).

22. S. Higuchi et al., "Effects of VDT Tasks with a Bright Display at Night on Melatonin, Core Temperature, Heart Rate, and Sleepiness," *Journal of Applied Physiology* 94, no. 5 (2003): 1773–76.

23. Owens et al., "Television-Viewing Habits."

24. D. A. Thompson and D. A. Christakis, "The Association between Television Viewing and Irregular Sleep Schedules among Children Less Than 3 Years of Age," *Pediatrics* 116 (2005): 851–56.

25. J. G. Johnson et al., "Association between Television Viewing and Sleep Problems during Adolescence and Early Adulthood," *Archives of Pediatrics & Adolescent Medicine* 158, no. 6 (2004): 562–68.

26. J. Cantor, *Mommy, I'm Scared: How TV and Movies Frighten Children and What We Can Do to Protect Them* (San Diego: Harcourt Brace, 1998).

Chapter 6

1. M. E. Eisenberg, D. Neumark-Sztainer, and M. Story, "Associations of Weight-Based Teasing and Emotional Well-Being among Adolescents," *Archives of Pediatrics & Adolescent Medicine* 157, no. 8 (2003): 733–38.

2. S. J. Olshansky et al., "A Potential Decline in Life Expectancy in the United States in the 21st Century," *New England Journal of Medicine* 352, no. 11 (March 17 2005): 1138–45.

3. Cherie Marcus, "The Thinning of Women on Television," University of Florida Interactive Media Lab project (Fall 2000), http://iml.jou.ufl.edu/projects/Fall2000/Marcus/overview.htm.

4. Ibid.

5. W. Feldman, E. Feldman, and J. T. Goodman, "Culture vs. Biology: Children's Attitudes toward Thinness and Fatness," *Pediatrics* 81 (February 1988): 190–94.

6. K. Harrison. "Television Viewing, Fat Stereotyping, Body Shape Standards, and Eating Disorder Symptomatology in Grade School Children," *Communication Research* 27 (October 2000): 617–40.

7. Ibid.

8. Ibid.

9. H. Lavine, D. Sweeney, and S. H. Wagner, "Depicting Women as Sex Objects in Television Advertising: Effects on Body Dissatisfaction," *Personality and Social Psychology Bulletin* 25, no. 8 (1999): 1049–58.

10. D. L. Borzekowski, T. N. Robinson, and J. D. Killen, "Does the Camera Add 10 Pounds? Media Use, Perceived Importance of Appearance, and Weight Concerns among Teenage Girls," *Journal of Adolescent Health* 26, no. 1 (2000): 36–41.

11. J. Van den Bulck, "Is Television Bad for Your Health? Behavior and Body Image of the Adolescent 'Couch Potato.'" *Journal of Youth & Adolescence* 29, no. 3 (1999): 273–88.

12. Feldman et al., "Culture vs. Biology."

13. J. A. Cattarin et al., "Body Image, Mood, and Televised Images of Attractiveness: The Role of Social Comparison," *Journal of Social & Clinical Psychology* 19, no. 2 (2000): 220–39.

14. A. J. Weiss and B. J. Wilson, "Emotional Portrayals in Family Television Series That Are Popular among Children," *Journal of Broadcasting & Electronic Media* 40 (Winter 1996): 1–29.

15. B. L. Fredrickson and K. Harrison, "Throwing like a Girl: Self-Objectification Predicts Adolescent Girls' Motor Performance," *Journal of Sport & Social Issues* 29 (February 2005): 79–101.

16. Ibid.

17. Cattarin et al., "Body Image, Mood, and Televised Images of Attractiveness."

18. T. N. Robinson, "Reducing Children's Television Viewing to Prevent Obesity: A Randomized Controlled Trial," *Journal of the American Medical Association* 282, no. 16 (1999): 1561–67.

19. R. C. Klesges, M. L. Shelton, and L. M. Klesges, "Effects of Television on Metabolic Rate: Potential Implications for Childhood Obesity," *Pediatrics* 91, no. 2 (1993): 281–86.

20. W. H. Dietz et al., "Effect of Sedentary Activities on Resting Metabolic Rate," *American Journal of Clinical Nutrition* 59, no. 3 (1994): 556–59.

21. D. R. Anderson, "The Effects of TV Program Comprehensibility on Preschool Children's Visual Attention to Television," *Child Development* 52 (1981): 151–57.

22. D. R. Anderson and S. R. Levin, "Young Children's Attention to *Sesame Street*," *Child Development* 47 (1976): 806–11.

23. B. A. Dennison et al., "An Intervention to Reduce Television Viewing by Preschool Children," *Archives of Pediatrics & Adolescent Medicine* 158, no. 2 (2004): 170–76.

24. X. Wang and A. C. Perry, "Metabolic and Physiologic Responses to Video Game Play in a Group of 7- to 10-Year-Old Boys," *Archives of Pediatrics & Adolescent Medicine* (in press).

25. D. A. Christakis et al., "Television, Video, and Computer Game Usage in Children under 11 Years of Age," *Journal of Pediatrics* 145 (November 2004): 652–56.

26. N. Stroebele and J. M. de Castro, "Television Viewing Is Associated with an Increase in Meal Frequency in Humans," *Appetite* 42 (February 2003): 111–13.

27. N. Signorielli and J. Staples, "Television and Children's Conceptions of Nutrition," *Health Communication* 9, no. 4 (1997): 289–301.

28. D. S. Acuff and R. H. Reiher, *Kidnapped: How Irresponsible Marketers Are Stealing the Minds of Your Children* (Chicago: Dearborn Trade Pub., 2005).

29. N. Cotugna, "TV Ads on Saturday Morning Children's Programming—What's New?" *Society for Nutrition Education* 20, no. 3 (1988): 125–27.

30. L. Quaid, "Nickelodeon, Kellogg Targets of Junk-Food Lawsuit," Associated Press, January 19, 2006.

31. Ibid.

32. M. E. Goldberg et al., "TV Messages for Snack and Breakfast Foods: Do They Influence Children's Preferences?" *Journal of Consumer Research* 5 (September 1978): 73–81.

33. M. E. Goldberg, "A Quasi-Experiment Assessing the Effectiveness of TV Advertising Directed to Children," *Journal of Marketing Research* (November 1990): 445–54.

34. Jenny Deam, "Targeting Kid Consumers," *Denver Post,* July 23, 2002.

35. McSpotlight.org, Justice Bell's 1997 decision in the "McLibel Suit" (www.mcspotlight.org/case/trial/verdict/verdict.html).

36. K. Harrison and A. L. Marske, "Nutritional Content of Foods Advertised during the Television Programs Children Watch Most," *American Journal of Public Health* 95, no. 9 (2005): 1568–74.

37. Goldberg et al., "TV Messages for Snack and Breakfast Foods."

38. J. P. Galst, "Television Food Commercials and Pro-Nutritional Public Service Announcements as Determinants of Young Children's Snack Choices," *Child Development* 51, no. 3 (1980): 935–38.

39. A. E. Gallo, "Food Advertising in the United States," in Elizabeth Frazao, ed., *America's Eating Habits: Changes and Consequences*, USDA Economic Research Service agriculture information bulletin (1999): 173–80.

40. G. J. Gorn and M. E. Goldberg, "Behavioral Evidence of the Effects of Televised Food Messages on Children," *Journal of Consumer Research* 9, no. 2 (1982): 200–205.

41. F. P. Rivara et al., "Prevention of Smoking-Related Deaths in the United States," *American Journal of Preventive Medicine* 27, no. 2 (2004):118–25.

Chapter 7

1. "Melvin Lee" is a pseudonym to protect the boy's identity. His name was in the papers at the time of this incident, but we assume that he and his family have suffered enough from his infamy.

2. A. N. Meltzoff, "Imitation of Televised Models by Infants," *Child Development* 59 (October 1988): 1221–29.

3. R. A. King, "Adolescence," in M. Lewis, ed. *Child and Adolescent Psychiatry: A Comprehensive Textbook*, 3rd ed. (Philadelphia: Lippincott Williams & Wilkins, 2002): 332–43.

4. J. N. Giedd et al., "Brain Development during Childhood and Adolescence: A Longitudinal MRI Study," *Natural Neuroscience* 2 (October 1999): 861–63.

5. A. A. Baird et al., "Functional Magnetic Resonance Imaging of Facial Affect Recognition in Children and Adolescents," *Journal of the American Academy of Child and Adolescent Psychiatry* 38 (February 1999): 195–99.

6. A. Wyllie, "Responses to Televised Alcohol Advertisements Associated with Drinking Behaviour of 10- to 17-Year-Olds," *Addiction* 93, no. 3 (1998): 361–71.

7. E. Donnerstein and S. Smith, "Sex in the Media," in D. G. Singer and J. L. Singer, eds., *Handbook of Children and the Media* (Thousand Oaks, CA: Sage Publications, 2001): 289–308.

8. C. McLaren, "The Media Doesn't Influence Us—Except When It Does," *Stay Free!* 20 (Fall 2002): 40–52.

9. "The Media Made Them Do It," www.stayfreemagazine.org/archives/20/media_influencer.html, accessed 1/28/06.

10. C. de Jager, "'Fear' Accident Shocks Viewers," *Variety,* January 25, 2006.

11. R. Potts, M. Doppler, and M. Hernandez, "Effects of Television Content on Physical Risk-Taking in Children," *Journal of Experimental Child Psychology* 58 (1994): 321–31.

12. C. K. Atkin, "Mass Communication Effects on Drinking and Driving," *Surgeon General's Workshop on Drunk Driving: Background Papers* (Rockville, MD: U.S. Department of Health and Human Services, 1989).

13. J. D. Sargant et al., "Alcohol Use in Motion Pictures and Its Relation with Early-Onset Teen Drinking," *Journal of Studies on Alcohol* 67, no. 1 (January 2006): 54–66.

14. V. C. Strasburger, "Children, Adolescents, Drugs, and the Media," in Singer and Singer, *Handbook of Children and the Media* (Thousand Oaks, CA: Sage Publications, 2001): 415–46.

15. Ibid.

16. H. W. Perkins, M. P. Haines, and R. Rice, "Misperceiving the College Drinking Norm and Related Problems: A Nationwide Study of Exposure to Prevention Information, Perceived Norms, and Student Alcohol Misuse," *Journal of Studies on Alcohol* 66 (July 2005): 470–78.

17. C. Neighbors, M. E. Larimer, and M. A. Lewis, "Targeting Misperceptions of Descriptive Drinking Norms: Efficacy of a Computer-Delivered Personalized Normative Feedback Intervention," *Journal of Consulting & Clinical Psychology* 72 (June 2004): 434–47.

18. S. T. Walters and C. Neighbors, "Feedback Interventions for College Alcohol Misuse: What, Why, and for Whom?" *Addictive Behavior* 30 (July 2005): 1168–82.

19. Atkin, "Mass Communication Effects."

20. Sargant et al., "Alcohol Use in Motion Pictures."

21. J. G. Hull and C. F. Bond Jr., "Social and Behavioral Consequences of Alcohol Consumption and Expectancy: A Meta-Analysis," *Psychological Bulletin* 99 (May 1986): 347–60.

22. Wyllie, "Responses to Televised Alcohol Advertisements."

23. V. C. Strasburger and E. Donnerstein, "Children, Adolescents, and the Media: Issues and Solutions," *Pediatrics* 103, no. 1 (January 1999): 129–39.

24. S. Villani, "Impact of Media on Children and Adolescents: A 10-Year Review of the Research," *Journal of the American Academy of Child & Adolescent Psychiatry* 40, no. 4 (2001): 392–401.

25. A. Wyllie, "The Response of Young Men to Increased Television Advertising of Alcohol in New Zealand," *Health Promotion International* 6, no. 3 (1998): 191–97.

26. K. Fleming, E. Thorson, and C. K. Atkin, "Alcohol Advertising Exposure and Perceptions: Links with Alcohol Expectancies and Intentions to Drink or Drinking in Underaged Youth and Young Adults," *Journal of Health Communications* 9, no. 1 (January–February 2004): 3–29.

27. N. M. Malamuth and E. A. Impett, "Research on Sex in the Media: What Do We Know about Effects on Children and Adolescents?" in Singer and Singer, *Handbook of Children and the Media* (Thousand Oaks, CA: Sage Publications, 2001): 269–88.

28. King, "Adolescence."

29. L. M. Ward, "Talking about Sex: Common Themes about Sexuality in the Prime-Time Television Programs Children and Adolescents View Most," *Journal of Youth & Adolescence* 24, no. 5 (1995): 595–615.

30. D. Kunkel et al., *Sex on TV 4* (Menlo Park, CA: Kaiser Family Foundation, 2005).

31. J. P. Steyer, *The Other Parent: The Inside Story of the Media's Effect on Our Children* (New York: Atria Books, 2002).

32. A. J. Jacobs, "The XXX Files," *Entertainment Weekly* (August 6, 1999): 20–25.

33. Donnerstein and Smith, "Sex in the Media."

34. Kunkel et al., *Sex on TV 4.*

35. Donnerstein and Smith, "Sex in the Media."

36. Kunkel et al., *Sex on TV 4.*

37. D. Kunkel et al., *Sex on TV 3* (Menlo Park, Calif: Kaiser Family Foundation, 2003).

38. Kunkel et al., *Sex on TV 4.*

39. Donnerstein and Smith, "Sex in the Media."

40. Kunkel et al., *Sex on TV 4.*

41. S. Linn, *Consuming Kids: Protecting Our Children from the Onslaught of Marketing and Advertising* (New York: Anchor Books, 2005).

42. Donnerstein and Smith, "Sex in the Media."

43. Malamuth and Impett, "Research on Sex in the Media."

44. Ward, "Talking about Sex."

45. Kunkel et al., *Sex on TV 3.*

46. Ibid.

47. Ward, "Talking about Sex."

48. Kunkel et al., *Sex on TV 4.*

49. Malamuth and Impett, "Research on Sex in the Media."

50. R. L. Collins et al., "Watching Sex on Television Predicts Adolescent Initiation of Sexual Behavior," *Pediatrics* 114, no. 3 (September 2004): e280–89.

51. J. D. Brown et al., "Sexy Media Matter: Exposure to Sexual Content in Music, Movies, Television, and Magazines predicts Black and White Adolescents' Sexual Behavior," *Pediatrics* 117, no. 4 (April 2006): 1018–27.

52. D. F. Roberts and P. G. Christenson, "Popular Music in Childhood and Adolescence," in Singer and Singer, *Handbook of Children and the Media* (Thousand Oaks, CA: Sage Publications, 2001): 395–414.

53. R. H. duRant et al., "Tobacco and Alcohol Use Behaviors Portrayed in Music Videos: A Content Analysis," *American Journal of Public Health* 87, no. 7 (1997): 1131–35 (erratum appears in vol. 87, no. 9: 1514).

54. Donnerstein and Smith, "Sex in the Media."

55. M. Rich et al., "Aggressors or Victims: Gender and Race in Music Video Violence," *Pediatrics* 10 (April 1998, part 1): 669–74.

56. R. H. duRant et al., "Violence and Weapon Carrying in Music Videos: A Content Analysis," *Archives of Pediatrics & Adolescent Medicine* 151, no. 5 (1997): 443–48.

57. J. D. Johnson, L. A. Jackson, and L. Gatto, "Violent Attitudes and Deferred Academic Aspirations: Deleterious Effects of Exposure to Rap Music," *Basic & Applied Social Psychology* 16, no. 1–2 (1995): 17–41.

58. Ward, "Talking about Sex."

59. Donnerstein and Smith, "Sex in the Media."

60. Kunkel et al., *Sex on TV 3.*

61. Malamuth and Impett, "Research on Sex in the Media."

62. S. Villani, "Impact of Media on Children and Adolescents: A 10-Year Review of the Research," *Journal of the American Academy of Child & Adolescent Psychiatry* 40, no. 4 (2001): 392–401.

63. Kunkel et al., *Sex on TV 3.*

64. R. L. Collins et al., "Entertainment Television as a Healthy Sex Educator: The Impact of Condom-Efficacy Information in an Episode of *Friends,*" *Pediatrics* 112, no. 5 (2003): 1115–21.

65. Collins et al., "Watching Sex on Television."

Chapter 8

In addition to the sources for specific information cited below, the following books provided considerable useful background information.

B. Gunter, C. Oates, and M. Blades, *Advertising to Children on TV: Content, Impact, and Regulation* (Mahwah, NJ: Lawrence Erlbaum, 2005).

S. Linn, Consuming Kids: *Protecting Our Children from the Onslaught of Marketing and Advertising,* (New York: Anchor Books, 2005).

J. U. McNeal, *Kids as Customers: A Handbook of Marketing to Children* (New York: Lexington Books, 1992).

J. Schor, *Born to Buy: The Commercialized Child and the New Consumer Culture* (New York: Scribner's, 2004).

1. This anecdote was found at www.snopes.com, the online arbiter of true and false urban legends. The Soupy Sales story is true.

2. J. Ludden, "School Targets Older, Immigrant Students," NPR: *All Things Considered,* December 6, 2005.

3. American Association of Advertising Agencies and the Association of National Advertisers, *2001 Television Commercial Monitoring Report* (2002).

4. D. Kunkel, "Advertising and Children," in D. G. Singer and J. L. Singer, eds., *Handbook of Children and the Media* (Thousand Oaks, CA: Sage Publications, 2001): xvii, 765.

5. J. U. McNeal, *Kids as Customers: A Handbook of Marketing to Children* (New York: Lexington Books, 1992).

6. M. Warner, "Influencing Young Diets: Some Makers Say They'll Offer Healthier Products," *New York Times,* December 16, 2005.

7. J. Schor, *Born to Buy: The Commercialized Child and the New Consumer Culture* (New York: Scribner's, 2004).

8. Ibid.

9. D. Kunkel et al., *Report of the APA Task Force on Advertising and Children*, American Psychological Association, February 20, 2004.

10. C. Oates, "Children and Television Advertising: When Do They Understand Persuasive Intent?" *Journal of Consumer Behaviour* 1 (July 2001): 238–45.

11. Schor, *Born to Buy.*

12. Schor, *Born to Buy.*

13. D. S. Acuff and R. H. Reiher, *Kidnapped: How Irresponsible Marketers Are Stealing the Minds of Your Children* (Chicago: Dearborn Trade Publishers, 2005).

14. "Television Commercial," (http://en.wikipedia.org/wiki/Television_commercial).

15. Oates, "Children and Television Advertising."

16. B. Gunter, C. Oates, and M. Blades, *Advertising to Children on TV: Content, Impact, and Regulation* (Mahwah, NJ: Lawrence Erlbaum, 2005).

17. M. E. Goldberg and G. J. Gorn, "Children's Reactions to Television Advertising: An Experimental Approach, *Journal of Consumer Research* 1 (September 1974): 69–75.

18. T. A. Marshall et al., "Dental Caries and Beverage Consumption in Young Children," *Pediatrics* 112 (September 2003, part 1): e184–91.

19. G. Wyshak, "Teenaged Girls, Carbonated Beverage Consumption, and Bone Fractures," *Archives of Pediatrics & Adolescent Medicine* 154 (June 2000): 610–13.

20. V. C. Strasburger, "Children, Adolescents, Drugs, and the Media," in Singer and Singer, *Handbook of Children and the Media*: (Thousand Oaks, CA: Sage Publications, 2001) 415–46.

21. Center on Alcohol Marketing and Youth, *Alcohol Advertising on Television, 2001 to 2003: More of the Same* (Washington, DC: Center on Alcohol Marketing and Youth, 2004).

22. Strasburger, "Children, Adolescents, Drugs, and the Media."

23. Ibid.

24. Ibid.

25. Ibid.

26. Ibid.

27. K. Fleming, E. Thorson, and C. K. Atkin, "Alcohol Advertising Exposure and Perceptions: Links with Alcohol Expectancies and Intentions to Drink or Drinking in

Underaged Youth and Young Adults," *Journal of Health Communication* 9 (January-February 2004): 3–29.

28. V. C. Strasburger, "Children and TV Advertising: Nowhere to Run, Nowhere to Hide," *Journal of Developmental & Behavioral Pediatrics* 22 (June 2001): 185–87.

29. A. Wyllie, "Responses to Televised Alcohol Advertisements Associated with Drinking Behaviour of 10- to 17-year-olds," *Addiction* 93, no. 3 (1998): 361–71.

30. A. Wyllie, "The Response of Young Men to Increased Television Advertising of Alcohol in New Zealand," *Health Promotion International* 6, no. 3 (1998): 191–97.

31. C. K. Atkin, "Effects of Televised Alcohol Messages on Teenage Drinking Patterns," *Journal of Adolescent Health Care* 11 (January 1990): 10–24.

32. C. K. Atkin, "Mass Communication Effects on Drinking and Driving," *Surgeon General's Workshop on Drunk Driving: Background Papers* (Rockville, MD: U.S. Department of Health and Human Services, 1989).

33. Wyllie, "Responses to Televised Alcohol Advertisements."

34. Strasburger, "Children, Adolescents, Drugs, and the Media."

35. C. K. Atkin, K. Neuendorf, and S. McDermott, "The Role of Alcohol Advertising in Excessive and Hazardous Drinking," *Journal of Drug Education* 13 (1983): 313–25.

36. Strasburger, "Children, Adolescents, Drugs, and the Media."

37. H. Saffer and D. Dave, *Alcohol Advertising and Alcohol Consumption by Adolescents, Working Paper 9676* (Cambridge, MA: National Bureau of Economic Research, 2003).

38. W. H. Dietz and V. C. Strasburger, "Children, Adolescents, and Television," *Current Problems in Pediatrics* 21 (January 1991): 8–31; discussion 32.

39. B. Erbas at al., "Investigating the Relation between Placement of Quit Antismoking Advertisements and Number of Telephone Calls to Quitline: A Semiparametric Modelling Approach," *Journal of Epidemiology & Community Health* 60 (February 2006):180–82.

40. A. R. Lancaster and K. M. Lancaster, "Reaching Insomniacs with Television PSAs: Poor Placement of Important Messages," *Journal of Consumer Affairs* 36 (Winter 2002): 150–70.

41. Erbas at al., "Investigating the Relation."

42. W. DeJong and C. K. Atkin, "A Review of National Television PSA Campaigns for Preventing Alcohol-Impaired Driving, 1987–1992," *Journal of Public Health Policy* 16 (Spring 1995): 59–80.

43. W. DeJong, C. K. Atkin, and L. Wallack, "A Critical Analysis of 'Moderation' Advertising Sponsored by the Beer Industry: Are 'Responsible Drinking' Commercials Done Responsibly?" *Milbank Quarterly* 70, no. 4 (1992): 661–78.

44. C. K. Atkin, "Mass Communication Effects on Drinking and Driving."

45. T. N. Robinson et al., "Effects of Reducing Television Viewing on Children's Requests for Toys: A Randomized Controlled Trial," *Journal of Developmental & Behavioral Pediatrics* 22, no. 3 (2001): 179–84.

46. C. Grande, "Why Kids' Television Is No Longer Child's Play," *Financial Times,* February 3, 2004: 8.

47. Ibid.

48. Dietz and Strasburger, "Children, Adolescents, and Television."

49. J. P. Steyer, *The Other Parent: The Inside Story of the Media's Effect on Our Children* (New York: Atria Books, 2002).

50. Ibid.

51. Dietz and Strasburger, "Children, Adolescents, and Television."

52. D. L. Linebarger and D. Walker, "Infants' and Toddlers' Television Viewing and Language Outcomes," *American Behavioral Scientist* 46, no. 10 (2004):1–22.

53. Grande, "Why Kids' Television Is No Longer Child's Play."

54. Steyer, *The Other Parent.*

55. A. Quart, *Branded: The Buying and Selling of Teenagers* (Cambridge, MA: Perseus, 2003).

56. Schor, *Born to Buy.*

57. Gunter et al. *Advertising to Children.*

58. Schor, *Born to Buy,* p. 27.

59. Ibid.

60. CBC Marketplace, "Sex Sells: Marketing and 'Age Compression'" CBC News, January 9, 2005 (www.cbc.ca/consumers/market/files/money/sexy/marketing.html).

61. B. Schiffman, "The Most Expensive ZIP Codes in America," *Forbes,* September 26, 2003.

62. T. C. O'Guinn and L. J. Shrum, "The Role of Television in the Construction of Consumer Reality," *Journal of Consumer Research* 23 (March 1997):278–94.

63. J. Schor, *The Overspent American: Why We Want What We Don't Need* (New York: HarperPerennial, 1999).

64. Schor, *Born to Buy.*

65. T. Kasser, *The High Price of Materialism* (Cambridge, MA: MIT Press, 2002).

66. K. J. Pine, "Dear Santa: The effects of television advertising on young children." *International Journal of Behavioral Development.* 26, no. 6 (2002):529–539.

Chapter 9

1. G. Comstock and H. Paik, *Television and the American Child* (San Diego: Academic Press, 1991).

2. D. A. Christakis et al., "Television, Video, and Computer Game Usage in Children under 11 Years of Age," *Journal of Pediatrics* 145 (November 2004):652–56.

3. M. E. Eisenberg et al., "Correlations Between Family Meals and Psychosocial Well-Being among Adolescents," *Archives of Pediatrics & Adolescent Medicine* 158, no. 8 (August 2004):792–96.

4. K. W. Griffin, et al., "Parenting Practices as Predictors of Substance Use, Delinquency, and Aggression among Urban Minority Youth: Moderating Effects of Family Structure and Gender," *Psychology of Addictive Behavior* 14, no. 2 (June 2000):174–84.

5. Christakis et al., "Television, Video, and Computer Game Usage."

INDEX

Underscored page references indicate graphs and charts.

mindful viewing and, 216
risky behavior and, 174
sleep and, 106–16, 120
viewing television and, 216–17
weight and, 131, 135
Quantity of television
attention and, 32
child's development and, 25
as dimension of television, 11
education and, 38
mindful viewing and, 216
sleep and, 120
viewing television and, 211–13

R

Racial tolerance, 89–90
Radio shows, early, 23–24
Rambo, 193
Rand Corporation, 168
Ravussin, Eric, 133
Reading books, 27–28
Reagan, Ronald, 193
Reality television, 6, 70, 78–79, 199. *See also specific programs*
Real life, 24–25
Real World: Austin, 156
Relaxation, 104–6, 105
REM (rapid eye movement) sleep, 98–99, 104
Repetition, 47
Rescue 911, 114
Risky behavior
adolescent social tasks and, 152–54
alcohol abuse, 159–62, 170
brain development of teenagers and, 150–52
car chases and, 158–59
cartoons and, 158
drug abuse, 155, 170
imitation of, 149–50, 157–60
mindful viewing and, 177–78
in music videos, 170–71, 170
quality and content of television and, 174
quality of life issues and, 176–77
scripts for behavior and, 154–57
sex
in advertising, 126–27, 182
aggression and violence and, 168–72
attitudes about, 167–68
girls' vulnerability to, 172
information about, 162–67
in music videos, 170–71, 170
open communication about, 175–76

peer groups and, 172–74
positive effects of television and, 174–76
television scripts for, 155
smoking, 170
social learning and, 152–54
of teenagers, 149–51
television and, 159–60, 170
Road Runner, 73, 83
Robinson, Tom, 130–31, 134–35
Rogers, Fred, 24
Ronald McDonald (restaurant mascot), 139
Roots (miniseries), 58
R-rated films, 165
Rugrats, 165

S

Sales, Soupy (Milton Supman), 179–81
Salomon, Gavriel, 40
Sarnoff, David, 17
Saving Private Ryan (film), 228
Schor, Juliet, 196, 199
Scooby-Doo, 2, 27, 228
Scott, Ridley, 185
Scream (film), 73
Seinfeld, 173, 200
Selection and attention, 19
Self-direction, verbal, 29, 31
Self-esteem, 126–29
Self-image, 126–29
Self-objectification, 127–28
Self-perceptions, 128–29
Sesame Street
age appropriateness and, 49
attention studies and, 21–22
education and, 7, 11, 22, 27, 41–46, 221, 229
8-month-old's viewing of, 17
entertainment and, 52, 229
financial development of, 191–92
idea for, 44–45
image changes on, 27
impact of, 45–46
interaction of parent and, 55
language development and, 29
merchandising and, 192
nutrition and, 145
prosocial behaviors and, 90, 94
skills emphasized on, 51
testing groups for, 45
3-year-old's viewing of, 216–17
Sesame Workshop, 192